Learn Red Hat® Linux® Server Tips

George M. Doss

Wordware Publishing, Inc.

Library of Congress Cataloging-in-Publication Data

Doss, George M.
Learn Red Hat Linux server tips / by George M. Doss.
p. cm.
ISBN 1-55622-714-0 (pbk.)
1. Linux. 2. Client/server computing. I. Title.
QA76.9.C55 D67 2000
005.4'4769--dc21 99-059496
CIP

2320 Los Rios Boulevard
Plano, Texas 75074

Printed in the United States of America

ISBN 1-55622-714-0
10 9 8 7 6 5 4 3 2 1
0001

All inquiries for volume purchases of this book should be addressed to Wordware Publishing, Inc., at the above address. Telephone inquiries may be made by calling:

(972) 423-0090

This book is dedicated to Charles R. Estes, Professor Extraordinaire. Charles taught me nothing about Linux, but he did teach me that it is important to ask the correct question of meaning if one expects to get a logical answer that is meaningful. Charles became my mentor, and then more importantly a friend. Charles, thanks for trusting in me.

This is the second book in this series on Red Hat Linux. I would like to thank the very fine people at Wordware Publishing in their professional efforts to take my draft and make it a pleasurable viewing experience. The two people responsible for this are Martha McCuller, interior design; and Alan McCuller, cover design. In addition, editers Beth Kohler and Kellie Henderson have to be thanked many times over for catching my unfortunate word faux pas. Finally, thanks to Jim Hill, the publisher, who had enough faith in my writing skills to offer me a contract.

Any omissions or technical misinterpretations are, of course, mine.

George M. Doss

Contents at a Glance

Chapter		
1	Server Type Tips	1
2	E-mail Server Tips	11
3	File Server Tips	19
4	Internet Server Tips	47
5	News Server Tips	61
6	Remote Administration Server Tips	71
7	Security Server Tips	83
8	Miscellaneous Server Tips	89
9	TCP/IP Tips	97
10	Point-to-Point Protocol (PPP) Tips	111
11	Network Information System (NIS) Tips	115
12	Network File System (NFS) Tips	121
13	Network Administrative Tips	129
14	General Networking Tips	151
15	Shell Tips	165
16	GNU Project Tips	169
17	Packaging Tips	177
18	Apache Server Tips	185
19	Words and Acronyms Tips	191
20	System Call Tips	201
21	Server/System Administration Tips	207
22	Red Hat Package Manager Tips	215
23	Red Hat Tools Tips	221
24	Hardware Tips	227
25	Filesystem Structure Tips	237
Appendix A	HOWTOs Table of Contents	257
Appendix B	Listing of Man Pages for Networking Administration and Maintenance	333
Appendix C	Networking Request for Comments (RFCs)	345
Appendix D	List of Linux 6.0 Server Packages	351
Appendix E	Listing of Man Pages for Linux 6.0	359

Contents

Chapter 1—**Server Type Tips** 1
What is a server? 1
What is a three-tier client/server? 1
What is a Linux server? 1
What is a service? 1
What are examples of services? 1
What is an application server? 2
What is a caching-only server? 2
What is a database server? 2
What is a domain name server? 2
What is an e-mail server? 2
What is a file server? 2
What is an Internet server? 3
What is an FTP server? 3
What is a messaging server? 3
What is a network file server (NFS)? 3
What is a network information server (NIS)? 3
What is a newsgroup server? 4
What is a print server? 4
What is a proxy server? 4
What is a remote administration server? 4
What is a security server? 4
What is a gateway server? 4
What is a firewall server? 5
What is an SMB server? 5
What is an inetd server? 5
What is a UUCP server? 5
What are the hard drive requirements? 5
What are the network adapter requirements? 5
What is the SCSI controller requirement? 6
What is the difference between a server and a workstation? 6
How do I create mount points? 6
How do I set up an X server? 6
What is an archie server? 6
What are some man pages on the Apache Web server? 7
What are some man pages on news servers? 7
What are some man pages on a NetWare server? 7
What are some man pages on a remote server? 7
What are some man pages on server daemons? 8
What are some man pages on Samba? 8

What are some man pages on the Internet server? 9
What are some man pages on the NIS server?. 9
What are some man pages on various types of servers?. 9

Chapter 2—**E-mail Server Tips 11**
What is electronic mail? 11
What are the two basic e-mail agents? 11
What is required to get e-mail?. 11
What is the basic functionality of POP? 11
What are some of the available mail commands? 12
How does elm work? 12
Is there a HOWTO available on e-mail? 12
What is the purpose of the aliases file?. 12
What packages support mail? 13
What is sendmail? 13
What are the important functions of sendmail? 13
What is the first step in compiling sendmail? 14
What is a critical step in installing sendmail? 14
What are the important functions of the sendmail configuration file? 14
What is the final step in installing sendmail? 14
What if sendmail cannot be configured? 14
What if sendmail hangs? 15
Why should I upgrade my sendmail package? 15
Is there any method for stopping spamming with sendmail? 15
What is MIME? 15
Is there a way to filter e-mail? 15
What are the functions of an alias? 16
What is SMTP? 16
What is the basic RFC for SMTP?. 16
What is the Domain Name System (DNS)?. 16
What are the specific Red Hat Linux packages for e-mail?. 16
What is the importance of bulletins for e-mail? 17
What are some available RFCs on e-mail? 17

Chapter 3—**File Server Tips 19**
What is file management? 19
What is a file? 19
What are five common types of files? 19
Where are some of the executable files found? 20
Where are some of the special files found? 20
How do I make a file? 20
How do I display a list of files?. 20
How do I display a list of hidden files?. 20
How do I get information on a file? 20

How do I copy a file? 20
How do I rename a file? 21
How do I move a file? 21
How do I delete a file? 21
How do I change a file's time stamp? 22
How do I get symbolic link information? 22
How do I change file permissions? 22
How do I change file ownership? 23
How do I search for files? 23
How do I find a command in a given directory? 24
How do I find files not accessed in a given period? 24
How do I find files accessed in a given period? 24
How do I find files not modified in a given period? 24
How do I find files modified in a given period? 25
How do I find the location of the find command and its man pages? . 25
How do I find a file by size? 25
How do I find files by type? 25
How do I use the locate command? 26
How are text files displayed? 26
How are compressed files displayed? 27
How can I process text files? 28
How do I use cut? 28
How do I use dd? 28
How do I use diff? 29
How do I use expand? 30
How do I use fold? 30
How do I use grep? 30
How do I use lpr? 31
How do I use nl? 31
How do I use paste? 31
How do I use patch? 32
How do I use sed? 32
How do I use sort? 33
How do I use split? 33
How do I use tac? 33
How do I use tr? 34
How do I use uniq? 34
How do I use wc? 34
How do I archive and compress files? 35
How do I use compress? 35
How do I use cpio? 35
How do I use gunzip? 36
How do I use gzip? 36
How do I use tar? 36
How do I use uncompress? 37

How do I use unzip? 37
How do I use zip?. 37
How do I handle MS-DOS files? 37
What are five basic file suffixes for designating programming languages or scripts? 38
What is a symbolic link? 38
What does a filename that begins with the prefix in. mean? 38
How do I create a directory? 38
How do I copy a directory?. 38
How do I delete a directory? 38
How do I find a list of directories? 39
How do I find the pathname of my home directory?. 39
How do I navigate through the directories? 39
How do I change directory permissions?. 39
How do I change the name of the root directory? 39
How do I list contents of directories? 39
How can I display the pathname of the working directory? 39
What is / (a single backslash)?. 40
What is /bin? 40
What are basic programs found in the /bin directory?. 40
What is /dev?. 40
What are some of the files found in the /dev directory?. 40
What is /dev/null? 41
What is /dev/printer? 41
What is /etc? 41
What are some of the files found in the /etc directory? 41
What is /etc/fstab? 41
What is /etc/group? 41
What is /etc/hosts?. 42
What is /etc/profile? 42
What is /etc/passwd? 42
What is /etc/services? 42
What is /etc/sysconfig?. 42
What is /etc/X11? 43
What is /home?. 43
What is /lib? 43
What is /mnt? 43
What is /sbin? 43
What is /tmp? 43
What is /usr? 44
What is /usr/bin?. 44
What is /usr/lib? 44
What is /usr/lib/rhs?. 44
What is /usr/local? 44
What is /usr/local/bin? 44

What is /usr/local/lib? 44
What is /usr/local/src? 44
What is /usr/man? 44
What is /usr/spool? 45
What is /usr/src? 45
What is /usr/X11R6? 45
What is /var? 45
What is /var/lib/rpm? 45
What is /var/log? 45
What are some of the files found in the /var/log directory? 45
How do I install Shadow Suite? 46

Chapter 4—**Internet Server Tips** **47**
What is an Internet server? 47
What is an intranet server? 47
What is a primary concern in having an Internet server? 48
What are the basic steps in setting up an Internet server? 48
What is PPP? 48
What is SLIP? 49
What is CSLIP? 49
What is a dummy interface? 49
What are the special requirements for adding a dummy interface? . . 49
How can I check the localhost dummy interface? 49
How do I set up serial communication devices? 50
What types of programs for the Internet are available? 50
What is dip? 51
How do I use dip? 51
What is the Domain Name Service? 51
What is a domain name server? 51
What is a name server? 51
What are the types of name servers? 51
What is URL? 52
Is there a package that supports browsing? 52
Is there a package that supports chat (IRC)? 52
Is there a package that supports faxing? 52
What is an FTP service? 52
What are the basic steps in an FTP request? 52
How can the FTP server be made securer than normal? 53
What are the FTP commands that can be used to control user access? 53
What are the commands that control FTP logging? 53
What are the commands that control FTP permissions? 53
What are the packages that support FTP? 54
What are some important FTP administrative utilities? 54
What HOWTOs are available to support Internet functionality? 55
Is there a program that supports Web searches? 55

How do I set up a Domain Name Service (DNS)? 55
What tools are required to configure a DNS? 55
How do I configure Ethernet network adapters? 56
How do I connect to my Internet service provider? 56
How do I set up serial communication devices? 56
How do I find files that show host name and IP address associations? 56
What fields are found in the /etc/hosts file? 56
What types of entries should be in the /etc/hosts file? 57
How do I find files that show service name and port number associations? 57
What is the port number for a WWW service? 57
What is the port number for FTP service? 57
Where can I find an access control facility for Internet services? . . . 58
Where are the IP addresses of name servers kept? 58
Where is the host name kept? 58
Where do I find network names and their IP addresses? 58
What files allow and deny host access to Internet services? 58
How do I check the routing status to another host? 58
How do I find information on setting up for the WWW? 58
What is the first step in the WWW server setup? 58
What is the second step in the WWW server setup? 59
What are some of the Red Hat Linux packages that support the Internet? 59
Are there RFCs available to assist in setting up a WWW server? 60

Chapter 5—**News Server Tips** **61**
What is a news server? 61
What is Usenet? 61
What are the logical parts of Usenet news? 61
What are the two types of Usenet programs? 62
What are some of the available Linux newsgroups? 62
What are some of the available Red Hat newsgroups? 62
What are some of the available mail newsgroups? 63
What must I decide first as a system administrator? 63
What is a first step in newsgroup selection? 63
What is a logical policy on having newsgroups? 64
What is a basic requirement in configuring a news reader? 64
What are the essential questions I must ask to have Usenet? 64
What are the hardware requirements? 64
What is an NNTP server? 64
What is an alternative to NNTP? 65
How do I install the INN package? 65
What are some important INN files? 65
What files have to be configured for INN? 65

What are the hardware requirements for INN? 65
What are the daemons used with INN? 65
Where is INN documentation? 66
What are the basic functions of a news reader? 66
What are some basic news readers for handling news? 66
Is there a full-screen news reader? 66
What is the purpose of the .newsrc file? 66
What are the basic characteristics of the pine news reader?. 67
What are the basic characteristics of the tin news reader?. 67
What are the basic characteristics of the slrn news reader? 68
What are the basic characteristics of the trn news reader? 68
How do I install the trn RPM? 69
What is Netnews?. 69
What is the Netnews Transport Protocol? 69
How do I configure Network Information Service (NIS)? 69
How do I set up to use Usenet news? 69
What is a basic administrative requirement?. 69
What is an important news distribution policy? 70
Who is the newsgroup controlling authority? 70
What are the essential administrative tasks for the news server? . . . 70

Chapter 6—**Remote Administration Server Tips 71**
What is a remote administration server?. 71
What is the primary function of the telnet command?. 71
What are the available options that can be used at the telnet> prompt? 71
What are some of the basic telnet commands?. 72
What is the tftpd user interface? 72
What is fingerd? 72
What is innxmit? 72
What is ntpget? 73
What is passwd.nntp? 73
What is talkd? 73
What is uux? 73
What is xon? 73
What does Net::Ping do? 73
What is RPC? 73
What RPC daemons do I need? 74
How do I start these daemons?. 74
What does rpc.portmap do? 74
What does rpc.mountd do? 74
What does rpc.nfsd do?. 74
How does the /etc/exports file work? 74
What are possible mount options for /etc/exports? 75
What is important about RPC program versions? 75

What are the r- commands? 75
What is the rlogin command? 76
What is the rsh command? 76
What is the rcp command? 76
What is the rusers command? 77
What is rdist? 77
What is ristd? 77
What is rquota? 77
What is rquotad? 77
What is rup? 77
What is the RPM for FTP? 77
What is an FTP server? 78
What is an FTP service? 78
How do I install anonymous FTP? 78
What is the port number for FTP service? 78
What are the basic steps in an FTP request? 78
How do I use the ftpd daemon? 79
What files need to be edited to customize FTP configuration? 79
How can the FTP server be made securer than normal? 79
What is found in the /etc/ftpaccess file? 79
What are the FTP commands that can be used to control user access? 79
What are the commands that control FTP logging? 80
What are the commands that control FTP permissions? 80
What are the packages that support FTP? 81
What are some important FTP administrative utilities? 81

Chapter 7—**Security Server Tips** **83**
What is a firewall server? 83
What are the types of firewalls? 83
What are four essential components of a firewall? 83
What is a rule set (policy)? 84
What is an authentication mechanism? 84
What is a filter? 84
What is a router/gateway program? 84
How does an IP filtering firewall work? 84
How does a proxy server serve as a firewall? 84
What are some of the advantages of a proxy server? 84
What is ipfwadm? 85
Where can I get ipfwadm? 85
What is a gateway server? 85
What is masquerading? 85
What is a major disadvantage of a firewall? 85
Where on the Internet can I get information on firewalling? 85
How do I set up a firewall? 86

What are the basic steps in making a firewall with masquerading? . . 86
What are accounting rules? 86
What are input rules?. 87
What are output rules? 87
What are forwarding rules? 87
Are there RFCs on firewalling? 87
What is the importance of the networking options? 87
What does CONFIG_FIREWALL do? 88
What does CONFIG_NET_ALIAS do?. 88
What does CONFIG_IP_FORWARD do? 88
What does CONFIG_IP_ACCT do? 88
What does CONFIG_IP_ROUTER do? 88
What does CONFIG_IP_NOSR do? 88

Chapter 8—**Miscellaneous Server Tips. 89**
What is an application server? 89
What is a messaging server? 89
What is a print server? 89
What is a proxy server?. 90
What is a printer?. 90
What is the /etc/printcap file? 90
Where is an entry on a physical printer kept? 90
What are the basic commands for handling printing? 90
What is spool? 91
How do I do offline printing? 91
How can the line printer system be managed?. 91
What is the printer daemon? 92
How can I query the printing spool? 92
How do I remove a document from the spool queue? 93
What print configuration tool is available?. 93
How do I get more information on printing?. 93
Why can't I configure my printer? 94
How can I reconfigure my printer?. 94
How do I define a printer using printtool?. 94
How do I set the print system's host ID? 94
How can I keep up with printer usage? 94
What are some important printer troubleshooting tips? 95
What man pages are available to assist with printer problems? 95
How can I set up a scanner? 95

Chapter 9—**TCP/IP Tips 97**
What is TCP/IP? 97
What is an IP address? 97
What is a loopback address? 97
What is IPv6? 98

How can I install IPv6? . . . 98
Are there RFCs that discuss IPv6? . . . 98
Are there RFCs that discuss TCP/IP? . . . 98
What is netcfg? . . . 99
What do I use to hand-configure my network interface? . . . 99
What are some of the basic TCP/IP commands? . . . 99
Besides the basic TCP/IP commands, what others are available? . . . 99
How do I use the ftpd daemon? . . . 100
How do I use the gated daemon? . . . 100
How do I use the host command? . . . 100
How do I use the ifconfig command? . . . 100
How do I use the named command? . . . 100
How do I use the netstat command? . . . 101
How do I use the nslookup command? . . . 101
How do I use the pppd daemon? . . . 101
How do I use the route command? . . . 101
How do I use the routed daemon? . . . 101
What does arp do? . . . 102
What does bootpd do? . . . 102
What does bootptest do? . . . 102
What does fingerd do? . . . 102
What does gdc do? . . . 102
What does icmpinfo do? . . . 102
What does identd do? . . . 102
What does imapd do? . . . 102
What does ftpd do? . . . 103
What is imap? . . . 103
What is inn? . . . 103
What does inetd do? . . . 103
What does logger do? . . . 103
What does lpd do? . . . 103
What does netdate do? . . . 103
What does rdate do? . . . 103
What does rexecd do? . . . 103
What does rlogind do? . . . 104
What does rmail do? . . . 104
What does rsh do? . . . 104
What does rstat do? . . . 104
What does ruptime do? . . . 104
What does rusers do? . . . 104
What does rwall do? . . . 104
What does rwhod do? . . . 104
What does slattach do? . . . 105
What does syslogd do? . . . 105
What does talkd do? . . . 105

What does tcpd do? . . . 105
What does tcpdchk do? . . . 105
What does tcpdmatch do? . . . 105
What does telnetd do? . . . 105
What does tftpd do? . . . 105
What does traceroute do? . . . 106
What is the Serial Line Internet Protocol? . . . 106
How do I know if I have SLIP support in my kernel? . . . 106
How do I load a SLIP module? . . . 106
How can I automate a SLIP connection? . . . 106
What is ICMP? . . . 106
What is DNS? . . . 106
What are some of the important RFCs on DNS? . . . 107
What is a domain? . . . 108
What is a domain name server? . . . 108
What is the IP address for a standalone host? . . . 108
What are some of the basic steps for IP interface configuration? . . . 108
What is PLIP? . . . 108
How do I add the PLIP interface? . . . 108
How do I add an Ethernet interface? . . . 109
What is DHCP? . . . 109

Chapter 10—**Point-to-Point Protocol (PPP) Tips . . . 111**
What is the Point-to-Point Protocol? . . . 111
What are the basic components of PPP? . . . 111
How does my PPP connection run? . . . 111
How do I set up PPP? . . . 111
What are the basic steps in getting PPP to work? . . . 112
How do I know if I have PPP support in my kernel? . . . 112
How do I get status on my PPP connection? . . . 112
How do I use the pppd command? . . . 112
How can I make my PPP more secure? . . . 113
What RFCs are available on PPP? . . . 113

Chapter 11—**Network Information System (NIS) Tips . . . 115**
What is NIS? . . . 115
Why is NIS associated with YP? . . . 115
What is the importance of NIS? . . . 115
What is the importance of NIS+? . . . 115
How does NIS work? . . . 116
What is a requirement for one NIS domain? . . . 116
What is the RPC protocol? . . . 116
Where are the RPCs located? . . . 116
How do I find RPC information? . . . 116
What types of NIS servers are available? . . . 116

What are the two types of NIS servers? 117
What is an NIS domain? 117
What is an NIS map? 117
How do I administer NIS? 117
How do I administer NIS group access? 117
What types of NIS accounts exist? 117
Is there a HOWTO on NIS? 118
What are some of the NIS commands? 118
How do I allow a specific user to log in to NIS? 118
How do I stop just anyone from logging in to NIS? 118
How do I troubleshoot NIS? 119

Chapter 12—**Network File System (NFS) Tips** **121**
What is the Network File System? 121
What is a use for NFS? 121
What is the core characteristic of NFS? 121
What may be the weakest feature of NFS? 121
What are the basic NFS components? 122
Is there a special requirement for mounting NFS? 122
What are some of the NFS commands? 122
What NFS daemons do I need? 122
How do I start these daemons? 123
What does rpc.portmap do? 123
What does rpc.mountd do? 123
What does rpc.nfsd do? 123
How does the /etc/exports file work? 123
What are possible mount options for /etc/exports? 123
What are the basic NFS mount options? 124
What is the difference between a hard and soft mount? 124
Is there is an automatic check on the integrity of NFS? 124
Is there a manual way to check the integrity of NFS? 125
How do I check for the presence of NFS daemons? 125
How do I start and stop NFS services? 125
Is there a HOWTO for NFS? 125
What ports do I use to firewall NFS? 125
Is there a man page for NFS? 126
What is mountd? 126
What is nfsd? 126
What does rpcinfo do? 126
What does showmount do? 127
What are the available RFCs on NFS? 127

Chapter 13—**Network Administrative Tips** **129**
What is a network? 129
What are some of the expected network services? 129

What is a daemon? 130
What is an intranet?. 130
What are some of the basic TCP/IP commands? 130
What are the important command operators? 130
How do I use online help? 131
How can one make long commands easier? 132
What is the meaning of [] in command syntax? 132
What are some network commands to handle files? 132
How do I find files? 133
How do I archive and compress files?. 134
What commands display processing status? 136
What commands are available to manage processes? 137
What commands handle user management? 139
What commands handle job management?. 140
How can I make a banner? 140
How do I set date and time? 140
How do I power down the system? 141
What are some networking commands? 141
When should I use a HOWTO? 142
Where do I find HOWTOs? 142
What is a man page? 142
How do I find a man page? 142
What is the syntax for the man command? 142
How do I print a man page? 143
How do authors divide the man pages?. 143
How does Red Hat divide the man pages? 143
How do I find multiple man page sections for a command or call? . 144
Where are man pages found online? 144
How can I search the man pages for a string? 144
How do I see the source of a man page? 144
Can I write my own man page? 145
What happens when I access a man page? 145
How do I move about in a man page? 145
What are some keywords for searching man pages? 145
How do I find out about compatible hardware? 146
What types of editors are available? 146
What types of graphic programs are available?. 147
What types of programs are available to do programming? 147
What types of utilities are available? 147
What package supports basic networking? 148
What man pages are available for networking administration? . . . 148
What package supports network debugging? 148
How do I load balance a router? 148
How do I configure Ethernet network adapters? 148
How do I create an intranet server? 149

How do I set up Network File System (NFS)? 149
How do I set up a Linux User Group? 149
Where do I find names for network devices? 149
What program do you use to do network configuration? 149
Where is the host name kept? 149
Where do I find network names and their IP addresses? 150
How do I check the routing status to another host? 150
How do I check on a network's status? 150
What is a UUCP network? 150
What is a major disadvantage of a UUCP network? 150
Who are the primary users of a UUCP network? 150
What is a major contribution to the Internet from UUCP? 150

Chapter 14—**General Networking Tips 151**
What is a general networking tip? 151
How do I start and stop a service? 151
How can I get reports on the status of the processes? 151
Is there a method for getting even more process information? 152
What is the importance of rc.sysinit? 152
What is the default run level of the /etc/init file? 153
How do I display the etc/inittab file? 153
How do I find more information on the inittab file? 153
What is the importance of the rc.local script? 153
What are some of the archiving commands? 153
What are some of the essential networking daemons? 154
What are the basic commands for clock management? 154
What are some of the commands for handling the hardware? 155
What are some of the basic commands for managing the kernel? . . 155
What are the basic user networking commands called? 155
How can I automate tasks? 155
What is an issue concerning more than one Ethernet board? 156
What is the first Ethernet device called? 156
What are some of the network devices supported in the kernel? . . . 156
Is there a HOWTO available on Ethernet? 156
What is the importance of the linuxconf tool? 157
How do I shut down a network? 157
How do I prepare for system crashes? 157
What are some actions I need to take to avoid a crash? 158
What are some actions I should not do to avoid a crash? 158
How can I do a quick check of the storage space? 158
What are some important filesystem tools? 159
How do I use badblocks? 159
How do I use debugfs? 159
How do I use dumpe2fs? 159
How do I use e2fsck? 160

How do I use fsck? 160
How do I use mke2fs? 160
How do I use tune2fs? 160
What does the traceroute command do? 160
What is the w utility? 161
What does perror do? 161
What is Samba? 161
What are some of the important components of Samba? 161
What are some of the important Samba files ? 161
Where can I find more information on Samba? 162
What is RPM? 162
What is the basic strategy for keeping a system up to date? 162
Where can I get the latest kernel upgrade? 162
How do I upgrade using a stock kernel by Red Hat? 162
What is the importance of Linux kernel 2.2.x? 163
What are some important kernel 2.2 enhancements? 163
What is a major difference between kernel 2.2 and 2.3? 163
What general networking RFCs are available? 164

Chapter 15—**Shell Tips** **165**
What is a shell? 165
What is bash? 165
Are there other shells besides bash? 165
What is sh-utils? 165
What are the basic shell operators? 167
How can I find a shell command? 167
What is a script? 167
How do I run a script? 167

Chapter 16—**GNU Project Tips** **169**
What is the GNU Project? 169
Where do I find information on the GNU Project? 169
How do I find information about installed GNU
Project distributions? 169
What are some of the GNU Project distributions? 169
What are some general GNU utilities? 171
What are some file GNU utilities? 172
How do I use chgrp? 172
How do I use chmod? 173
How do I use chown? 173
How do I use cp? 174
How do I use df? 174
How do I use dir? 174
How do I use ls? 175
How do I use mkdir? 175

How do I use mknod? 175
How do I use mv? 175
How do I use rm? 176
How do I use rmdir? 176

Chapter 17—**Packaging Tips 177**
What is a package? 177
What does RPM stand for? 177
What is RPM? 177
Where do I get more information on RPM?. 178
How do I find a package using RPM? 178
How do I see if I have an installed package? 178
How do I find all packages on my machine? 178
How do I find detailed information on a package? 178
How do I find filenames for an installed package? 178
How do I find a package associated to a file?. 179
How do I install a package? 179
How do I uninstall a package? 179
How do I upgrade a package?. 179
How do I verify a package? 179
What packages support archiving? 179
What package supports browsing? 179
What package supports chat (IRC)? 180
What package supports compiling? 180
What packages support debugging? 180
What packages support editing? 180
What package supports faxing? 180
What packages support file management? 180
What package supports ftp?. 180
What packages support GIF files? 181
What packages support JPEG files? 181
What packages support mail? 181
What package supports network debugging? 181
What package supports basic networking? 181
What packages support newsgroup? 182
What package supports scheduling? 182
What packages support scripting? 182
What package supports security? 182
What packages support sound? 182
What packages support text manipulation?. 182
What packages support TIF files? 183
What package supports Usenet news? 183
What packages support version control? 183

Chapter 18—**Apache Server Tips** **185**
What is an Apache server? 185
What is a Web server? 185
What features or functions does an Apache server support? 185
How do I install Apache RPM? 186
How do I upgrade the Apache RPM? 186
What is httpd? 186
What are the essential Apache configuration files? 186
Where does the Apache RPM install files? 187
What are the golden rules for server configuration maintenance? . . 187
What are some of the specific types of information found in httpd.conf? 187
How can I test my server? 187
What are some of the specific types of information found in srm.conf? 188
What are some of the specific types of information found in access.conf? 188
What is the difference between a standalone and an inetd server? . 188
Why might I want an inetd server configuration? 188
How do I run an inetd server? 188
Is there any essential requirement of the inetd configuration? 189
How do I start a standalone server? 189
How do I start an inetd server? 189
How can I stop the Apache server? 189
What are two important URLs to find information? 189
What are some of the books written on the Apache server? 190

Chapter 19—**Words and Acronyms Tips** **191**
What is API? 191
What is ARP? 191
What is ARPA? 191
What is a backbone? 191
What is BBS? 191
What is BGP? 192
What is a bridge? 192
What is CSLIP? 192
What is a daemon? 192
What is dip? 192
What is DNS? 192
What is a domain? 192
What is EGP? 192
What is electronic mail? 193
What is Ethernet? 193
What is a file? 193
What is file management? 193

What is a filesystem? 193
What is a firewall? 193
What is FTP? 193
What is a gateway? 194
What is the GNU Project? 194
What is a host? 194
What is ICMP?. 194
What is an internet (small i)? 194
What is the Internet? 194
What is IP? 194
What is an IP address? 195
What is IRC? 195
What is a kernel? 195
What is a LAN? 195
What is a library? 195
What is a man page? 195
What is masquerading? 195
What is MIME? 195
What is a module? 196
What is NFS? 196
What is NIS?. 196
What is NNTP? 196
What is a package? 196
What is PLIP? 196
What is a port? 197
What is PPP? 197
What is a printer? 197
What is a proxy? 197
What is quota? 197
What is RARP? 197
What is a resolver? 197
What is an RFC?. 198
What is RIP?. 198
What is a route?. 198
What is routing?. 198
What is RPC? 198
What is RPM? 198
What is sendmail?. 198
What is a server? 199
What is a service? 199
What is SLIP? 199
What is SMTP? 199
What is spool?. 199
What is TCP? 199
What is TCP/IP?. 199

What is TFTP? . . . 199
What is URL? . . . 200
What is Usenet? . . . 200
What is UUCP? . . . 200
What is WWW? . . . 200

Chapter 20—**System Call Tips . . . 201**
What is a system call? . . . 201
What is the first step in creating a new system call? . . . 201
What do I need to create a prototype? . . . 201
Is there a simple method for creating a prototype? . . . 201
What are some of the system calls for file management? . . . 202
What are some of the system calls for directory management? . . . 202
What are some of the system calls for call processing management? . . . 203
What are some of the system calls for managing sockets? . . . 203
What are some of the system calls for timers? . . . 204
What are some of the system calls for filesystem management? . . . 204
What are some of the system calls for access management? . . . 205
What are some of the system calls for user management? . . . 205
What are some of the system calls for group management? . . . 205
What are some of the system calls to handle domains? . . . 205

Chapter 21—**Server/System Administration Tips . . . 207**
What is a system administrator? . . . 207
What are the broad requirements of a system administrator? . . . 207
What are some of the specific tasks of a system administrator? . . . 208
Where in the filesystem does a system administrator manage? . . . 208
What is a major security risk for the root? . . . 208
What is account management? . . . 209
What is customer service? . . . 209
What is the planning process? . . . 209
What types of communication tools are available? . . . 210
How do I get assistance to be a system administrator? . . . 210
What is a major tool for solving problems? . . . 210
What might be the most important task of a system administrator? . . . 211
How do I add a user to the system? . . . 211
How do I edit /etc/passwd? . . . 211
How do I edit /etc/group? . . . 212
How do I create a home directory? . . . 212
How do I copy files from /etc/skel to the new home? . . . 212
How do I change ownerships and permissions? . . . 212
How do I set the password? . . . 213

Chapter 22—**Red Hat Package Manager Tips** **215**
What is a package? 215
What are the fundamental features of RPM? 215
What are the basic modes for using RPM? 215
How do I get the version number of RPM? 216
How can I get online help about RPM? 216
What are the basic steps in building any RPM? 216
How do I find a list of all RPMs? 216
How do I find just RPMs for Red Hat Linux? 217
How do I find Red Hat documentation on RPM? 217
How do I install a package? 217
What are the options for rpm -i? 217
How can I install a package from an FTP site? 218
How can I reinstall a package that is corrupt? 218
How can I install files already installed by another package? 218
How do I uninstall a package? 218
How do I handle the "... break dependencies" error? 218
How do I update a package? 218
How do I use RPM to query about a package? 219
What are the options for query? 219
What kind of information do I get when I enter rpm –qi? 219
How do I use RPM to verify a package is installed properly? 220

Chapter 23—**Red Hat Tools Tips** **221**
What tools can I find in the control panel? 221
What can I do with helptool? 221
What can I do with kernelcfg? 222
What can I do with linuxconf? 222
What can I do with modemtool? 222
What can I do with netcfg? 222
What can I do with printtool? 222
What can I do with thsysv? 222
What can I do with timetool? 223
What other tools are available besides those in the control panel? . . 223
What does ab do? 223
What does apxs do? 223
What does comanche do? 223
What does fetchmailconf do? 224
What does glint do? 224
What does installit do? 224
What does kbdconfig do? 224
What does makehistory do? 224
What does mouseconfig do? 224
What does newsrequeue do? 224
What does ntsysv do? 224

What does readprofile do? 225
What does scsi_info do?. 225
What does setup do? 225
What does swat do?. 225
What does timeconfig do?. 225
What does usermount do? 225
What does userpasswd do? 225
What does Xconfigurator do? 226

Chapter 24—**Hardware Tips 227**
What is important to know about hardware?. 227
How do I find out about compatible hardware? 227
What type of processors will Linux run on?. 228
What is the /proc file? 228
What is the /proc/cpuinfo file? 228
What is the /proc/pci file? 228
What other types of information are available through /proc?. . . . 228
What types of information are found in /proc/interrupts? 229
What types of information are found in /proc/ioports? 229
What are some of the network devices supported in the kernel?. . . 229
What is /dev? 229
What are some of the files found in the /dev directory? 229
What is /dev/null? 230
What is /etc/fstab? 230
How do I determine keyboard rate? 230
How can I determine if the kernel identifies my mouse? 230
How is a generic mouse linked? 230
What is /dev/printer?. 230
Where is an entry on a physical printer kept? 231
What are essential files for the printer?. 231
What is the /etc/printcap file? 231
How do I define a printer using printtool? 231
How do I set up serial communication devices? 232
What is a rule about modems? 232
How do I check that the CD-ROM driver is in the kernel? 232
What is an issue with more than one Ethernet board? 232
What is the first Ethernet device called? 232
Is there a HOWTO available on Ethernet? 233
What are some of the commands for handling the hardware? 233
How do I find storage device space data?. 233
What are the purposes of mmap and munmap? 233
What does scsi_info do?. 234
What does setup do? 234
Are there any newsgroups on hardware for Linux?. 234
What RFCs are available on hardware devices? 234

Are there any HOWTOs on hardware devices? 234
Are there any man pages on hardware devices? 235

Chapter 25—**Filesystem Structure Tips 237**
How do I use ls?. 237
What are the original directories in the Red Hat distribution? 238
How do I display the basic contents of the filesystem? 238
How do I display the contents of the filesystem? 239
What are the basic contents of the /bin directory? 239
What are the basic contents of the /boot directory? 240
What are the basic contents of the /dev directory?. 240
What are the basic contents of the /etc directory? 250
What are the basic contents of the /home directory?. 251
What are the basic contents of the /lib directory? 253
What are the basic contents of the /lost+found directory?. 254
What are the basic contents of the /mnt directory? 254
What are the basic contents of the /proc directory? 254
What are the basic contents of the /root directory? 255
What are the basic contents of the /sbin directory? 255
What are the basic contents of the /tmp directory? 256
What are the basic contents of the /usr directory? 256
What are the basic contents of the /var directory? 256

Appendix A—**HOWTOs Table of Contents 257**
Linux Benchmarking HOWTO. 257
The Linux Busmouse HOWTO 258
The Linux CD-ROM HOWTO 259
Configuration HOWTO 261
DNS HOWTO 262
Linux Ethernet-HOWTO. 263
Firewall and Proxy Server HOWTO 270
Linux Hardware Compatibility HOWTO 271
The Linux Intranet Server HOWTO 274
Linux IPCHAINS-HOWTO. 276
Linux IPX-HOWTO 278
ISP-Hookup-HOWTO 280
The Linux Keyboard and Console HOWTO 281
Red Hat Linux KickStart HOWTO 282
The Linux Electronic Mail Administrator HOWTO 283
The Linux Mail User HOWTO 285
The Linux Modem-HOWTO 286
The Linux MP3 HOWTO 290
Multicast over TCP/IP HOWTO 290
HOWTO: Multi Disk System Tuning 292
Linux Networking-HOWTO (Previously the Net-3 HOWTO) 295

The Linux Networking Overview HOWTO 299
NFS HOWTO 300
The Linux NIS(YP)/NYS/NIS+ HOWTO 301
Linux PCMCIA HOWTO 302
The Linux Plug-and-Play-HOWTO 304
Linux PPP HOWTO 306
The Linux Printing HOWTO. 308
RPM HOWTO (RPM at Idle) 310
The Linux SCSI Programming HOWTO 311
Linux Security HOWTO 312
The Linux Serial HOWTO 314
Linux Shadow Password HOWTO. 318
SMB HOWTO 320
Building and Installing Software Packages for Linux 320
The Linux Sound HOWTO 321
The Linux UUCP HOWTO 323
Virtual Services HOWTO 324
Linux VPN Masquerade HOWTO 326
Linux WWW HOWTO 327
The X Window User HOWTO 329

Appendix B—**Listing of Man Pages for Networking Administration and Maintenance 333**

Appendix C—**Networking Request for Comments (RFCs) 345**

Appendix D—**List of Linux 6.0 Server Packages 351**

Appendix E—**Listing of Man Pages for Linux 6.0. . . . . 359**

Index 377

Introductory Remarks

This book is the second book I have written on the Red Hat Linux distribution. The emphasis is on Linux 6.0; however, one must recognize that Linux 6.0 is built on past distributions. It originates out of the reading of the various Linux newsgroups. For example, the last chapter on filesystem structure is based on the general question, "How do I find 'x' file?"

A smart system administrator knows how to find information, rather than thinking he or she knows it all. This book emphasizes where to find information and the types of content in sources. There is a long appendix dedicated to tables of contents of HOWTOs so the reader can quickly determine if a given HOWTO has the type of information required to answer a question or solve a problem. In addition, there is an appendix giving a listing of most of the man pages for the Red Hat distribution.

This book focuses on the server and system environment. The prior book gave emphasis to the OS commands; those are the ones that impact the kernel's configuration. This environment is the one of the network or an intranet, and Internet access. Also it was taken into account that an individual may choose to have a server, and is a limited node to the Internet but required to know about system administration.

The companion CD-ROM included with this book contains Red Hat Linux Publisher's Edition, version 6.1. For further information, see the page opposite the inside back cover.

Skill Level and Topic Table

This table has two parts: Part I is a listing of chapters and appendices according to skill levels (beginning, intermediate, and advanced), and Part II lists some major topics and associated chapters and appendices. The chapters are listed under each skill level and topic alphabetically.

Part I

Beginning Level

- Apache Server Tips (18)
- E-mail Server Tips (2)
- File Server Tips (3)
- Filesystem Structure Tips (25)
- General Networking Tips (14)
- GNU Project Tips (16)
- HOWTOs Table of Contents (A)
- Internet Server Tips (4)
- List of Man Pages for Linux 6.0 (E)
- Miscellaneous Server Tips (8)
- Network Administrative Tips (13)
- News Server (5)
- Packaging Tips (17)
- Red Hat Package Manager Tips (22)
- Red Hat Tools Tips (23)
- Security Server Tips (7)
- Server Packages (D)
- Server Type Tips (1)
- Shell Tips (15)
- Words and Acronyms Tips (19)

Intermediate Level

- E-mail Server Tips (2)
- File Server Tips (3)
- Filesystem Structure Tips (25)
- Hardware Tips (24)
- HOWTOs Table of Contents (A)
- Internet Server Tips (4)
- List of Man Pages for Linux 6.0 (E)
- Man Pages for Network Administration (B)

Network Administrative Tips (13)
Network File System (NFS) Tips (12)
Network Information System (NIS) Tips (11)
Point-to-Point Protocol (PPP) Tips (10)
Red Hat Tools Tips (23)
Remote Administration Server Tips (6)
Security Server Tips (7)
Server/System Administration Tips (21)
System Calls Tips (20)
TCP/IP Tips (9)

Advanced Level
File Server Tips (3)
Filesystem Structure Tips (25)
Hardware Tips (24))
HOWTOs Table of Contents (A)
List of Man Pages for Linux 6.0 (E)
Man Pages for Network Administration (B)
Network File System (NFS) Tips (12)
Network Information System (NIS) Tips (11)
Networking Request for Comments (RFCs) (C)
Point-to-Point Protocol (PPP) Tips (10)
Red Hat Tools Tips (23)
Remote Administration Server Tips (6)
Security Server Tips (7)
Server/System Administration Tips (21)
System Call Tips (20)
TCP/IP Tips (9)

Part II

Administration
File Server Tips (3)
Filesystem Structure Tips (25)
General Networking Tips (14)
GNU Project Tips (16)
Man Pages for Network Administration (B)
Miscellaneous Server Tips (8)
Network Administrative Tips (13)
Network File System (NFS) Tips (12)
Network Information System (NIS) Tips (11)
Networking Request for Comments (RFCs) (C)
Packaging Tips (17)
Point-to-Point Protocol (PPP) Tips (10)

- Red Hat Package Manager Tips (22)
- Red Hat Tools Tips (23)
- Remote Administration Server Tips (6)
- Security Server Tips (7)
- Server/System Administration Tips (21)
- Shell Tips (15)
- System Call Tips (20)
- TCP/IP Tips (9)
- Words and Acronyms Tips (19)

Documentation
- HOWTOs Table of Contents (A)
- List of Man Pages for Linux 6.0 (E)
- Man Pages for Network Administration (B)
- Networking Request for Comments (RFCs) (C)
- Red Hat Package Manager Tips (22)
- Server Packages (D)
- Server Type Tips (1)

Hardware
- General Networking Tips (14)
- Hardware Tips (24)

Internet/Networking
- Apache Server Tips (18)
- E-mail Server Tips (2)
- General Networking Tips (14)
- Hardware Tips (24)
- Internet Server Tips (4)
- Man Pages for Network Administration (B)
- Network Administrative Tips (13)
- Network File System (NFS) Tips (12)
- Network Information System (NIS) Tips (11)
- Networking Request for Comments (RFCs) (C)
- News Server Tips (5)
- Point-to-Point Protocol (PPP) Tips (10)
- Remote Administration Server Tips (6)
- Security Server Tips (7)
- System Call Tips (20)
- TCP/IP Tips (9)

Protocols
- Network File System (NFS) Tips (12)
- Network Information System (NIS) Tips (11)
- Point-to-Point Protocol (PPP) Tips (10)
- TCP/IP Tips (9)

Servers/Services
- Apache Server Tips (18)
- E-mail Server Tips (2)
- File Server Tips (3)
- Internet Server Tips (4)
- Miscellaneous Server Tips (8)
- News Server Tips (5)
- Remote Administration Server Tips (6)
- Security Server Tips (7)
- Server Packages (D)
- Server Type Tips (1)
- Server/System Administration Tips (21)

System
- File Server Tips (3)
- Filesystem Structure Tips (25)
- General Networking Tips (14)
- GNU Project Tips (16)
- Network Administrative Tips (13)
- Network File System (NFS) Tips (12)
- Network Information System (NIS) Tips (11)
- Networking Request for Comments (RFCs) (C)
- Point-to-Point Protocol (PPP) Tips (10)
- Red Hat Tools Tips (23)
- Server/System Administration Tips (21)
- Shell Tips (15)
- System Call Tips (20)
- TCP/IP Tips (9)

Chapter 1

Server Type Tips

This chapter looks at general questions about types of servers.

What is a server?

A server is a computer that is the centerpiece of a network (intranet) that can process one or more network services.

What is a three-tier client/server?

A three-tier client/server is a way to view data problems. The separate data problems are:

- Storage and retrieval
- Manipulation
- Presentation

What is a Linux server?

It is a server that runs on a Linux operating system.

What is a service?

A service is a process that implements a function for other processes.

What are examples of services?

The essential network services are application, e-mail, file, Internet, messaging, newsgroups, print, proxy, remote administration, and security (gateway and firewall).

What is an application server?

An application server runs the back end or server side of an application. It has been optimized to execute software at top speed. Two special servers of this type are Internet and databases that use a query language.

What is a caching-only server?

This server functions like a domain server except it handles the network level DNS queries for local running applications. It caches the information, thus its name.

What is a database server?

A database server is designed to handle databases such as Oracle or SQL. Client applications are used to connect to the server.

What is a domain name server?

This server holds all the information on hosts within an authoritative zone. It is also called a master name server.

What is an e-mail server?

An e-mail server provides routing and storing of electronic mail between any two e-mail accounts. One of the more common Linux mail transport programs is the University of California at Berkeley's sendmail originally authored by Eric Allman. Two e-mail protocols are Simple Mail Transfer Protocol (SMTP) and Post Office Protocol (POP, not to be confused with the Point of Presence Protocol).

What is a file server?

A file server provides the primary function of most networks. It is the location of the file manager.

What is an Internet server?

An Internet server is a special application server that handles Hypertext Transfer Protocol (HTTP, the basic World Wide Web protocol), File Transfer Protocol (FTP), and Gopher requests. Services include Web page publishing, posting information files and programs, and managing Uniform Resource Locators (URLs). This is usually referred to as a Web server.

What is an FTP server?

A File Transfer Protocol (FTP) server handles transfers among machines across a network. There are two types, private and anonymous. Private is for a user-only site. Anonymous is available for anyone, and thus has a high security risk level. This server type is discussed in more detail in Chapter 6.

What is a messaging server?

A messaging server manages the various messaging services such as a LAN package. It can be configured as an Internet e-mail gateway. It can be used for sorting news services for interest to corporate employees or for dialing into paging services.

What is a network file server (NFS)?

This type of server uses the Network File System (NFS) for connecting disks on a remote system to a local system and giving the appearance that they are located in the same physical site. It allows you to mount files from different computers over a TCP/IP network.

What is a network information server (NIS)?

This type of server uses the Network Information System (NIS) to provide generic database access facilities. It makes the network appear as a single system.

What is a newsgroup server?

A newsgroup server manages messaging using the Network News Transport Protocol (NNTP). InterNetNews (INN) is a news package commonly used on Linux machines. See RFC 977 for further details about NNTP.

What is a print server?

A print server manages all printing requests across the network for attached printers. It does not handle the printer requests of attached printers to individual nodes or terminals. Samba, a software product (protocol), is used by Microsoft operating systems to allow a Linux user to communicate to a printer.

What is a proxy server?

A proxy server is a server that acts for another server. This server is used in network security solutions.

What is a remote administration server?

A remote administration server manages incoming connections from a remote client. This is done using modems, ISDN interfaces, or Point-to-Point Tunneling Protocol (PPTP) connections.

What is a security server?

A security server is usually thought of as a firewall; however, it can come in at least two other flavors, gateway and administration. It is a server that includes such services as logon authentication, access control, and permissions.

What is a gateway server?

A gateway server is a server that manages outgoing messaging. It can be used to manage the internal uses of e-mail and newsgroups.

What is a firewall server?

A firewall server is a security server to manage incoming messaging. It is used to prevent accessing internal IP addresses from external computers on the Internet.

What is an SMB server?

A Session Message Block (SMB, or Samba) server uses a protocol to handle Microsoft Windows 95, 98, 2000, or NT file and printer requests. The next evolutionary step by Microsoft may be the Common Internet File System (CIFS).

What is an inetd server?

An Internet Daemon (inetd) server starts at system boot time and uses the startup file /etc/inetd.conf to manage the listed services performed by daemons. A daemon is a program that opens a port and accepts an incoming connection while the parent continues listing for the next request. This is a waste of resources.

What is a UUCP server?

A UNIX-to-UNIX CoPy server handles requests from remote sites over telephone lines. There are a number of varieties of UUCP. The version commonly distributed with Linux is Taylor UUCP.

What are the hard drive requirements?

The server needs 1.6 GB of minimum storage. Other factors include number of users, applications, and utilities.

What are the network adapter requirements?

A network adapter is a requirement if you have to be connected to an Ethernet network. Companies that have network adapters that support Linux include 3Com, Allied Telesis, Digital Equipment Corporation (DEC), Fujitsu, Hewlett-Packard (HP), Novell, and SMC (Western Digital).

What is the SCSI controller requirement?

The Small Computer System Interface (SCSI) controller requires support. Some of the companies that have supported controllers are Adaptec, BusLogic, DPT, Future Domain, ICP-Vortex, Seagate, Sound Blaster, Trantor, and Western Digital.

What is the difference between a server and a workstation?

A server handles messaging requests on a network for groups of people, while a workstation (node or terminal) handles similar types of messaging on an individual basis. A workstation can be a standalone machine.

How do I create mount points?

You need to have mount points for the server and other devices. For example, the following creates mount points for a DOS/Win floppy, the CD-ROM, the Windows partition, the parallel port Zip drive, and an NFS directory:

```
# cd /mnt
    /mnt# mkdir floppy; mkdir cdrom; mkdir win; mkdir zip; mkdir server
```

Now edit the file /etc/fstab and add the following entries:

```
/dev/fd0         /mnt/floppy    vfat       user,noauto 0 1
/dev/cdrom       /mnt/cdrom     iso9660    ro,user,noauto 0 1
/dev/hda1        /mnt/win       vfat       user,noauto 0 1
/dev/sda4        /mnt/zip       vfat       user,noauto,exec 0 1
server:/export   /mnt/server    nfs        defaults
```

How do I set up an X server?

See Configuration HOWTO v1.2.6; January 19, 1999, by Guido Gonzato (guido@ibogeo.df.unibo.it).

What is an archie server?

In the early days of anonymous FTP archie, a database query program was developed to contact anonymous FTP sites worldwide. It indexes a site's information into the local site and then does the querying. It is still a popular service. The counterpart to archie is veronica, which searches gopher servers.

What are some man pages on the Apache Web server?

Here are four man pages on the Apache Web server:

ab	benchmarking tool for Apache Web server
apachectl	control interface for the Apache Web server
httpd	Apache Hypertext Transfer Protocol server
rotatelogs	rotates Apache logs without killing the server

What are some man pages on news servers?

Here are six man pages on the news servers:

Cleanfeed	spam filter for Usenet new server
getlist	gets a list from an NNTP server
innxbatch	sends xbatched Usenet articles to a remote NNTP server
innxmit	sends Usenet articles to a remote NNTP server
nnrpd	NNTP server for on-campus hosts
nntpget	gets Usenet articles from a remote NNTP server

What are some man pages on a NetWare server?

Here are seven man pages on the NetWare server:

nwfsctrl	performs NetWare server control command
nwfsinfo	prints NetWare file server information
nwfstime	displays and sets a NetWare server's date and time
nwsfind	finds a NetWare server
nwuserlist	lists logged users on a NetWare server
pserver	NetWare print server
slist	lists available NetWare servers

What are some man pages on a remote server?

Here are seven man pages on the remote server:

fingerd	remote user information server
rdistd	remote file distribution server program
rexecd	remote execution server
rlogind	remote login server
rquotad	remote quota server
rshd	remote shell server
talkd	remote user communication server

What are some man pages on server daemons?

Here are 19 man pages on server daemons:

fingerd	remote user information server
ftpd	File Transfer Protocol server
httpd	Apache Hypertext Transfer Protocol server
identd	TCP/IP IDENT protocol server
inetd	Internet super server
named	Internet domain name server (DNS)
nnrpd	NNTP server for on-campus hosts
rdistd	remote file distribution server program
rexecd	remote execution server
rlogind	remote login server
rquotad	remote quota server
rshd	remote shell server
rstatd	kernel statistics server
rwhod	system status server
smbd	server to provide SMB/CIFS services to clients
talkd	remote user communication server
telnetd	Telnet protocol server
tftpd	Trivial File Transfer Protocol server
timed	time server daemon

What are some man pages on Samba?

Here are three man pages on Samba:

samba	a Windows SMB/CIFS fileserver for UNIX
smbclient	FTP-like client to access SMB/CIFS resources on servers

smbd	server to provide SMB/CIFS services to clients

What are some man pages on the Internet server?

Here are five man pages on the Internet server:

identd	TCP/IP IDENT protocol server
inetd	Internet super server
inetd.conf	Internet server's database
named	Internet domain name server (DNS)
nslookup	queries Internet name servers interactively

What are some man pages on the NIS server?

Here are three man pages on the NIS server:

yypoll	returns version and master server of an NIS map
ypset	binds ypbind to a particular NIS server
ypwhich	returns name of NIS server or map master

What are some man pages on various types of servers?

Here are 14 man pages on various types of servers:

dig	sends domain name query packets to name servers
dnsquery	queries domain name servers using resolver
ftpd	File Transfer Protocol server
ftpshut	closes down an FTP server at a given time
host	looks up host names using domain server
ncpmount	mounts all volumes of a specified Novell file server
rstatd	kernel statistics server
rwhod	system status server
telnetd	Telnet protocol server
tftpd	Trivial File Transfer Protocol server
timed	time server daemon
xferlog	FTP server logfile
Xconfigurator	configures XFree server and display
Xserver	X Window System display server

Chapter 2

E-mail Server Tips

This chapter focuses on an electronic mail (e-mail) server and its functions. This chapter also discusses different types of mail applications and mail agents.

What is electronic mail?

It is the service that permits you to exchange messages with another user on a remote host without requiring you to know how to access that host.

What are the two basic e-mail agents?

The two agents are transport and user. A mail transport agent (MTA) is the program that sends a mail file from one computer to another. A mail user agent (MUA) is the program that manages an e-mail message.

What is required to get e-mail?

The basic requirements are the IP address or name of an ISP's mail server when sendmail is used. The **popclient** program in the **/usr/bin** directory is used to get the e-mail. In addition, the type of Post Office Protocol (POP) the ISP uses, username, and a password are required.

What is the basic functionality of POP?

The Post Office Protocol (POP) works at a system-independent level to handle e-mail. It allows a client machine to connect to a mail server and transfer the mail. The latest version is POP3. The latest RFC on POP3 is RFC 1957, "Some Observations on Implementations of the Post Office Protocol (POP3)" by R. Nelson (June 1996). A new RFC comes out on POP every several years (there have been at least five prior RFCs on POP3 since 1988).

Note: Do not confuse this POP with Point-of-Presence.

What are some of the available mail commands?

The commands listed here are the initial commands to call various mail programs:

elm	a mail-handling program that you use to create, compose, edit, and send mail and organize the mail into different folders
fetchmail	uses a Point-to-Point (PPP) connect for you to get your mail from your Internet service provider (ISP)
mail	a minimal mail interface for sending, handling, or reading mail
pine	does Internet Usenet news and e-mail and uses pico as its text editor
procmail	processes incoming mail by searching messages for specified strings and handles the mail according to filters

How does elm work?

Upon elm's startup it reads a set of configuration variables found in the elm.rc file in /usr/lin/elm. It next attempts to read the .elm/elnrc file in the home directory. This file is created when one of the "save options" is selected from the elm options menu.

Note: Elm is no longer under development.

Is there a HOWTO available on e-mail?

See Mail-HOWTO.gz. This HOWTO shows how to set up and maintain e-mail. It is occasionally posted to comp.os.linux.announce.

What is the purpose of the aliases file?

There are three basic reasons for using an alias:

- Pass e-mail to an application for processing
- Redirect mail to a file

- Remap an e-mail address to another username

What packages support mail?

At least nine application packages support mail in Red Hat Linux distribution (version number and release number on version 6.0):

elm	terminal mode mailer (2.5.0.0.2pre8)
exmh	graphical interface to the MH mail system (2.0.2-7)
fetchmail	remote mail service (5.0.0-1)
mailx	/bin/mail program, the basic program (8.1.1-8)
metamail	implementation of Multipurpose Internet Mail Extensions (MIME) (2.7-20)
mutt	full-screen Linux mailer (0.95.4us-4)
nmh	mailer with a command-line interface only (0.27-8)
pine	text-based mail and news client that uses the editor pico (4.10-2)
xmailbox	notification of received mail program on the X Window System (2.5-7)

Note: To find the latest version and release numbers of any above package on your filesystem, enter rpm –q package-name.

What is sendmail?

It is a very powerful and complex mailing program. In the simplest of terms, it is a mail router. Its configuration file is sendmail.cf. The definitive book on sendmail.cf is nearly 800 pages. The mail agent's RPM's version and release is 8.9.3-10 for Red Hat Linux 6.0.

Note: For additional information, see http://www.sendmail.org/faq.

What are the important functions of sendmail?

There are three important functions of sendmail:

- Mail router—mail transport agent (MTA)
- SMTP client—delivers mail to SMTP server
- SMTP server—mail daemon

Note: sendmail is not a final delivery agent.

What is the first step in compiling sendmail?

Before compiling sendmail, one should read the following documents:

- FAQ
- Readme
- Release notes
- Known bugs

What is a critical step in installing sendmail?

A critical step in installing sendmail is backing up any files to be replaced. Do not forget the old sendmail daemon. These files are used to restore sendmail if something goes wrong in the installation.

What are the important functions of the sendmail configuration file?

There are three important functions of a sendmail configuration file:

- Sets the sendmail environment
- Defines the mailer's characteristics
- Specifies the rulesets for managing addresses and selected mailers

What is the final step in installing sendmail?

The final step in installing sendmail is test, test, and test again. People get somewhat angry when their mail does not work.

What if sendmail cannot be configured?

Try http://www.sendmail.org.

Do you want to send e-mail or do you want to use sendmail? If you want to send e-mail, perhaps you should consider another package that is less difficult to configure such as smail or zmailer. There is also qmail found at http://www.qmail.org. If sendmail is the package you want to use, look at http://www.harker.com/webgencf. A user interface asks questions and a sendmail.cf is sent based on your answers.

What if sendmail hangs?

At the lilo prompt try linux init s. This input puts you in a single user mode. If sendmail does not start when trying to make a connection, the possible problem is the local host name is unresolved.

Ensure that your host name is the second entry in /etc/hosts. Use <ctrl>d to boot to the multi-user mode and do an edit if required.

Why should I upgrade my sendmail package?

The two obvious reasons for upgrading your sendmail package periodically are enhanced features and functions for security and spam.

Is there any method for stopping spamming with sendmail?

There are two changes you can make to /etc/sendmail.cf:

First, change the Privacy Options line to read:

PrivacyOptions=authwarnings,nexpn,novrfy

Second, change the SMTP Greeting Message line to read:

SmtpGreetingMessage=$j Sendmail $v/$Z; $b NO UCE C=country-code L=Location-code

Note: For further information on e-mail abuse, see http://www.mail-abuse.org.

What is MIME?

Multipurpose Internet Mail Extensions is an e-mail system that permits the attaching of binary files such as images, executable programs, and sound files.

Is there a way to filter e-mail?

The procmail program found under the /usr/bin directory can be used to filter e-mail such as spam.

What are the functions of an alias?

An alias has at least three functions:

- Maps e-mail addresses to other user names
- Directs mail to files
- Passes e-mail messages to other applications for processing

What is SMTP?

SMTP stands for Simple Mail Transfer Protocol. It is the standard for transferring e-mail over the Internet. It defines how programs exchange Internet e-mail. For Linux, the sendmail program supports SMTP connections.

Note: No matter the type of machine, whether it be a Sun workstation or an Apple computer, if both have SMTP, mail can be exchanged.

What is the basic RFC for SMTP?

The Request for Comments for SMTP is RFC 821, "Simple Mail Transfer Protocol," by J. Postel (August 1982).

What is the Domain Name System (DNS)?

The Domain Name System maps host names and IP addresses through a distributed database architecture. A host name is a name such as mycompany.com, while the IP address takes the form of nnn.nnn.nnn.nnn.

What are the specific Red Hat Linux packages for e-mail?

The following list is of nine Red Hat Linux packages that support e-mail:

- elm (Version 2.5.0.0.2pre8)
- exmh (Version 2.0.2-7)
- fetchmail (Version 5.0.0-1)
- mailx (Version 8.1.1-8)
- metamail (Version 2.7-20)

- mutt (Version 0.95.4us-4)
- nmh (Version 0.27-8)
- pine (Version 4.10-2)
- xmailbox (Version 2.5-7)

What is the importance of bulletins for e-mail?

Bulletins can be used to distribute mail immediately to all POP users without the requirement of making individual copies.

What are some available RFCs on e-mail?

Twenty-six available Request for Comments (RFCs) on e-mail are:

- 1056—PCMAIL: A Distributed Mail System for Personal Computers. M.L. Lambert. (June 1988)
- 1123—Requirements for Internet Hosts—Application and Support. R.T. Braden. (October 1989)
- 1168—Intermail and Commercial Mail Relay Services. A. Westine, A.L. DeSchon, J. Postel, and C.E. Ward. (July 1990)
- 1176—Interactive Mail Access Protocol: Version 2. M.R. Crispin. (August 1990)
- 1203—Interactive Mail Access Protocol: Version 3. J. Rice. (February 1991)
- 1211—Problems with the maintenance of large mailing lists. A. Westine and J. Postel. (March 1991)
- 1327—Mapping between X.400 (1988) / ISO 10021 and RFC 822. S. Hardcastle-Kille. (May 1992)
- 1339—Remote Mail Checking Protocol. S. Dornerand and P. Resnick. (June 1992)
- 1343—A User Agent Configuration Mechanism for Multimedia Mail Format Information. N. Borenstein. (June 1992)
- 1344—Implications of MIME for Internet Mail Gateways. N. Borenstein. (June 1992)
- 1421—Privacy Enhancement for Internet Electronic Mail: Part I: Message Encryption and Authentication Procedures. J. Linn. (February 1993)
- 1422—Privacy Enhancement for Internet Electronic Mail: Part II: Certificate-Based Key Management. S. Kent. (February 1993)

- 1423—Privacy Enhancement for Internet Electronic Mail: Part III: Algorithms, Modes, and Identifiers. D. Balenson. (February 1993)
- 1424—Privacy Enhancement for Internet Electronic Mail: Part IV: Key Certification and Related Services. B. Kaliski. (February 1993)
- 1506—A Tutorial on Gatewaying between X.400 and Internet Mail. J. Houttuin. (September 1993)
- 1711—Classifications in E-mail Routing. J. Houttuin. (October 1994)
- 1844—Multimedia E-mail (MIME) User Agent Checklist. E. Huizer. (August 1995)
- 1869—SMTP Service Extensions. J. Klensin, N. Freed, M. Rose, E. Stefferud, and D. Crocker. (November 1995)
- 1893—Enhanced Mail System Status Codes. G. Vaudreuil. (January 1996)
- 2033—Local Mail Transfer Protocol. J. Myers. (October 1996)
- 2045—Multipurpose Internet Mail Extensions (MIME) Part One: Format of Internet Message Bodies. N. Freed and N. Borenstein. (November 1996)
- 2046—Multipurpose Internet Mail Extensions (MIME) Part Two: Media Types. N. Freed and N. Borenstein. (November 1996)
- 2047—MIME (Multipurpose Internet Mail Extensions) Part Three: Message Header Extensions for Non-ASCII Text. K. Moore. (November 1996)
- 2048—Multipurpose Internet Mail Extension (MIME) Part Four: Registration Procedures. N. Freed, J. Klensin, and J. Postel. (November 1996)
- 2049—Multipurpose Internet Mail Extensions (MIME) Part Five: Conformance Criteria and Examples. N. Freed and N. Borenstein. (November 1996)
- 2110—MIME E-mail Encapsulation of Aggregate Documents, such as HTML (MHTML). J. Palme and A. Hopmann. (March 1997)

Note: When an RFC is revised, it is given a new number. For example, the Post Office Protocol has been revised about once every two years since 1988. Each time it gets a new number: 1081, 1225, 1460, 1725, and so forth.

Chapter 3

File Server Tips

3

This chapter looks at the basic server of any filesystem, the file server. The comprehension of how to manage and organize the files is critical so that you can have a file server and other types of servers that are also in the filesystem be as effective and efficient as possible. One needs to know the organization of the directories and associated files or file types. The file server has a file system within the Red Hat Linux filesystem.

Note: To see all available options for any command discussed in this chapter, you need to do a man command-name command. Also, see Chapter 25.

What is file management?

It is the process of managing and controlling file services on a server, that is, giving to users on a network the capabilities to read, write, delete, and copy files.

What is a file?

A file is an object in a path that has no further branching.

What are five common types of files?

- Directory
- Executable
- Special
- System
- User

Where are some of the executable files found?

Some of the executable files are found in the /bin, /usr/bin, and /usr/sbin directories.

Where are some of the special files found?

Some of the special files are found in the devices /dev directory.

How do I make a file?

Do a cd for change of directory and then use the command mkdir filename. Example filenames are bin and text.

How do I display a list of files?

Use the command ls to list all non-hidden files in your current directory.

How do I display a list of hidden files?

Use the command ls -a to list all hidden (invisible) files in your current directory. An example of an invisible file is any startup file.

How do I get information on a file?

Use the command info to display online help information for a specified command.

info	gives detailed information.	
	-f infofile	gives specific information; for example, info -f dev displays only "Is a directory"

Note: The syntax is info [options] command.

How do I copy a file?

cp	lets you copy a file (cp file1 file2)	
	-a	preserves file attributes
	-b	makes a backup
	-d	copies only a link

-i	prompts for permission before overwriting a file
-l	creates only hard disk links
-p	preserves file ownership, permissions, and time stamp
-R	recursively copies files in all subdirectories
-s	creates only soft links
-u	copies a file if its time stamp is later than that at the destination
-v	displays wordy messages as copying processes

How do I rename a file?

ln assigns a new name to a file

-b	backs up file change
-d	creates a hard link to a directory only
-f	removes the newly named file
-s	creates a symbolic link
-v	displays wordy messages

How do I move a file?

mv lets you move a file (limited to two arguments)

-b	makes a backup
-f	removes the file without a prompt
-i	prompts for permission before overwriting a file
-v	displays filename before moving it

Note: This command may be used to rename or move a file, depending on syntax used.

How do I delete a file?

rm lets you delete (remove) a file (rm * deletes all files in the current directory)

-f	removes the file without a prompt

-i	prompts for permission before overwriting a file
-R	recursively removes files in all subdirectories and directories
-v	displays filename before moving it

How do I change a file's time stamp?

touch — lets you create a file or update its time stamp

-a	changes access time only
-c	stops touch if file does not exist
-d time	uses time specified
-m	changes modification time only
-r file	uses the time from file instead of current time

How do I get symbolic link information?

stat — prints a variety of file information and can be used to verify symbolic links

How do I change file permissions?

chmod — lets you change file permissions

u	user
g	group
o	other
r	read
w	write
x	execute
+	adds
-	deletes
=	sets the permissions as specified
Example:	chmod ug+rx file1 means to add read and execute permissions to user and group of file1.

Other options reflect action:

-c	lists only files whose permissions changed
-f	stops any error message displays

-v	shows wordy displays of permission changes
-R	recursively changes file permissions in all subdirectories

Note: The syntax is chmod [options] permission files.

How do I change file ownership?

chown lets you change file owner and group

-c	lists only files whose permissions changed
-f	stops any error message displays
-v	shows wordy displays of permission changes
-R	recursively changes file permissions in all subdirectories

Note: The syntax is chown [options] user-name.group-name files. This command requires that you be logged in at the root to make changes.

How do I search for files?

There are at least five key commands used for searching for files:

find finds files based on criteria such as name, size, etc.

Note: When find is used without arguments, the output is a listing of all files in the current directory including the subdirectories. The syntax is find path [options]. To display all files that end in .gz, you would enter find . -name "*.gz". To see available options, use the man find command.

locate finds files based on a periodically updated database

Note: No options. The syntax is locate [string … stringN] with each string separated by a space. The command updatedb builds the database used by the locate command.

look searches files for a string and also is used as a dictionary command for words found in the /usr/dict directory

whereis finds binary, man pages, and source for a command

-b	searches only for binaries

	-m	searches only for man pages
	-v	searches only for sources
which	finds in the directories listed in the PATH environment the variable for a command	

Note: There are no options.

How do I find a command in a given directory?

To find the quota command under the /usr/bin directory you would enter find /usr/bin –name quota.

To find all the occurrences of the commands beginning with the letter q in the /usr directory you would enter find /usr –name q*.

How do I find files not accessed in a given period?

To find files in /usr/bin directory not accessed in the last ten days you would enter find /usr/bin –type f –atime +10.

This command reads "find in /usr/bin directory the regular files accessed more than ten days from this time."

How do I find files accessed in a given period?

To find files in /usr/bin directory not accessed in the last ten days you would enter find /usr/bin –type f –atime -10.

This command reads "find in /usr/bin directory the regular files accessed in less than ten days from this time."

How do I find files not modified in a given period?

To find files in /usr/bin directory not modified in the last ten days you would enter find /usr/bin –type f –mtime +10.

This command reads "find in /usr/bin directory the regular files modified more than ten days from this time."

How do I find files modified in a given period?

To find files in /usr/bin directory not modified in the last ten days you would enter find /usr/bin –type f –mtime -10.

This command reads find in /usr/bin directory the regular files modified in less than ten days from this time.

How do I find the location of the find command and its man pages?

To find the location of the find command and its man pages enter whereis find. The return is find: /usr/bin/find /usr/man/man1/find.1.

How do I find a file by size?

To find a file by size you would use find directory –size n[bckw] where n is the size and the letters stand for:

b	512-byte block (default)
c	bytes
k	kilobytes (1,024 bytes)
w	2-byte words

If you used find –size 10 it would find files of ten 512-byte blocks in the local directory.

How do I find files by type?

To find a file by type you would use find directory –type [bcdpfls] where the letters stand for:

b	block (buffered) special
c	character (unbuffered) special
d	directory
p	name pipe (FIFO)
f	regular file
l	symbolic link
s	socket

If you used find –type f it would find regular files in the local directory.

How do I use the locate command?

You can specify any list of files separated by a space. The **locate** command runs through the database files and displays a list of matches. You might enter **locate bit byte**. The results include the following:

/usr/include/bits/byteswap.h
/usr/include/byteswap.h
/usr/lib/tix4.1/demos/bitmaps/network.xbm
/usr/man/man1/kibitz.1
/usr/man/mann/bitmap.n
/usr/man3/byorder.3
/usr/src/linux-2.2.5/include/byteorder
/usr/src/linux-2.2.5/linux/bitops.h
/etc/charsets/t-61-8bit
/lib/modules/2.2.5-15/misc/pcbit.o

Note: The wildcard option works for this command. For example, you might enter **locate *ash**. Some of the results include:

/bin/bash
/bin/ash
/sbin/sash

How are text files displayed?

There are at least five basic commands for displaying files:

cat scrolls a file's contents across the screen

-b	numbers nonblank lines
-e	shows end of line as $ and all nonprinting characters
-n	numbers output lines beginning with number 1
-s	replaces multiple blank lines with a single blank line
-t	shows tabs as ^I
-v	shows nonprinting characters
-A	shows all characters including nonprinting ones

Note: The syntax is **cat [option] files**. This command can display contents or concatenate several files into one. For example, **cat file1 file2 > file3** combines the first two files into **file3**.

file	displays the type of data in a file	
	-c	displays a parsed form of the magic file
	-m	specifies other magic files
	-v	displays version number and exits
	-z	looks inside compressed files

Note: Uses the rules found in /usr/lib/magic.

less	displays a file one page at a time backward	
	-?	displays a list of commands that can be used with **less**
	-p text	displays the first line where **text** is found
	-s	reduces multiple blank lines to a single blank line
more	displays a file one page at a time forward	
	+N	displays the file starting at line **N**
	+/text	displays two lines before the **text**
	-s	reduces multiple blank lines to a single blank line
tail	displays part of a file	
	-n	displays **n** lines from file end
	+n	displays **n** lines from file start
	-f	reads the file at regular intervals and displays all new lines

How are compressed files displayed?

There are at least three commands for displaying compressed files:

zcat	displays a compressed file after decompressing
zless	displays a compressed file one page at a time backward
zmore	displays a compressed file one page at a time forward

Note: These commands can directly read files compressed with **gzip** or **compress** without requiring the use of **gunzip**. These commands are good for reading HOWTOs. Parallel commands are **cat**, **less**, and **more**.

How can I process text files?

There are at least 17 commands for text processing:

- cut
- dd
- diff
- expand
- fold
- grep
- lpr
- nl
- paste
- patch
- sed
- sort
- split
- tac
- tr
- uniq
- wc

How do I use cut?

cut — extracts specified sections from a line of text in a file

Option	Description
-b list	extracts the characters at positions specified in the list
-d char	specifies the character that delimits the fields (default is tab)
-f list	extracts the fields specified in a list using the default
-s	skips lines that do not contain delimited fields

Note: The syntax is cut [options] file.

How do I use dd?

dd — copies blocks of data from one file to another

Option	Description
bs=nbytes	reads and writes blocks of n bytes at a time
cbs=nbytes	converts blocks of n bytes at a time
count=nblocks	converts n blocks from input to output
bs=nbytes	reads and writes blocks of n bytes at a time
conv=code	converts code when it is one of the following:

	ascii	coverts EBCDIC to ASCII (IBM mainframes)
	ebcdic	converts ASCII to EBCDIC
	lcase	converts to lowercase
	noerror	continues after read errors
	swab	swaps every pair of input bytes
	ucase	converts to uppercase
ibs=nbytes	reads blocks of n bytes at a time	
if=file	reads from specified file instead of standard input	
obs=nbytes	writes blocks of n bytes at a time	
of=file	reads from specified file instead of standard output	

Note: Syntax is dd option1=value1 option2=value2 .... This command is usually used for copying data directly from one device to another.

How do I use diff?

diff — compares two text files for differences

-a	treats all files as text
-b	ignores blank lines and repeated blank spaces
-c	produces output in a different format
-d	tries to find a smaller set of changes
-e	produces a script for ed editor to convert from_file to to_file
-f	acts like -e, but in reverse order
-i	ignores case
-l	passes the output to the pr command (performs basic formatting of text documents) to paginate it
-n	works like -f but counts number of changed lines
-r	recursively compares files with same name in all subdirectories

-s	reports when two files are the same
-t	expands tabs to spaces in the output
-u	uses the unified output format
-v	displays versions of diff
-v	ignores spaces and tabs when comparing lines

Note: The syntax is diff [options] from_file to_file.

How do I use expand?

expand — converts all tabs into spaces

-i	converts only the initial tab into spaces
-n	sets the tabs n spaces apart
-n l ...	sets the tab stops

Note: The syntax is expand [options] files.

How do I use fold?

fold — wraps each line of text to fit a specified width (default is 80 characters)

-b	counts bytes instead of columns (backspaces and tabs are also counted)
-s	breaks lines at word boundaries
-w N	sets line width N characters

Note: The syntax is fold [options] files.

How do I use grep?

grep — searches for a regular expression within a text file

-N	displays N lines around the expression
-c	shows the number of lines that contain the expression
-f file	reads options from specified file
-i	ignores case
-l	displays the filenames that contain the expression
-n	displays the line number next to the lines that contain the expression

-q	returns a status code only
-v	displays the lines that do not contain the expression
-w	matches whole words only

Note: The syntax is grep [options] expression files.

3

How do I use lpr?

lpr prints files (line printer)

-P printer	prints to the printer specified in /etc/printcap
-#N	prints N copies of each file
-h	suppresses the first page with first user data (burst page)
-m	sends mail upon completion of print job
-r	removes the file after printing
-J jobname	prints the job name on the burst page
-U username	prints the user name on the burst page

Note: The syntax is lpr [options] files.

How do I use nl?

nl numbers all non-blank lines in a text file and prints the lines to standard output

-ba	numbers all lines
-bt	numbers text lines only (default)
-sc	separates text from line numbers with the character c (tab is the default)
-wn	uses n columns to show the line numbers

Note: The syntax is nl [options] file.

How do I use paste?

paste concatenates corresponding lines for several files

-d delim	uses delimiters from a list of characters instead of a tab

-s	pastes the lines from one file at a time instead of one line from each file

Note: The syntax is paste file1 file2 ....

How do I use patch?

patch — updates a text file using the differences between the original and the revised copy of the file

-c	causes patch file to be interpreted as a context diff
-e	forces patch file to interpret the patch as an ed script
-f	forces patch file to be applied regardless of any inconsistencies
-n	causes patch file to be interpreted as a normal diff
-pN	strips everything up to N slashes in the pathname
-R	indicates that patch file was created with new and old files swapped
-u	causes patch file to be interpreted as a unified diff
-v	displays the version number

Note: The syntax is patch [options] patch-file.

How do I use sed?

sed — copies a file to standard output while applying specified editing commands

-e	applies the editing commands to the files
-f	applies editing commands from the scriptfile
-n	suppresses default output

Note: The syntax is sed [options] [editing_commands] [file].

How do I use sort?

sort sorts lines in a text file

-b	ignores leading blanks
-c	checks files to see if already sorted and prints an error message if not
-d	sorts as a phone directory
-f	treats lowercase letters as uppercase letters
-g	sorts numerically but uses conversions to real numbers
-i	ignores unprintable characters
-k	specifies the sort field as characters between two positions
-m	merges files by sorting them as groups
-n	sorts numerically (for cases where lines begin with numbers)
-o file	writes output to specified file
-r	reverses the sort order
-tC	specifies the character separator
-+N	only considers characters from position N forward (first is zero)

Note: The syntax is sort [options] [files].

How do I use split?

split breaks up a file into smaller files with a specified size

-l N	puts N lines in each file
-b Nk	splits the file into N kilobytes
-c Nk	puts in as many lines as possible without exceeding the N kilobyte argument

Note: The syntax is split [options] file [prefix].

How do I use tac?

tac reverses a file so that the last line becomes first

-b	places the separator at the beginning of each line

3

-r	treats the separator string specified by **-s** as a regular expression
-s sep	specifies a separator rather than the default new line character

Note: The syntax is tac file.

How do I use tr?

tr — substitutes one group of characters for another throughout the file

-c	complements characters in string1 with ASCII codes 001-377
-d	deletes from the input all characters specified in string1
-s	replaces repeated sequences of any characters in string1 with a single character

Note: The syntax is tr [options] string1 [string2].

How do I use uniq?

uniq — eliminates duplicate lines for a text file

-N	ignores the first N fields on each line
+N	ignores the first N characters on each line
-c	writes number of times each line occurs
-d	writes only duplicate lines
-u	writes only unique lines (default)

Note: The syntax is uniq [options] file.

How do I use wc?

wc — counts the number of lines, words, and characters in a text file

-c	displays only the character count
-l	displays only the line count
-w	displays only the word count

Note: The syntax is wc [options] [files].

How do I archive and compress files?

There are at least eight commands for archiving and compressing files:

- compress
- cpio
- gunzip
- gzip
- tar
- uncompress
- unzip
- zip

How do I use compress?

compress — compresses files using Lempel-Ziv compression

Option	Description
-c	compresses file to standard output and retains original
-d	decompresses the file
-r	recursively compresses files in subdirectories
-v	verifies by a message that each file is compressed
-V	prints a version number and exits

Note: The syntax is compress [options] files. A .Z is appended as a suffix to the filename.

How do I use cpio?

cpio — copies files to and from an archive

Option	Description
-a	resets access times of input files
-B	copies using 5,120 bytes per record (default equals 512)
-c	reads or writes header information as ASCII
-d	creates directories as needed
-i	extracts files whose names match the expression
-m	retains previous file modification time

-o	copies to archive files whose names are provided on standard output
-p	copies files to another directory on the same system
-v	prints a listing of filenames

Note: The syntax is cpio [options] expression.

How do I use gunzip?

gunzip uncompresses files compressed with either **compress** or **gzip**

Note: The options are the same as the **gzip** command. The file suffix can be either **.gz** or .Z.

How do I use gzip?

gzip compresses files better than **compress**

-c	writes file to standard output and retains the original file
-d	uncompresses the file
-h	displays a help message
-l	lists contents of a compressed file
-n	does not save original name and stamp
-r	recursively compresses files in all subdirectories
-v	displays wordy output
-V	displays version number

Note: The syntax is gzip [options] files.

How do I use tar?

tar creates an archive of files in one or more directories

-c	creates a new archive
-C dir	extracts files into the specified directory
-d	compares files in an archive with files in the current directory
-f file	uses the specified file as the archive
-L n	specifies capacity as n kilobytes

-N date	archives files newer than the specified date
-r	extends the archive with more files
-t	displays a listing of the contents of an archive
-T file	archives or extracts the filenames specified in file
-v	displays wordy messages
-x	extracts from the archive
-z	compresses or uncompresses archive with gzip

Note: The syntax is tar [options] files_or_directories.

How do I use uncompress?

uncompress uncompresses files compressed with compress

-c	writes file to standard output and retains the original file
-r	recursively uncompresses files in all subdirectories
-v	displays a message as each is uncompressed
-V	displays version number and exits

Note: The syntax is uncompress [options] files. It removes the .Z suffix.

How do I use unzip?

unzip extracts (default), lists, or tests a zipped file

How do I use zip?

zip adds (default), lists, or tests a zipped file

How do I handle MS-DOS files?

All these commands are a part of mtools. A selection of commands is:

mcopy	copies files to and from MS-DOS disks without mounting the disk drive
mdel	deletes files from MS-DOS disks without mounting the disk drive

mdir	lists files on a MS-DOS disk
mren	renames a file

What are five basic file suffixes for designating programming languages or scripts?

file.C	C++ source code
file.c	C source code
file.f	Fortran source code
file.s	Assembly source code
file.sh	Shell scripts

What is a symbolic link?

A symbolic link is an indirect pointer to a file.

What does a filename that begins with the prefix in. mean?

A file with the prefix in. usually designates an Internet service daemon.

How do I create a directory?

Do a cd for change of directory and then use the command mkdir directoryname. Example filenames are bin and text.

-a mode	assigns the specified permission
-p	creates parent directories when they do not exist

How do I copy a directory?

cp	lets you copy a directory (cp directory1 directory2)

How do I delete a directory?

rmdir deletes (removes) a directory

-f	removes files without prompting
-i	prompting is done before removing a file

-r	recursively removes files in all subdirectories and directories
-v	displays each filename before removing it

How do I find a list of directories?

Use the command ls -d. This command lists directories like files rather than directory content.

How do I find the pathname of my home directory?

Use the command pwd.

How do I navigate through the directories?

cd — changes your current directory

cd ..	lets you move up a directory level
cd -	lets you move to the home directory
cd directory name	lets you move to a specific directory

How do I change directory permissions?

chgrp — changes the permissions of the directory to a new group

Note: The syntax is chgrp new-group directory.

How do I change the name of the root directory?

chroot — makes the root directory something else on the filesystem

Note: The syntax is chroot old-location new-location.

How do I list contents of directories?

Use the command dir, which is similar to the ls command.

How can I display the pathname of the working directory?

pwd — displays the current directory (print working directory)

Note: There are no options.

What is / (a single backslash)?

A single backslash means the root directory.

What is /bin?

It is the directory for binary executable commands.

What are basic programs found in the /bin directory?

The commonly used executable programs that are also binary files that are found in the /bin directory include the following:

- login
- Editors (ed, vi)
- File utilities (cp, mv, rm, ln, tar)
- Filesystem utilities (dd, df, mount, umount, sync)
- Shells (bash, csh, ksh)
- System utilities (arch, hostname, uname)

What is /dev?

This is the directory for device special files.

What are some of the files found in the /dev directory?

Some of the device files found in the /dev directory include:

- xdaN (1-8)
- xdbN (1-8)
- zqftN (0-3)
- MAKEDEV
- mouse
- cdrom

What is /dev/null?

This is commonly called the bit bucket, the place for non-required output.

What is /dev/printer?

This is the local print requests socket.

What is /etc?

It is the directory for local and configuration files that are not binary.

What are some of the files found in the /etc directory?

This is the normal storage directory for system-wide configuration files such as these ten files:

- HOSTNAME
- lilo.conf.rpmsave
- mtab
- passwd
- pine
- ppp
- profile
- protocols
- shadow
- uucp

What is /etc/fstab?

This file contains a list of all devices that can be mounted automatically by the filesystem. The file contains the device name, where the device is to be mounted, type of filesystem, and options.

What is /etc/group?

This file has information about groups and their users.

What is /etc/hosts?

This file contains a list of IP addresses and the corresponding host names and optional aliases. A critical IP address here is the one used for the local host when Internet connections and services are to be tested. It is as follows:

```
127.0.0.1     localhost
```

What is /etc/profile?

This file contains common shell information for all users. It is the default initialization file for users whose shell is either bash, ksh, or sh.

What is /etc/passwd?

It is the directory for password table. It contains all information on the user except the encrypted password, which is found in /etc/shadow.

What is /etc/services?

It is the directory for networking services under TCP/IP. It has a list of services and their ports. Each service requires a line of information that includes the following:

- Official service name
- Port number
- Protocol name
- Services alias (optional)

Each entry is separated by a space. For example, the httpd entry might look as follows:

```
http 8080/tcp httpd httpd
```

The port 8080 is used because an inetd server runs better on this port than the one for the standalone server, which is port 80.

What is /etc/sysconfig?

It is a directory unique to Red Hat for boot time configuration files.

What is /etc/X11?

It is the directory for X11 configuration files.

What is /home?

It is the directory for all home directories of users, including the root user.

What is /lib?

It is the directory for library files that are needed to execute /bin and /sbin.

What is /mnt?

It is the directory for removable media such as CD-ROMs.

What is /sbin?

It is the directory for system administration commands used by the root user, and is limited to executables to boot and to mount /usr and to perform system recovery. It includes the following system programs:

- fdisk
- fsck
- init
- lilo
- mkfs
- shutdown

Note: Most of the programs under the /sbin directory are executed only from the root.

What is /tmp?

It is the directory for temporary files.

What is /usr?

It is the directory for a site's sharable files. It usually has its own partition and should be mountable read only. This is the location for the storage of common programs and files used by the system users.

What is /usr/bin?

It is the directory for additional binary executable commands.

What is /usr/lib?

It is the directory for libraries and package configuration files.

What is /usr/lib/rhs?

It is the directory unique to Red Hat for control panel and related tool files.

What is /usr/local?

It is the directory for local (personal) use files, and has a structure similar to /usr. In addition, the man pages and libraries are located here.

What is /usr/local/bin?

It is the directory for local system administration binary commands.

What is /usr/local/lib?

It is the directory for locally added libraries.

What is /usr/local/src?

It is the directory for local command source files.

What is /usr/man?

It is the directory for system online manual pages.

What is /usr/spool?

Various spool directories

What is /usr/src?

It is the directory for the Linux kernel source files.

What is /usr/X11R6?

It is the directory for XFree86 files.

What is /var?

It is the directory for log (/var/log) and spool (/var/spool) files.

What is /var/lib/rpm?

It is the directory unique to Red Hat for Red Hat Program Manager (RPM) files.

What is /var/log?

This directory contains most of the system messages.

What are some of the files found in the /var/log directory?

Ten of the files that are found in the /var/log directory are the following:

- boot.log
- cron
- htmlaccess.log
- maillog
- messages
- netconf.log
- news
- samba
- sendmail.st
- spool

How do I install Shadow Suite?

See Shadow-Password-HOWTO.gz. This HOWTO tells how to obtain, install, and configure the password Shadow Suite. Shadow Suite provides a more secure password system than the original Linux installation. It also covers why you should use shadow, related programs, putting it to use, and adding shadow support to a C program. The author is Michael H. Jackson (mhjack@tsnet.com).

Chapter 4

Internet Server Tips

4

This chapter focuses on the Internet server as compared to a Web server. An Internet server handles a full set of services from Archie to news and more.

Note: To see available options for the commands discussed in the chapter, you need to do a man command-name command. In addition, any methodologies discussed here may not be applicable to Linux distributions other than Red Hat. Also see Chapters 9 and 10.

What is an Internet server?

An Internet server is not a Web server. A Web server serves Web pages to Web browsers. An Internet server includes the services of the World Wide Web, mail, news, chat, Gopher, Archie, and FTP. Many of the services may have their own server such as mail and news.

What is an intranet server?

An intranet server has the functionality of an Internet server, but handles server requests with a self-contained network. This functionality includes these capabilities:

- E-mail
- Newsgroups
- Phone lists
- Employee or departmental Web pages
- Corporate policy information
- Training information
- Company documentation

What is a primary concern in having an Internet server?

The primary concern is security. With an Internet server you open your intranet (network) to an uncontrolled, ubiquitous, and unmanageable environment. This is where firewalls and gateways come into play.

What are the basic steps in setting up an Internet server?

There are at least ten starting or basic steps (outline or framework), including the following determinations:

- Type of server
- Method of connection
- Security level and method
- Browser standards
- E-mail configuration
- Usenet configuration
- Gopher capabilities
- FTP capabilities
- Web page standards
- Content indexing capabilities

Note: This list is not inclusive. Setting up an Internet server is not done after reading a chapter in a book or skimming through a complete book to get the highlights. Fortunately, there are a number of HOWTOs available on setting up your options for an Internet server. There is at least one book on the market that discusses the technical implication of creating an Internet server, not Red Hat, that is over 500 pages.

What is PPP?

The Point-to-Point Protocol is link-layer protocol used in association with the Internet Protocol. It is one of two primary connection protocols, the other being SLIP. PPP is the faster of the two. See Chapter 10 for further details.

What is SLIP?

The Serial Line Internet Protocol exchanges IP packets over a serial line. It is usually installed automatically as a part of the Linux kernel. It has a modification called CSLIP (Compressed SLIP).

What is CSLIP?

Compressed Serial Line Internet Protocol exchanges IP packets over a serial line. It uses the header compression of most TCP/IP datagrams.

What is a dummy interface?

An IP address has been reserved to test your server and services connection. It is 127.0.0.1. When you install Linux without network support you should have in the /etc/hosts file the single line:

```
127.0.0.1 localhost
```

Note: This line tells TCP/IP that there is a special interface called localhost, a dummy interface. It is a loopback interface. The above line should be in the /etc/hosts file to do any local interface testing. If it is not on your system, then you should create the file and add the line. This is the IP address for every local host Linux machine.

What are the special requirements for adding a dummy interface?

After creating the /etc/hosts file and adding the line 127.0.0.1 localhost you need to be at the root level and issue the two following commands:

```
ifconfig lo 127.0.0.1
route add 127.0.0.1
```

How can I check the localhost dummy interface?

If you enter ping localhost at the root and you do not get the message unknown host, then you are configured correctly.

How do I set up serial communication devices?

See Serial-HOWTO.gz. This HOWTO explains setting up serial communication devices. It covers supported serial hardware, serial port names, some interesting programs, dialing out and in with your modem, setting up a terminal connection, communication programs and utilities, tips, and troubleshooting. The author is Greg Hankins (gregh@cc.gatech.edu).

See Serial-Programming-HOWTO.gz. This HOWTO explains how to program the serial port. It covers getting started and some program examples. The author is Peter H. Baumann (Peter.Baumann@dlr.de).

What types of programs for the Internet are available?

This is a selection of nine programs for working with the Internet that may be available to you:

dip	The Dial-up IP Protocol Driver (dip) allows for the automation of the steps in setting up a SLIP connection to a remote system.
elm	This is a mail-handling program. You can compose, edit, and send mail, and place your mail in different folders.
imap	It is an Internet Message Access Protocol server.
inn	InterNetNews is a TCP/IP-based news server.
pine	It is a mail and Usenet news program. It has an editor called pico. You can store your mail in different folders.
pppd	The Point-to-Point daemon runs programs in the background while you are using a PPP connection. It handles data transmission.
sendmail	It is a sophisticated mail-transport agent.
tin	This is a full-screen Usenet newsreader. It uses a menu system and permits browsing, saving, posting, and replying to messages.
trn	It is a full-screen news reader.

Note: The mail programs elm, pine, and sendmail are discussed in more detail in Chapter 2. The news programs inn, pine, tin, and trn are discussed in more detail in Chapter 5. To determine if these files are installed, enter rpm –q filename.

What is dip?

The Dial-up IP Protocol Driver (dip) handles Serial Line Interface Protocol (SLIP) and Point-to-Point (PPP) connections for IP addresses. Enter man dip for details on the options. It handles incoming and outgoing connections. It does include a certain level of security for incoming connections that includes user name and password.

How do I use dip?

The dip command can be used to establish either incoming or outgoing connections for users. Commands can be either interactive or scriptfile. In addition, it can be used as a shell to establish dial-in connections. It then can be executed by either diplogin or diplogini. The syntax is dip [options] [chat scriptfile].

What is the Domain Name Service?

The Domain Name Service (DNS) is the system whereby each site maintains its map of IP addresses to machine names. This is for human convenience. It is easier for a human to remember a name rather than a complex number that can be larger than a telephone number. It is easier to remember redhat.com rather than, say, 206.12.41.999 (not the actual Red Hat IP address).

What is a domain name server?

A domain name server is used to convert the Internet machine name (myname.com) to the IP (Internet Protocol) numeric address (123.123.123.255).

What is a name server?

A name server is the server (computer) that translates a human-readable name such as www.mycompany.com into a numeric address such as 000.123.000.456. It uses the protocols of TCP/IP.

What are the types of name servers?

There are three types of name servers:

- Caching—normally used
- Primary—your site is to be connected directly to the Internet
- Secondary—load is too large to be handled by primary

What is URL?

Uniform Resource Locator is the method for specifying the protocol, format, login (usually for ftp rather than http), and location of materials on the Internet.

Is there a package that supports browsing?

The lynx package supports HTML, text formatting, forms, and tables.

Is there a package that supports chat (IRC)?

Internet Relay Chat (IRC) uses ircii and ircii-help.

Is there a package that supports faxing?

Efax supports faxing.

What is an FTP service?

FTP service permits a user to access files on a machine without having a user account. This is done using one of two special usernames, anonymous or ftp. The FTP service is controlled from the /etc/inetd.conf file.

What are the basic steps in an FTP request?

The eight steps for a public FTP request are:

1. Client connects to FTP port, usually 21.
2. When connection is detected, the FTP daemon (/usr/sbin/in.ftpd) is invoked.
3. Server is initiated.
4. Client provides a user name and password.
5. User placed in the home directory for FTP users (default is /home/ftp).
6. Server executes a chroot system call.

7. Client gets files.
8. Server disconnects.

How can the FTP server be made securer than normal?

You can make the FTP server securer than normal by editing the access rights found in these files:

- /etc/ftpaccess
- /etc/ftpconversions
- /etc/ftphosts
- /var/log/xferlog

What are the FTP commands that can be used to control user access?

There are seven FTP commands that can be used to control user access:

autogroup	Automatically assigns users to a certain group permission
class	Defines a user class
deny	Denies explicitly a user to certain hosts
guestgroup	Restricts real users to only FTP privileges
limit	Controls the number of users by class and time of day
loginfails	Sets the number of login failures permitted to a user
private	Permits user to FTP files without having a public FTP server

What are the commands that control FTP logging?

There are two FTP commands for controlling logging:

log commands	Logs each command invoked by a user
log transfers	Logs file transfers by user

What are the commands that control FTP permissions?

There are eight FTP commands that can control FTP permissions:

chmod	Determines whether a client can change a permission on the server's files
delete	Determines whether a client can delete a file on the server

overwrite	Determines whether a client can replace a file on the server
passwd-check	Determines the level of security for a string to be submitted as an anonymous user's e-mail address
path-filter	Determines the acceptable filenames for any upload to the server
rename	Determines whether a rename request is valid
umask	Determines whether a client can change default permissions
upload	Determines what permissions the client has to place files in directories and the types of permissions the file can hold

What are the packages that support FTP?

In Red Hat Linux 6.0 there are at least four packages that support FTP. They are the following:

anonftp (version 2.8.1)	Permits downloads from your machine without having a user account; anonymous access
ftp (version 0.10-22)	Provides the standard UNIX command-line FTP client
gftp (version 1.13)	Provides a multithreaded FTP client for X Windows. It permits such actions as simultaneous downloads and file transfer queries.
ncftp (version 3.0beta18-3)	Provides an enhanced FTP client that includes support for command line editing, command histories, recursive gets, and automatic anonymous logins.

What are some important FTP administrative utilities?

There are three important FTP administrative utilities that give server status and shutdown capabilities:

ftpcount	Shows total current users count and maximum possible
ftpwho	Shows all active connected users
ftpshut	Permits a continuously running server to be shut down

What HOWTOs are available to support Internet functionality?

Some of the HOWTOs available on Internet functionality are:

- DNS
- Firewall and Proxy Server
- ISP-Hookup
- Linux Electronic Mail
- NFS
- Linux PPP
- Linux WWW

Is there a program that supports Web searches?

See the PostSQL HOWTO and its section 27 for Web search tips.

How do I set up a Domain Name Service (DNS)?

See DNS-HOWTO.gz. This HOWTO tells how to configure Linux for setting up a DNS. It covers a caching-only name server, a simple domain, a real domain example, and maintenance, and has an FAQ. The author is Nicolai Langfeldt (janl@math.uio.no).

What tools are required to configure a DNS?

There are four tools you should have knowledge of before trying to configure a DNS. These tools are the following:

- The resolver library—enables client programs to perform queries
- named—daemon that handles queries
- nslookup—utility used to ensure the resolver and server are configured correctly
- traceroute—determines a packet path across your network and onto other networks

Note: A resolver is a library routine or program that extracts information from the name server in response to a query.

How do I configure Ethernet network adapters?

See Ethernet-HOWTO.gz. This HOWTO explains how to configure and use Linux Ethernet network adapters. It covers card selection criteria, includes an FAQ, gives performance tips, and considers configuration issues. The majority of the HOWTO has vendor, manufacturer, and model specific information. The editor is Paul Gortmaker (Paul.Gortmaker@anu.edu.au).

How do I connect to my Internet service provider?

See ISP-Hookup-HOWTO.gz. This HOWTO shows how to connect Linux to an Internet service provider (ISP) using a dial-up modem. It covers connection, surfing, sending and receiving e-mail, and automating the connection. The author is Egil Kaveberg (egil@sn.no).

How do I set up serial communication devices?

See Serial-HOWTO.gz. This HOWTO explains how to set up serial communication devices. It covers supported serial hardware, serial port names, some interesting programs, dialing out and in with your modem, setting up a terminal connection, communication programs and utilities, tips, and troubleshooting. The author is Greg Hankins (gregh@cc.gatech.edu).

See also Serial-Programming-HOWTO.gz. This HOWTO explains how to program the serial port. It covers getting started and some program examples. The author is Peter H. Baumann (Peter.Baumann@dlr.de).

How do I find files that show host name and IP address associations?

See the /etc/hosts file. This directory can speed up the lookup time of frequently used IP addresses. This is the location of the IP-address-to-host name mapping.

What fields are found in the /etc/hosts file?

There are three fields found in the /etc/hosts file:

- IP address number

- Host name
- Alias (optional)

What types of entries should be in the /etc/hosts file?

The should be at least four entries in the **/etc/hosts** file:

- Localhost
- The host itself
- ISP server (NIS server)
- Any systems from which you mount disks

How do I find files that show service name and port number associations?

See the file **/etc/services**. Each service requires a line of information that includes the following:

- Official service name
- Port number
- Protocol name
- Services alias (optional)

Each entry is separated by a space. For example, the **httpd** entry might look as follows:

```
http 8080/tcp httpd httpd
```

The port 8080 is used because an **inetd** server runs better on this port than the one for the standalone server, which is port 80.

What is the port number for a WWW service?

Standalone server should be port 80. An **inetd** server should use 8080.

What is the port number for FTP service?

Port 21.

Where can I find an access control facility for Internet services?

See directory /usr/sbin/tcpd.

Where are the IP addresses of name servers kept?

See the /etc/resolv.conf file.

Where is the host name kept?

See the HOSTNAME variable in /etc/sysconfig/network.

Where do I find network names and their IP addresses?

See /etc/networks. Red Hat Linux does not automatically install this file.

What files allow and deny host access to Internet services?

See /etc/hosts.allow and /etc/hosts.deny.

How do I check the routing status to another host?

Use the command /sbin/route and specify the host's IP address.

How do I find information on setting up for the WWW?

For technical details on setting up clients and servers for the World Wide Web, see Linux WWW HOWTO by Wayne Liester (n3mtr@qis.net).

What is the first step in the WWW server setup?

You need a server and sufficient knowledge to handle HTTP server software packages and the related tools. There are many servers available, but the most popular server may be the Apache. One of the advantages of the Apache server is that it is modular.

What is the second step in the WWW server setup?

You need to set up a browser. The Red Hat distribution includes Netscape.

Note: There are other browsers one can use including Lynx, Emacs-W3, and Kfm.

What are some of the Red Hat Linux packages that support the Internet?

The following 24 packages support Internet services:

elm (Version 2.5.0)
exmh (Version 2.0.2)
fetchmail (Version 4.7.0, Version 5.0.0)
finger (Version 0.10)
ftp (Version 0.10)
fwhois (Version 1.00)
mailx (Version 8.1.1)
metamail (Version 2.7)
mutt (Version 0.95.4us)
ncftp (Version 3.0beta18)
netscape-common (Version 4.51)
netscape-communicator (Version 4.51)
nmh (Version 0.27)
pine (Version 4.10)
rsh (Version 0.10)
slrn (Version 0.9.5.4)
talk (Version 0.10, Version 0.11)
tcpdump (Version 3.4)
telnet (Version 0.10)
tin (Version 1.4_990216)
traceroute (Version 1.4a5)
trn (Version 3.6)
xmailbox (Version 2.5)
xrn (Version 9.01)

Are there RFCs available to assist in setting up a WWW server?

When one is ready to get one's fingers dirty, there are a number of Request for Comments available on such subjects as HTML, Hypertext Transfer Protocol, and URLs. Here is a short list of potentially useful RFCs (longer list found in Appendix C):

791	Internet Protocol (1981)
799	Internet Name Domains (1981)
950	Internet Standard Subnetting Procedure (1985)
1011	Official Internet Protocols (1987)
1173	Responsibilities of Host and Network Managers: A Summary of the "Oral Tradition" of the Internet (1990)
1180	TCP/IP Tutorial (1991)
1332	The PPP Internet Protocol Control Protocol (IPCP) (1992)
1349	Type of Service in the Internet Protocol Suite (1992)
1661	The Point-to-Point Protocol (PPP) (1994)
1704	On Internet Authentication (1994)
1738	Uniform Resource Locators (URL) (1994)
1883	Internet Protocol, Version 6 (IPv6) Specification (1995)
1958	Architectural Principles of the Internet (1996)
1963	PPP Serial Data Transport Protocol (SDTP) (1996)
1983	Internet Users' Glossary (1996)
2026	The Internet Standards Process—Revision 3 (1996)
2057	Sources Directed Access Control on the Internet (1996)
2084	Considerations for Web Translation Security (1997)
2151	A Primer on Internet and TCP/IP Tools and Utilities (1997)

Chapter 5

News Server Tips

This chapter looks at the news server, Usenet, NNTP server, and the characteristics of various new readers.

Note: To see available options for the commands discussed in the chapter, you need to do a man command-name command. In addition, RPM install syntax may require the architecture such as i386.

5

What is a news server?

Usually a Linux news server uses the protocols of Usenet, the world's largest bulletin board. Usenet is organized into newsgroups. These newsgroups usually are for special interest groups.

What is Usenet?

It is the largest electronic bulletin board in the world. It is a message storing and forwarding network service. It is a dial-up system that originally used the UNIX-to-UNIX CoPy (UUCP) protocol for message transfer. The news, however, uses the Network News Transfer Protocol (NNTP). For further technical details, see RFC 977, "Network News Transfer Protocol" by B. Kantor and P. Lapsley (1986).

What are the logical parts of Usenet news?

There are two logical parts: protocols and programs. The system administrator has to be involved in both, while a network user needs to work with programs. A standalone user is also a system administrator on a limited basis.

What are the two types of Usenet programs?

The two types of Usenet programs (software) are the news reader and the processing applications for the articles. An article is any single posted message.

What are some of the available Linux newsgroups?

This list excludes those newsgroups with the name Red Hat in them. They are listed in the next question. There are ten general Linux newsgroups:

- alt.linux.projects
- alt.os.linux
- aus.computers.linux
- comp.os.linux.announce
- comp.os.linux.answers
- comp.os.linux.hardware
- comp.os.linux.misc
- comp.os.linux.networking
- comp.os.linux.security
- comp.os.linux.setup

Note: Any one of these groups may not have messages at any given time. In addition, they may not be available through your Internet service provider (ISP).

What are some of the available Red Hat newsgroups?

Here are ten of the available Red Hat newsgroups:

- linux.redhat.applixware
- linux.redhat.axp
- linux.redhat.devel
- linux.redhat.digest
- linux.redhat.install
- linux.redhat.list
- linux.redhat.misc
- linux.redhat.pam
- linux.redhat.ppp
- linux.redhat.rpm

What are some of the available mail newsgroups?

Here are eight of the available mail newsgroups:

- comp.mail.elm
- comp.mail.imap
- comp.mail.mime
- comp.mail.misc
- comp.mail.pine
- comp.mail.sendmail
- comp.mail.smail
- comp.mail.uucp

What must I decide first as a system administrator?

You must first decide whether or not Usenet will be offered on your system. This is a major task and responsibility. A single day's posting, depending on the newsgroups offered, might run to at least half a gigabyte, probably more. It also takes a large amount of bandwidth.

Note: An educated guess is that eighty percent of what might be found in a newsgroup, not necessarily those listed above, might be balderdash. One needs to consider the use of an ISP as the source for newsgroups.

What is a first step in newsgroup selection?

You can first use the basic hierarchy name to select your newsgroup. The "original" first-level identifiers included:

biz	Business
comp	Computers
misc	Miscellaneous
news	Usenet issues and information
rec	Recreational information
sci	Scientific
soc	Social
talk	Conversation
alt	Anything else

However, in recent times, there are first-level identifiers such as Linux and Microsoft to represent information on companies. In addition, there are country identifiers such as de.* for Germany (Deutschland) that are prefixed to the above identifiers. The newsgroup list becomes much shorter when you eliminate the newsgroups that begin the first-level identifiers of alt, talk, soc, rec, misc, and countries where your company does not do business. At the time of this writing there are 333 newsgroups that begin de.*.

What is a logical policy on having newsgroups?

There is precedence from the Internet service providers. The policy is called "user-defined." The policy means that you only carry the newsgroups requested by the users. You can also add the requirement that a newsgroup has to be approved as a work related activity.

What is a basic requirement in configuring a news reader?

One major consideration in configuring a news reader such as tin is to identify the shell type, whether it is ksh or bash or C or tcsh.

What are the essential questions I must ask to have Usenet?

There are four essential questions you must answer to your satisfaction to have a Usenet feed:

- Is enough hard disk storage available?
- Is there sufficient network bandwidth?
- What level of newsgroup feed is required?
- Is there an available computer for handling just the newsgroup feed?

What are the hardware requirements?

There are no specific hardware requirements; however, it is strongly recommended to have a separate computer to run the Usenet feed.

What is an NNTP server?

A Network News Transfer Protocol (NNTP) server is the news server of an Internet service provider (ISP).

What is an alternative to NNTP?

An alternative to NNTP is INN (InterNetNews). It is more complex to configure than NNTP; however, it is more flexible and was designed for large systems. It handles news requests for both TCP/IP and UUCP.

How do I install the INN package?

Check first to see if it is installed by entering rpm –q inn. If it is not installed, enter rpm –i inn-2.2.8.rpm.

What are some important INN files?

Two important INN files are as follows:

/etc/rc.d/init.d/innd—used to start the INN package by entering file-name start
/etc/rc.d/rc.news

What files have to be configured for INN?

The /etc/news/hosts.nntp file has the available newsfeeds. The /etc/news/nnrp.access file allows remote machines to access the local host.

What are the hardware requirements for INN?

There is a need for a fast process, not super fast, and disk space. The disk space is the same requirement as for any news reader. The number and types of newsgroups determine the requirements. The faster the modem, the better.

What are the daemons used with INN?

There are two daemons used with INN, innd and nnrpd.

Where is INN documentation?

The online documentation with the Red Hat Linux distribution is found in the /usr/doc directory. The files are INN-faq_part1 through INN-faq_part9.

What are the basic functions of a news reader?

There are six basic news reader functions or capabilities:

- Subscribe or unsubscribe
- Browse individual messages and their threads
- Reply to author of the message
- Post a new or follow-up message
- Print a message
- Save a message to home directory

What are some basic news readers for handling news?

Here are four basic news readers for getting the news:

pine	handles Internet Usenet news and e-mail and uses pico as its text editor
slrn	handles Internet Usenet news and has some advantages over tin that include the ability to color code various message parts and use the mouse
tin	lets you read Usenet news and uses a menu system
trn	supports threaded news

Is there a full-screen news reader?

A full-screen Usenet news reader is tin. It uses a menu system and permits browsing, saving, posting, and replying to messages. Another full-screen news reader is trn.

What is the purpose of the .newsrc file?

The purpose of the .newsrc file, located in the home directory, acts as a newsgroup index. This is an individual selection rather than retrieving the full newsgroup list (depending on your ISP the number can be somewhere 40,000 plus). This file is used by both the tin and slrn news reader. This file is created using a text editor. Some possible newsgroups that can be entered are given earlier in this chapter. The list does not have to be in alphabetical order, but each entry needs to end with a colon. If the newsgroup is not supported by the ISP, then it is simply ignored. Here is an example:

```
alt.os.linux:
aus.computers.linux:
comp.os.linux.announce:
linux.redhat.ppp:
linux.redhat.rpm:
comp.mail.pine:
comp.mail.sendmail:
linux.redhat.install:
linux.redhat.list:
alt.linux.projects:
```


What are the basic characteristics of the pine news reader?

Here are nine characteristics of the pine (Program for Internet and News and E-mail) news reader:

- Located in the /usr/bin directory
- An interactive mail and news reader
- Reads newsgroup list in the .newsrc file
- Editor called pico
- Needs ISP news server name to be located in the /etc/nntpserver file
- Screen-oriented
- Automatic mail checker
- Personal defaults are in the .pinerc file under the home directory
- Initiated with the command pine –i

What are the basic characteristics of the tin news reader?

Here are seven characteristics of the tin (threading) news reader:

- Located in the /usr/bin directory
- Full-screen
- Reads newsgroup list in the .newsrc file
- Cursor navigation
- Needs ISP news server name to be located in the /etc/nntpserver file

- Defaults are in the .tinrc file under the .tin directory
- Initiated with the command tin –r

Note: The command tin –r means read the news remotely from the default NNTP server whose variable is found in the /etc/nntpserver file.

What are the basic characteristics of the slrn news reader?

Here are eight characteristics of the slrn (S-Lang read news) news reader:

- Located in the /usr/bin directory
- Full-screen that includes both headers and messages
- Reads newsgroup list in the .newsrc file
- Mouse-cursor aware mode
- Needs ISP news server name to be located in the /etc/nntpserver file
- Different NNTP servers might be specified on the command line
- Defaults are in the .slrnrc file under the /usr/lib/slrn directory
- Initiated with the command slrn –h nntp-server-name

Note: To customize the .slrnrc file, copy it into the home directory and make changes.

What are the basic characteristics of the trn news reader?

Here are eight characteristics of the trn (threaded read news) news reader:

- Standalone program
- Located in the /usr/bin directory
- Improved version of rn news reader
- Reads newsgroup list in the .newsrc file
- Threaded news reader
- Needs ISP news server name to be located in the /etc/nntpserver file
- Defaults are in the .trnrc file
- Can be initiated with the command trn –r

How do I install the trn RPM?

Since the trn RPM is included with the Red Hat distribution, you install it like any other RPM. You enter rpm –i trn-3.6-16.rpm.

Note: The entries for three other news readers are:
rpm –i pine-4.10-2.rpm
rpm –i slrn-0.9.5.4-5.rpm
rpm –i tin-1.4_990216-3.rpm

What is Netnews?

Netnews is a loosely controlled collection of discussion groups.

What is the Netnews Transport Protocol?

Netnews Transport Protocol transmits Netnews or Usenet messages over the top of TCP/IP.

How do I configure Network Information Service (NIS)?

See NIS-HOWTO.gz. This HOWTO tells how to configure Linux for NIS. It has a glossary and a FAQ. It covers the requirements for setting up the NIS and the NIS+, and discusses the setting up of a NIS server. The author is Thorsten Kukuk (kukuk@vt.uni-paderborn.de). See Chapter 11 for a further discussion.

How do I set up to use Usenet news?

See News-HOWTO.gz. This HOWTO tells the method for setting up and maintaining Usenet news or discussion groups. An important URL on how to become a Usenet site is ftp://ftp.uu.net in the directory /usenet/news.announce.newusers.

What is a basic administrative requirement?

The system administrator needs to prepare an informational for new users so they know how to send and receive mail. The minimum includes the following:

- Name (first and last)
- E-mail address (userid@hostname.domain)
- SMTP mail server's name

While this information should be set up in the mail reader software, something might go wrong. This information should be defined in a sigfile (signature file).

What is an important news distribution policy?

There should be a policy that users use a distribution line in the message header. This might eliminate some unnecessary flaming. The distribution values are the following:

local	Local news servers
state postal abbreviation	Specified state servers
us	United States
na	North America
world	Worldwide

Who is the newsgroup controlling authority?

The controlling authority is you, the system administrator.

What are the essential administrative tasks for the news server?

The following six tasks are required of a news server administrator:

- Install the original service
- Maintain the service that includes installing upgrades
- Monitor the service's performance
- Add and delete users from the service
- Develop a policy for availability of newsgroups
- Create a user informational file on headers including distribution line

Chapter 6

Remote Administration Server Tips

This chapter focuses on three methods for handling remote access, Telnet, Remote Procedure Call (RPC), and File Transfer Protocol (FTP). Remote access as a PPP client is discussed in Chapter 10. A very simple definition of remote access used for this chapter is a dial-up network connection.

Note: To see available options for the commands discussed in the chapter, you need to do a **man command-name** command. For some of the commands under the **/etc/ftpaccess** one might also use **info command-name** command. In addition, RPM install syntax may require the architecture such as i386.

6

What is a remote administration server?

A remote administration server is a server that handles the **telnet** command.

What is the primary function of the telnet command?

The Telnet protocol is used by the telnet user interface to communicate with another host. The syntax is

telnet [options] [host [port]]

When entered without the **host** argument, its prompt **telnet>** is invoked. The **host** argument is the official host name. The **port** argument indicates a port number (default is the Telnet port).

What are the available options that can be used at the telnet> prompt?

Ten available options can be used at the **telnet>** prompt:

-a	automatic login into the remote site
-d	turns on socket-level debugging
-e [escape_char]	sets initial Telnet escape character
-E	disables the escape character functionality
-l user	sends **user** to the remote if the remote site understands ENVIRON
-L	specifies the 8-bit data path on output
-n tracefile	opens **tracefile** for recording the trace information
-r	emulates **rlogin**
-S tos	sets the IP type-of-service (TOS) option for the Telnet connection
-8	requests 8-bit operation

What are some of the basic telnet commands?

Here are six basic **telnet** commands:

CTRL-Z	suspends **telnet**
close	closes the session
display argument ...	displays **set** and **toggle** values
logout	closes the session
status	shows current connection and mode status
quit	closes and exits the session

What is the tftpd user interface?

It is a user interface to the Trivial File Transfer Protocol (TFTP). It allows users to transfer files to and from a remote machine.

What is fingerd?

It is a remote user information server (daemon). It is based on RFC 1196, "Finger User Internet Protocol." This RFC has been obsoleted by RFC 1288 by D. Zimmerman (December 1991).

What is innxmit?

It sends Usenet articles to a remote NNTP server. It is usually invoked by a script.

What is ntpget?

It gets Usenet articles to a remote NNTP server. The articles are sent in a standard format.

What is passwd.nntp?

It is used for passwords for connecting to a remote NNTP server. This file is usually interpreted by the NNTPsendpassword routine.

What is talkd?

It notifies a user that someone else wants to initiate a conversation.

What is uux?

It is a remote command executed over UUCP. It is not executed immediately, but by the uuxqt daemon.

What is xon?

It starts an X program on a remote machine. It runs the specified command (default is –ls) using rsh, remsh, or remed.

What does Net::Ping do?

It checks a remote host for reachability.

What is RPC?

RPC stands for Remote Procedure Call. An RPC enables procedures to be executed on a server, referred to as an RFC server, generated by a client request. RPC is a collection of tools and library functions originally developed by Sun Microsystems. Built on top of RPC are the Network File System (NFS) and the Network Information System (NIS). See Chapters 11 and 12 for more details on these two systems.

What RPC daemons do I need?

You need to have rpc.mountd and rpc.nfsd running on your server.

How do I start these daemons?

You need two lines in a script located in /etc/rc.d/init/nfs. They are:

```
daemon rpc.mountd
daemon rpc.nfsd
```

Note: These daemons must start only after rpc.portmap is running. In the configuration file /etc/exports you identify the NFS that must be entered. NFS is discussed in Chapter 12.

What does rpc.portmap do?

It maps calls from clients to the appropriate NFS daemon. This called "portmapper" daemon registers a port selected by any RPC application.

Note: When the portmapper dies, all port information is lost. You either restart all RPC services or reboot.

What does rpc.mountd do?

Mount and unmount requests are handled by this daemon.

What does rpc.nfsd do?

This daemon translates the NFS requests to actual requests on the local filesystem server.

How does the /etc/exports file work?

It is used by rpc.mountd and rpc.nfsd to determine the files that are to be exported and their restrictions. It consists of a list of file systems, one per line. Each line consists of:

- Mount points for a local file system
- Allowable computers that might be mounted
- Mount options separated by commas

What are possible mount options for /etc/exports?

The 16 options are:

all-squash	Maps to the anonymous user all user IDs (UIDs) and group IDs (GIDs)
anongid	Sets the GID for the anonymous account
anonuid	Sets the UID for the anonymous account
insecure	Permits non-authenticated access
link_absolute	Does not convert absolute symbolic links to relative links
link_relative	Converts absolute symbolic links to relative links
map_daemon	Maps local and remote names and numeric IDs
no_root_squash	Does not do mapping from the root (default)
noaccess	Excludes subdirectories from a client
no-all-squash	Opposite of all-squash (default)
ro	Mounts the file system as read-only (default)
root-squash	Does mapping from the root
rw	Mounts the file system as read-write
secure	Requires authenticated access
squash-gids	Specifies the GIDs subject to anonymous mapping
squash-uids	Specifies the UIDs subject to anonymous mapping

6

What is important about RPC program versions?

This methodology permits several versions of an application to run on a server to prevent incompatibility with RPC-based services. A client's request indicates the program version number to be used. These program numbers are mapped against RPC-based services and are usually kept in /etc/rpc.

What are the r- commands?

The r- commands are for executing requests on remote hosts. They propagate a shell on the remote host and allow the user to execute commands. For these commands to work the user must be authorized, that is, have an account, on the host machine. The remote host checks in the /etc/host.equiv file to see if a local host is listed.

Note: While you might disable authorization, it is not recommended. Only administrative users should be given this privilege in an advisable manner.

What is the rlogin command?

The **rlogin** command connects the current local terminal to a designated remote host. It is similar to the **telnet** command. The syntax is **rlogin rhost [options]**

where the options are

-ec	specifies escape character c
-E	does not interpret any character as an escape character
-d	starts the debugging mode
-k	attempts to get tickets from remote host
-K	suppresses Kerberos authentication
-l username	specifies a **username** other than the default, which is the same as your local username
-L	allows an **rlogin** session without any output postprocessing
-x	turns on DES encryption

What is the rsh command?

The **rsh** (remote shell) command is an execution command on a remote host, that is, it starts a shell on the specified remote host to carry out the request execution. If no argument is specified, it begins an interactive shell on the remote host using **rlogin**. It uses the options of **rlogin**.

What is the rcp command?

The **rcp** (remote copy) command is used to copy between machines, with either being on a remote host. There are two syntax forms for this command:

```
rcp [-px] [-k realm] filename1 filename2
rcp [-px] [-r] [-k realm] file(s) directory
```

where the options are:

-p	preserves the modification times and modes of the source file

-x	turns on DES encryption
-k	requests a Kerberos ticket for the remote host
-r	recursively copies the source directory tree into the destination directory

What is the rusers command?

The **rusers** command lists clients logged in on the local machines (RPC version).

What is rdist?

It is a remote file distribution client program. It maintains identical copies of files over multiple hosts.

What is ristd?

It is a remote file distribution server (daemon) program.

What is rquota?

It implements quotas on remote machines. It is used in conjunction with NFS (see Chapter 12).

What is rquotad?

It is an RPC remote quota server. It returns quotas over NFS for a remote machine.

What is rup?

It displays remote status of the status of one or more hosts.

What is the RPM for FTP?

The package for Red Hat Linux 6.0 is FTP (0.10-22). It includes the standard UNIX command-line FTP client. When you have a network, this package should be installed to handle file transfers.

What is an FTP server?

A File Transfer Protocol (FTP) server handles transfers among machines across a network. There are two types, private and anonymous. Private is for a user-only site. Anonymous is available for anyone, and thus has a high security risk level.

What is an FTP service?

FTP service permits a user to access files on a machine without having a user account. This is done using one of two special usernames, anonymous or ftp. The FTP service is controlled from the /etc/inetd.conf file.

How do I install anonymous FTP?

The package, anonftp, should be installed if you install the standard Red Hat Linux distribution. To check installation, enter rpm –q anonftp. If not installed at the root, enter rpm –i anonftp-2.8.1.rpm.

What is the port number for FTP service?

Port 21.

What are the basic steps in an FTP request?

The eight steps for a public FTP request are:

1. Client connects to FTP port, usually 21.
2. When connection is detected, the FTP daemon (/usr/sbin/in.ftpd) is invoked.
3. Server is initiated.
4. Client provides a user name and password.
5. User placed in the home directory for FTP users (default is /home/ftp).
6. Server executes a chroot system call.
7. Client gets files.
8. Server disconnects.

How do I use the ftpd daemon?

The ftpd daemon is started by inetd. There must be an entry in the /etc/inetd.conf file. The syntax is in.ftpd [dlTt].

What files need to be edited to customize FTP configuration?

Three files you can edit to customize your FTP configuration are as follows:

- /etc/ftpaccess—defines access controls, etc.
- /etc/ftpusers—lists all users not allowed to use FTP
- /etc/ftphosts—determines accessibility from other hosts

How can the FTP server be made securer than normal?

You can make the FTP server securer than normal by editing the access rights found in these files:

- /etc/ftpaccess
- /etc/ftpconversions
- /etc/ftphosts
- /var/log/xferlog

What is found in the /etc/ftpaccess file?

The /etc/ftpaccess file is the primary method for establishing FTP control parameters. There are five areas of controls:

- Access
- Type of information to client
- Logging
- General (such as shutdown)
- Permissions

What are the FTP commands that can be used to control user access?

There are seven FTP commands that can be used to control user access:

autogroup	Automatically assigns users to a certain group permission
class	Defines a user class
deny	Explicitly denies a user to certain hosts
guestgroup	Restricts real users to only FTP privileges
limit	Controls the number of users by class and time of day
loginfails	Sets the number of login failures permitted to a user
private	Permits user to FTP files without having a public FTP server

What are the commands that control FTP logging?

There are two FTP commands for controlling logging:

log commands	Logs each command invoked by a user
log transfers	Logs file transfers by user

What are the commands that control FTP permissions?

There are eight FTP commands that can control FTP permissions:

chmod	Determines whether a client can change a permission on the server's files
delete	Determines whether a client can delete a file on the server
overwrite	Determines whether a client can replace a file on the server
passwd-check	Determines the level of security for a string to be submitted as an anonymous user's e-mail address
path-filter	Determines the acceptable filenames for any upload to the server
rename	Determines whether a rename request is valid
umask	Determines whether a client can change default permissions
upload	Determines what permissions the client has to place files in directories and the types of permissions the file can hold

What are the packages that support FTP?

In Red Hat Linux 6.0 there are at least four packages that support FTP. They are the following:

anonftp (version 2.8.1)	Permits downloads from your machine without having a user account; anonymous access
ftp (version 0.10-22)	Provides the standard UNIX command-line FTP client
gftp (version 1.13)	Provides a multithreaded FTP client for X Windows. It permits such actions as simultaneous downloads and file transfer queries.
ncftp (version 3.0beta18-3)	Provides an enhanced FTP client that includes support for command line editing, command histories, recursive gets, and automatic anonymous logins.

What are some important FTP administrative utilities?

There are three important FTP administrative utilities or tools that give server status and shutdown capabilities:

ftpcount	Shows total current users count and maximum possible
ftpwho	Shows all active connected users
ftpshut	Permits a continuously running server to be shut down

Chapter 7

Security Server Tips

This chapter looks at the firewall server, which is the centerpiece of a network security system when the network can be accessed from another network, usually the Internet or remotely. Having a firewall does not mean your system is secure. It takes more than a firewall to have a security system, including such things as the correct use of remote host access commands (Chapter 6) and a tight permissions system on your file server (Chapter 3).

Note: To see available options for the commands discussed in the chapter, you need to use a man command-name command.

7

What is a firewall server?

A firewall server is a controlled entry point to the internal network from an external network such as the Internet. The opposite of a firewall is a gateway. It uses a set of rules to determine what is allowed and what is barred. It protects as well as monitors traffic.

What are the types of firewalls?

There are two basic types of firewalls:

- IP filtering—Blocks unspecified access
- Proxy—Indirect access

What are four essential components of a firewall?

The four essential firewall components are the following:

- Rule set (policy)
- Authentication mechanism
- Packet filters

- Router/gateway application

What is a rule set (policy)?

A rule set might be called a policy, which is a high-level administrative goal set. In this instance, it is a set of high-level rules that specify the accessibility of the host, permitting or barring.

What is an authentication mechanism?

An authentication mechanism in its simplest form is a password. In a more complex form it is a smart card.

What is a filter?

A filter is a low-level policy, a practice, in that the filter actually carries out the specified rules of the policy.

What is a router/gateway program?

A router/gateway program or application is one in which the router acts as a funnel into the gateway application, which in turn handles a robust authentication and logging system.

How does an IP filtering firewall work?

This type of firewall uses absolute filters. A common use of filters is to protect e-mail from spam. However, this firewall type lacks a needed function, logging.

How does a proxy server serve as a firewall?

In the living world a proxy is an authorized agent that works for another person. The proxy speaks indirectly for another. Thus the two essential characteristics of a proxy server are authorized and indirect.

What are some of the advantages of a proxy server?

The following are advantages of a proxy server:

- Logs all actions
- No direct IP address
- Secure when configured correctly

What is ipfwadm?

The IP Firewall Administration is ipfwadm.

Note: If you want just a filtering firewall you only need Linux's basic networking packages.

Where can I get ipfwadm?

Since you do not get the Linux firewall package, ipfwadm, with the Red Hat Linux distribution you can go to http://www.xos.nl/linux/ipfwadm

What is a gateway server?

A gateway server is a controlled exit point to the external network. The opposite of gateway is a firewall. It uses a set of rules to determine what is allowed and what is barred. It protects as well as monitors traffic.

What is masquerading?

It is the presenting of one IP address to the world while having multiple internal addresses.

Note: For more information on masquerading, see IP Masquerade mini-HOWTO by Ambrose Au (ambrose@writeme.com).

What is a major disadvantage of a firewall?

The major disadvantage is also the major advantage. A firewall limits access to your intranet (network) from the Internet. Services are filtered.

Where on the Internet can I get information on firewalling?

There are many vendor sites, but two sites of interest might be:

http://whatis.com/firewall.htm

ftp://ftp.sunet.se/security/docs/nistpubs/800-10/node44.html

How do I set up a firewall?

See Firewall-HOWTO.gz. This HOWTO tells how to set an Internet firewall on a Linux system. It covers the definition of a firewall, firewalling software, preparing the Linux system, installing the TIS proxy server, setting up the SOCKS proxy server, and advanced configurations. The author is Mark Grennan (markg@netplus.net).

Note: Additional information on an IP firewall is found in the Linux NET-3-HOWTO by Terry Dawson (terry@perf.no.itg.telstra.com.au).

What are the basic steps in making a firewall with masquerading?

1. Compile firewall support into the kernel by running make config and selecting the following options:
   - Network firewalls
   - TCP/IP networking
   - IP: firewalling
   - IP: firewall packet logging
   - IP: masquerading
   - IP: ipautofw masq support
   - IP: ICMP masquerading
2. Define the firewall rules for:
   - Accounting
   - Input
   - Output
   - Forwarding

What are accounting rules?

Accounting rules are the rules against which all packets, received or sent, are compared. For every match there is an increment in a packet counter and a byte counter.

What are input rules?

Input rules determine the acceptance of an incoming packet. For every match there is an increment in a packet counter and a byte counter. First rule matched determines the policy of use.

What are output rules?

Output rules determine if an outgoing packet is allowed to be sent. For every match there is an increment in a packet counter and a byte counter. First rule matched determines the policy of use.

What are forwarding rules?

Forwarding rules determine packet movement between remote hosts. For every match there is an increment in a packet counter and a byte counter. First rule matched determines the policy of use. Only traffic traveling across the firewall is affected by forwarding rules.

Are there RFCs on firewalling?

The one Request for Comments on firewalls is RFC 1579 "Firewall—Friendly FTP" by S. Bellovin (February 1994).

What is the importance of the networking options?

The networking options need to be configured in a certain manner to ensure your machine can act as a firewall. You need to enable at least the following options:

- Firewall (CONFIG_FIREWALL)
- Network Aliasing (CONFIG_NET_ALIAS)
- IP: Forwarding/Gatewaying options (CONFIG_IP_FORWARD)
- IP: Accounting (CONFIG_IP_ACCT)
- IP: Optimize as Router Not Host (CONF_IP_ROUTER)
- IP: Drop Source Routed Frame (CONFIG_IP_NOSR)

Note: Ensure all machines talk TCP/IP. In addition, all the above are used in configuring the kernel for TCP/IP.

What does CONFIG_FIREWALL do?

A **Yes** lets the kernel allows networking software to enable or disable selectively access to groups of TCP/IP ports.

What does CONFIG_NET_ALIAS do?

A **Yes** lets the kernel allow multiple IP addresses for a network interface.

What does CONFIG_IP_FORWARD do?

A **Yes** lets the kernel forward TCP/IP packets to another network.

What does CONFIG_IP_ACCT do?

A **Yes** lets the kernel count and record incoming and outgoing traffic in bytes on a per-address and per-port basis.

What does CONFIG_IP_ROUTER do?

A **Yes** lets the kernel act as a router.

What does CONFIG_IP_NOSR do?

A **Yes** lets the kernel drop routed source frames.

Chapter 8

Miscellaneous Server Tips

This chapter notes certain types of miscellaneous server types such as application and messaging, but the focus is on print servers. Most application and messaging services are merged into many of the other servers discussed in this book.

Note: To see available options for the commands discussed in the chapter, you need to do a man command-name command.

What is an application server?

An application server runs the "back end," or server side, of an application. It has been optimized to execute software at top speed. Two special servers of this type are Internet (Chapter 4) and databases that use a query language.

8

What is a messaging server?

A messaging server manages the various messaging services such as a LAN package. It can be configured as an Internet e-mail gateway. It can be used for sorting news services for interest to corporate employees or for dialing into paging services.

What is a print server?

A print server manages all printing requests across the network for attached printers. It does not handle the printer requests of attached printers to individual nodes or terminals.

What is a proxy server?

A proxy server is a server that acts for another server. This server is used in network security solutions (Chapter 7).

What is a printer?

A printer is a set of printer capabilities defined in /etc/printcap. A physical printer can be defined a number of times in /etc/printcap as to how it handles fonts (type or size) and paper size.

What is the /etc/printcap file?

This file contains the specifications, perhaps too extensive for one's taste, for each named printer in the system. This text file can be edited with your editor of choice. It should be in the root and have the permissions –rw-r- -r- -. Some of the data kept in /etc/printcap include the following:

- Print device name
- Spool directory name
- Error file
- Remote printing host
- Remote printer name

Note: The permissions entry translates as owner with read and write, the group with read, and all others none.

Where is an entry on a physical printer kept?

A physical printer is a device, so information on it is kept in the /dev directory.

What are the basic commands for handling printing?

The five basic commands for print administration are as follows:

lpr	prints files (line printer)
lpc	used by the system administrator to manage line printer operations
lpd	line printer daemon, normally invoked at boot

lpq	queries the spool and reports job status
lprm	removes a document from the queue

What is spool?

Spool stands for Simultaneous Peripheral Operation Off Line. It allows for offline printing so the computer is tied up with a long print. It is referred to as background printing.

How do I do offline printing?

To do offline printing use the command:

lpr Basic syntax is lpr [options] [files].

Some of the options are:

-P printer	prints to the printer specified in /etc/printcap	
	-#N	prints N copies of each file
	-h	suppresses the first page with first user data (burst page)
-m	sends mail upon completion of print job	
-r	removes the file after printing	
	-J jobname	prints the job name on the burst page
	-U username	prints the user name on the burst page

The associated files and directories include:

etc/passwd	personal identification
/etc/printcap	printer description file
/usr/sbin/lpd*	line printer daemons
/var/spool/output/*/cf*	control file daemons
/var/spool/output/*/df*	data files specified in the cf files
/var/spool/output/*/tf*	temporary file copies

How can the line printer system be managed?

To manage the line printer system use the command:

lpc Syntax is lpc [command [argument ...]]

This command controls any printer configured in /etc/printcap.

This command has four functions:

8

- Disable or enable a printer
- Disable or enable a printer spool queue
- Reorder the printer spool queue
- Display status reports of printers and queues

Note: If arguments are used, the first is considered a command and the rest are arguments.

Three common commands are the following:

start [printer]	starts a previously stopped spool
stop [printer]	stops a spool
status [printer]	displays printer status

The associated files and directories include the following:

/etc/printcap	printer description file
/var/spool/*	spool directories
/var/spool/*/lock	lock file for queue control

What is the printer daemon?

The printer daemon is normally invoked at boot and is:

lpd	Syntax is lpd [-l] [port#]	
	-l	logs valid network requests
	port#	Internet port number

The essential associated files and directories are:

/dev/lp*	line printer devices
/dev/printer	local request socket
/etc/hosts.equiv	lists machine names allowed for printer access
/etc/hosts.lpd	lists machine names allowed for printer access, but under another administrator
/etc/printcap	printer description file
/var/spool/*	spool directories
/var/spool/*/minfree	minimum free space to leave

How can I query the printing spool?

To query the printing spool and get job status reports use the command:

lpq	Syntax is lpq [-l] [-P printer] [job# ...] [user ...]	
	-l	job information

-P	specifies a printer

The essential associated files and directories are:

/etc/printcap	printer description file
/usr/share/misc/termcap	for screen manipulation
/var/spool/*	spool directories
/var/spool/*/cf*	control files for jobs
Pa/var/spool/*/lock	lock file for the current active job

How do I remove a document from the spool queue?

To remove a document or documents from the print spool queue use the command:

lprm Syntax is [-P printer] [- job # ...] [user ...]

-P	specifies the printer
-	removes all jobs in queue
user	removes all specified users
job #	removes specified job

The basic files and directories include:

/etc/printcap	printer description file
/var/spool/*	spool directories
/var/spool/*/lock	lock file for the current daemon

8

What print configuration tool is available?

The Red Hat Linux printer configuration tool is printtool, and it is found under XFree86.

How do I get more information on printing?

See Printing-HOWTO.gz. This HOWTO tells how to set up printing.

In addition, see Printing-Usage-HOWTO.gz. This HOWTO tells how to use the print spooling system. It also covers how to print various types of files. The author is Matt Foster (markk@auratek.com).

Why can't I configure my printer?

You may need a ghostscript. Go to http://www.users.dircon.co.uk/~typhoon/.

How can I reconfigure my printer?

Under XFree86 you should use # printtool.

How do I define a printer using printtool?

The printtool program detects parallel printer devices. If /dev/lp0, /dev/lp1, or /dev/lp2 is not displayed, either your printer is not turned on or you do not have printing support. If there is no support, click the OK button. Next, give your printer a unique name that is not lpr. Follow the configuration instructions. Finally, do an ASCII or PostScript test from the Tests menu.

How do I set the print system's host ID?

To set the print system's host ID enter the command:

hostid	Syntax is hostid [-v] {decimal-id}	
	-v	prints the decimal and hexadecimal forms of the ID

Note: Only the system administrator can state the argument. The value is kept in the /etc/hostid file.

How can I keep up with printer usage?

To get the information on the number of pages used by each user enter the command:

pac	Syntax is [-P printer] [-c] [-m] [-p price] [-s] [-r] [name ...]	
	-P printer	specifies printer
	-c	sorts output by costs
	-m	groups a user's usage for multiple printers
	-p price	give dollar cost based on the value in /etc/printcap
	-r	reverses sort order

-s	summarizes the accounting file
name	statistics for specified name or names

What are some important printer troubleshooting tips?

The following five printer troubleshooting tips may seem obvious, but:

- Ensure the printer cable is connected correctly
- Ensure the printer is on
- Ensure the kernel daemon is active
- Ensure the lp.o module is available
- Ensure you have the correct printer filter

What man pages are available to assist with printer problems?

The following six man pages may assist in resolving printer problems:

- lpd
- lpq
- lprm
- printcap
- printmail
- tunelp

How can I set up a scanner?

To get documentation and software go to http://www.sunsite.unc/edu/pub/Linux/app/graphic/capture.

Chapter 9

TCP/IP Tips

This chapter focuses on the protocol suite that is the basis for the Internet and an intranet, Transport Control Protocol/Internet Protocol (TCP/IP).

Note: To see available options for the commands discussed in the chapter, you need to use a man command-name command.

What is TCP/IP?

The Transport Control Protocol/Internet Protocol (TCP/IP) is a suite of over 100 protocols and tools that form the basis for the Internet and an intranet. Its origins are from a research project funded by the U.S. Defense Advanced Research Projects Agency (DARPA) in 1969. The idea was to have the ability to move data quickly in case of a nuclear war. This project network was called ARPANET. In 1983, the TCP/IP suite was adopted as a network standard.

What is an IP address?

An IP address is a method for identifying the network interfaces on individual computer systems. The format is nnn.nnn.nnn.nnn. The range for each block is 0 to 255. Any connection to the Internet must be unique. The standard is IPv4.

What is a loopback address?

A loopback address is a reserved IP address, 127.0.0.1. It is usually called localhost. This is a network address, which points to the originating host. It is used for establishing and testing network services without a real Internet connection.

What is IPv6?

IPv6 is the successor to IPv4. It is an attempt to resolve problems caused by IPv4:

- More addresses (128 bits)
- Security (authentication and privacy mechanisms)
- Simpler structure (router packet manipulation)
- More options
- Service tags (multimedia)

How can I install IPv6?

There is an IPv6 network found at http://www-6bone.lbl.gov.

For technical details on installation, try the site http://sloth.wcug.wwu.edu/ipv6/faq/.

Are there RFCs that discuss IPv6?

There are a number of Request for Comments that discuss IPv6 including:

1883	Internet Protocol, Version 6 (IPv6) Specification. S. Deering and R. Hinden. (December 1995)
1884	IP Version 6 Addressing Architecture. R. Hinden and S. Deering, editors. (December 1995)
1885	Internet Control Message Protocol (ICMPv6) for the Internet Protocol Version 6 (IPv6). A. Conta and S. Deering. (December 1995)
1886	DNS Extensions to support IP version 6. S. Thomson and C. Huitema. (December 1995)
1887	An Architecture for IPv6 Unicast Address Allocation. Y. Rekhter, and T. Li, editors. (December 1995)
1888	OSI NSAPs and IPv6. J. Bound, B. Carpenter, D. Harrington, J. Houldsworth, and A. Lloyd. (August 1996)

Are there RFCs that discuss TCP/IP?

There are a number of Request for Comments that discuss TCP/IP including:

1792	TCP/IPX Connection Mib Specification (1995)
0896	Congestion Control in IP/TCP Internetworks (1984)

1155	Structure and Identification of Management Information for TCP/IP-based Internets (1990)
1180	TCP/IP Tutorial (1991)
1791	TCP and UDP over IPX Networks with Fixed Path MTU (1995)
2151	A Primer on Internet and TCP/IP Tools and Utilities (1997)

What is netcfg?

The **netcfg** tool is used to configure basic networking interfaces and services. It is used to set up a PLIP interface, an Ethernet interface, and a PPP connection.

What do I use to hand-configure my network interface?

You need to use the **ifconfig** command to set up the IP address, network mask, and broadcast address.

What are some of the basic TCP/IP commands?

Here are ten of many TCP/IP networking commands and daemons:

ftpd	Daemon for file transfers
gated	Daemon (gateway) for table route management
host	Print host and zone information
ifconfig	Configure network interface parameters
named	Daemon for domain name and IP address translation
netstat	Print network status
nslookup	Query domain servers
pppd	Daemon to create domain PPP serial connection
route	Manage routing tables
routed	Daemon to dynamically update routing tables

Besides the basic TCP/IP commands, what others are available?

arp	bootpd	bootptest	fingerd
ftpd	gdc	icmpinfo	identd
imapd	inetd	logger	lpd

netdate	rdate	rexecd	rlogind
rmail	rsh	rstat	ruptime
rusers	rwall	rwhod	slattach
syslogd	talkd	tcpd	tcpdchk
tcpdmatch	telnetd	tftpd	traceroute

How do I use the ftpd daemon?

The ftpd daemon is started by inetd. There must be an entry in the /etc/inetd.conf file. The syntax is in.ftpd [dlTt].

How do I use the gated daemon?

This gateway routing daemon handles multiple routing protocols including Routing Information Protocol (RIP), Border Gateway Protocol (BGP), and External Gateway Protocol (EGP). It is a replacement for the routed daemon. The syntax is gated [cfnt[options]CN].

How do I use the host command?

The host command prints information about specified hosts or zones in DNS. There are two forms of the syntax:

```
host [options] host [server]
host [options] zone [server]
```

How do I use the ifconfig command?

The ifconfig command assigns an address to a network interface and may be used to configure its parameters. At boot time, it defines each network interface's address on the machine. In addition, it can be used to redefine an interface's address and parameters. There are two forms of the syntax:

```
ifconfig [interface]
ifconfig [interface address_family parameters addresses]
```

How do I use the named command?

The named command is used by the resolver libraries to provide access to the Internet distributed naming database. When no argument is used, named uses /etc/named.boot for its initial data. For further technical details, see RFC 2065, "Domain Name System Security Extensions," by D. Eastlake, 3rd and C. Kaufmann (January 1997). The syntax is named [options].

How do I use the netstat command?

The netstat command shows network status. The syntax is netstat [acinortuvwx].

How do I use the nslookup command?

The nslookup command is used to query Internet domain name servers in one of two modes: interactive or non-interactive. In the interactive mode, the user queries name servers for host and domain information. In the non-interactive mode, the user prints just the name and requested host or domain information. The syntax is nslookup [-option...] [host] | [- [server]].

How do I use the pppd daemon?

The pppd daemon attempts to configure tty for the Point-to-Point Protocol (searching /dev), or by default the controlling terminal. The speed argument is baud rate. The syntax is pppd [options] [tty] [speed].

How do I use the route command?

The route command is used to manipulate manually the routing tables. The syntax is route [options] [command].

How do I use the routed daemon?

The routed daemon is used to manipulate automatically the routing tables. The syntax is route [dgqst] [logfile].

Note: This daemon can be replaced by the gated daemon.

What does arp do?

This command adds to, clears, or dumps the kernel's Address Resolution Protocol (ARP) cache.

What does bootpd do?

This daemon is normally run by **/etc/inetd**. It is the Internet Boot Protocol server.

What does bootptest do?

This command tests a server's **bootpd** daemon by sending a request every second for ten seconds or until the server responds.

What does fingerd do?

It is a remote user information server (daemon). It is based on RFC 1196, "Finger User Internet Protocol." This RFC has been obsoleted by RFC 1288 by D. Zimmerman (December 1991).

What does gdc do?

This command administers the **gated** daemon.

What does icmpinfo do?

This command intercepts and interprets ICMP packets.

What does identd do?

This command provides the username at the specified connection.

What does imapd do?

This is the Interactive Mail Access Protocol (IMAP) server daemon.

What does ftpd do?

This is the Internet File Transfer Protocol (FTP) server daemon.

What is imap?

It is an Internet Message Access Protocol server.

What is inn?

InterNetNews (inn) is a TCP/IP-based news server.

What does inetd do?

This is the Internet service daemon.

What does logger do?

This command adds entries to the system log using the daemon **syslogd**.

What does lpd do?

This is the line printer daemon.

What does netdate do?

This command sets the system time according to the time on a specified host.

What does rdate do?

This command notifies the time server that the date has changed.

What does rexecd do?

This daemon provides remote authentication facilities.

What does rlogind do?

This daemon provides a remote login facility.

What does rmail do?

This command handles remote mail received through UUCP.

What does rsh do?

The rsh command is an execute command on a remote host. If no argument is specified, it begins an interactive shell on the remote host using rlogin.

What does rstat do?

This command gives a summary of the specified host's system status. This summary includes the current time, uptime, and load averages.

What does ruptime do?

This command provides information on how long each local network machine has been up and which users are logged to each other.

What does rusers do?

The rusers command lists users logged in on the local machines (Remote Procedure Call (RPC) version).

What does rwall do?

This command prints a message to all users logged on to the specified host.

What does rwhod do?

This daemon maintains the database used by the rwho and ruptime programs.

What does slattach do?

This command attaches a serial line as a network interface.

What does syslogd do?

This daemon logs system messages into a set of files described by the configuration file /etc/syslog.conf.

What does talkd do?

It notifies a user that someone else wants to initiate a conversation.

What does tcpd do?

This daemon monitors incoming TCP/IP requests.

What does tcpdchk do?

This command displays a list of all problems with the TCP wrapper configuration.

What does tcpdmatch do?

This command predicts the TCP's wrapper response to a specific request.

What does telnetd do?

This is the Telnet protocol server (daemon).

What does tftpd do?

It is a user interface to the Trivial File Transfer Protocol (TFTP). It allows users to transfer files to and from a remote machine.

What does traceroute do?

The command traces the route taken by packets to reach the network host.

What is the Serial Line Internet Protocol?

Serial Line Internet Protocol (SLIP) is for the use of a serial modem (line). It is a part of the TCP/IP suite of protocols.

How do I know if I have SLIP support in my kernel?

Enter dsmesg | more. If you get a message that includes the following, you have SLIP support:

```
CSLIP: code copyright ...
SLIP: version ...
```

How do I load a SLIP module?

At the root, enter the command modprobe slip. To verify it has loaded, enter lsmod.

How can I automate a SLIP connection?

The Dial-up IP Protocol Driver (dip) allows for the automation of the steps in setting up a SLIP connection to a remote system.

What is ICMP?

The Internet Control Message Protocol is a companion protocol of the Internet Protocol. It is used by the kernel networking code to manage error messages and other message types, such as Redirect, among the hosts. While the Redirect message idea sounds good, it actually presents a network security risk.

What is DNS?

The Domain Name System is a network address resolution scheme. It was adopted in 1984.

What are some of the important RFCs on DNS?

Two of the original RFCs on DNS, 1034 and 1035, have been obsoleted by later RFCs.

1033	Domain administrators operations guide. M. Lottor. (November 1987)
1101	DNS encoding of network names and other types. P.V. Mockapetris. (April 1989)
1183	New DNS RR definitions. C.F. Everhart, L.A. Mamakos, R. Ullmann, and P.V. Mockapetris. (October 1990)
1383	An Experiment in DNS Based IP Routing. C. Huitema. (December 1992)
1535	A Security Problem and Proposed Correction With Widely Deployed DNS Software. E. Gavron. (October 1993)
1536	Common DNS Implementation Errors and Suggested Fixes. A. Kumar, J. Postel, C. Neuman, P. Danzig, and S. Miller. (October 1993)
1611	DNS Server MIB Extensions. R. Austein and J. Saperia. (May 1994)
1612	DNS Resolver MIB Extensions. R. Austein and J. Saperia. (May 1994)
1706	DNS NSAP Resource Records. B. Manning and R. Colella. (October 1994)
1712	DNS Encoding of Geographical Location. C. Farrell, M. Schulze, S. Pleitner, and D. Baldoni. (November 1994)
1713	Tools for DNS debugging. A. Romao. (November 1994)
1886	DNS Extensions to support IP version 6. S. Thomson and C. Huitema. (December 1995)
1912	Common DNS Operational and Configuration Errors. D. Barr. (February 1996)
2052	A DNS RR for specifying the location of services (DNS SRV). A. Gulbrandsen, and P. Vixie. (October 1996)
2065	Domain Name System Security Extensions. D. Eastlake, 3rd, and C. Kaufman. (January 1997)
2136	Dynamic Updates in the Domain Name System (DNS UPDATE). P. Vixie, Ed., S. Thomson, Y. Rekhter, and J. Bound. (April 1997)

What is a domain?

A domain is a collection of sites with a common dominator. It can be location, purpose, or interest.

What is a domain name server?

A domain name server holds all the host information for a zone. It is called either an authoritative or a master name server.

What is the IP address for a standalone host?

The IP address that is used for a loopback interface is always 127.0.0.1.

What are some of the basic steps for IP interface configuration?

There are five basic steps for IP interface configuration:

1. Activate the loopback interface
2. Configure the Ethernet interfaces
3. Configure a gateway
4. Route through a gateway
5. Link with a PLIP, SLIP, or PPP interface

What is PLIP?

PLIP stands for Parallel Internet Protocol. It provides a high-speed point-to-point connection. It is one of the two solutions for a permanent connection, the other solution being an Ethernet connection.

How do I add the PLIP interface?

To add the PLIP interface with X Window up, launch **netcfg**. The basic responses are:

1. Click the INTERFACES button
2. Click the ADD button
3. Select PLIP
4. Enter the local host's IP address
5. Enter the remote host's IP address

6. Enter the local host's network mask
7. Select Activate Interface at Boot Time, optional
8. Click DONE
9. Click YES to save
10. Click the Activate button

How do I add an Ethernet interface?

To add an Ethernet interface with X Window up, launch **netcfg**. The basic responses are:

1. Click the INTERFACES button
2. Click the ADD button
3. Select Ethernet
4. Enter the local host's IP address
5. Enter the local host's network mask
6. Select Activate Interface at Boot Time, optional
7. Click DONE
8. Click YES to save

What is DHCP?

DHCP stands for Dynamic Host Configuration Protocol. This automatically tries to configure the network interface. Red Hat uses **dhcpcd** (DHCP client daemon), which is compliant with RFC 2131, "Dynamic Host Configuration Protocol" by R. Droms (March 1997).

Chapter 10

Point-to-Point Protocol (PPP) Tips

This chapter looks at the Point-to-Point Protocol (PPP), which is the common method for transmitting datagrams over serial point-to-point links. It is the method for connecting to an Internet service provider (ISP), but it is not a general networking protocol such as TCP/IP.

Note: To see available options for the commands discussed in the chapter, you need to do a man command-name command.

What is the Point-to-Point Protocol?

Point-to-Point Protocol (PPP) is an Internet protocol for transmission over a serial modem (line).

What are the basic components of PPP?

The three basic components are as follows:

- Daemon—pppd
- Driver—HDLC (high-level data link control)
- Routine—chat

10

How does my PPP connection run?

The Point-to-Point daemon (pppd) runs programs in the background while you are using a PPP connection. It handles data transmission.

How do I set up PPP?

See PPP-HOWTO.gz. This HOWTO tells how to set up and use Point-to-Point Protocol (PPP) networking. It covers an overview of getting the PPP to work as a client, configuring the Linux kernel, getting information on the PPP server, configuring your modem and serial port, setting up Name to address resolution (DNS), and using root privileges. It also covers setting up the PPP connection files, using the Password Authentication Protocol (PAP), setting up the PPP connection manually, automating the PPP connection, debugging, and setting up the PPP server. The author is Robert Hart (hartr@hedland.edu.au).

What are the basic steps in getting PPP to work?

The four basic steps in getting PPP to work are the following:

1. Install PPP (use RPM)
2. Set up a PPP user account
3. Set up chat
4. Configure pppd

How do I know if I have PPP support in my kernel?

Enter dsmesg | more. If you get the message PPP: version ... then you have PPP support.

How do I get status on my PPP connection?

Enter the command pppstats.

How do I use the pppd command?

The pppd daemon attempts to figure tty for the Point-to-Point Protocol (searching /dev), or by default the controlling terminal. The speed argument is baud rate. The syntax is pppd [options] [tty] [speed].

Note: There are over seventy-five options for this daemon. The options involve such things as CHAP (Challenge Handshake Authentication Protocol), domain names, IPCP (IP Control Protocol), IPXCP (IP Transmission Control Protocol), routing, remote networking, LCP (Link Control Protocol), PAP (Password Authentication Protocol), ARP (Address Resolution Protocol), and compression

How can I make my PPP more secure?

There are two authentication protocols available to make your PPP connections more secure. They are the following:

- Password Authentication Protocol (PAP)
- Challenge Handshake Authentication Protocol (CHAP)

Note: In some documentation, CHAP is also called Cryptographic Handshake Authentication Protocol.

What RFCs are available on PPP?

Here is a very short list of five Request for Comments on PPP:

1332	The PPP Internet Protocol Control Protocol (IPCP). G. McGregor. (May 1992)
1618	PPP over ISDN. W. Simpson. (May 1994)
1661	The Point-to-Point Protocol (PPP). W. Simpson, Editor. (July 1994)
1877	PPP Internet Protocol Control Protocol Extensions for Name Server Addresses. S. Cobb. (December 1995)
2023	IP Version 6 over PPP. D. Haskin and E. Allen. (October 1996)

Chapter 11

Network Information System (NIS) Tips

This chapter discusses the Network Information System that was originally know as Sun Yellow Pages (YP); however, because of trademark issues that name was dropped by Sun Microsystems.

Note: To see available options for the commands discussed in the chapter, you need to do a man command-name command.

What is NIS?

The Network Information System is a generic client/server database system most commonly used for sharing password and group files across a network.

Why is NIS associated with YP?

The Network Information System was originally know as Sun Yellow Pages (YP); however, because of trademark issues that name was dropped by Sun. To this day, many of the NIS commands begin with yp. It is used to create a consistent information configuration across a network.

What is the importance of NIS?

Because Linux adheres to the NIS standard, it interacts easily with other versions of UNIX as either client or server.

What is the importance of NIS+?

NIS+ is an evolutionary step of NIS that addresses some of the security issues of NIS.

How does NIS work?

A master host is used for all system administration files and databases and it does the distribution of this information to all other hosts across the network. This is done by compiling information into databases called maps. It uses the RPC protocol.

What is a requirement for one NIS domain?

For NIS clients and servers to communicate, they must be in the same NIS domain. Both are bound to a NIS domain, thus a client can belong to only one domain.

What is the RPC protocol?

Remote Procedure Call (RPC) allows a host to do a remote call as though it were a local call. It uses a library of procedures and a network standard for ordering bytes and data structures.

Where are the RPCs located?

Most of the RPC files are located in two directories:

- /usr/bin
- /usr/src/linux-2.2.5/include/linux

How do I find RPC information?

To get information on the status RPC use this syntax rpcinfo [options] [host] [program] [version].

To get further option list, enter rpcinfo.

To show all register RPC service on the local machine, enter rpcinfo -p.

What types of NIS servers are available?

There are two commonly available servers:

- yps
- ypserv

What are the two types of NIS servers?

The two types of NIS servers are:

- Master—maintains and distributes the maps
- Slave—handles local processing requests

What is an NIS domain?

An NIS domain is a group of hosts with a common set of maps. These maps are contained in a subdirectory of /var/yp with the domain name. The domainname command is used to set up this NIS structure.

What is an NIS map?

A map consists of two dbm database files:

- Directory of keys
- Data values

How do I administer NIS?

To administer NIS ensure the RPC portmap program is installed. You then need to set a NIS server and NIS clients.

How do I administer NIS group access?

To control access you can put a group into a netgroup. The netgroup information is found in the /etc/netgroup file.

What types of NIS accounts exist?

The two types of NIS accounts are:

- Distributed—must be administered from the master machine and uses uniform NIS domain information
- Local—administered from the local machine and uses information unique to a specific machine

Is there a HOWTO on NIS?

See the Linux NIS (YP)/NIS HOWTO. This HOWTO tells how to configure Linux to support server and client using NIS. The author is Thorsten Kukuk (kukuk@vt.unipadrborn.de).

What are some of the NIS commands?

domainname	sets or displays name of current domain
rpc.portmap	RPC program number to IP mapper
rpc.yppasswdd	server for modifying the password file
rpcinfo	reports RPC information
showmount	shows information about the server
ypbind	daemon that lets client processes on a single node communicate with a ypserv process
ypcat	prints values in a database specified by mname
ypinit	builds and installs a database on a server
ypmatch	prints value of one or more keys from a map specified by mname
yppasswd	changes login password in network information system
yppoll	determines map version on server
yppush	forces propagation of changed server
ypset	points ypbind at a particular server

How do I allow a specific user to log in to NIS?

To allow a specific user to log in to NIS, add a line in the /etc/passwd file as follows:

```
+username::::::shell-name
```

The shell name is optional.

How do I stop just anyone from logging in to NIS?

To limit the NIS users in the /etc/passwd file, change +:::::: to +::::::/bin/false. This means that only people with actual entries in the /etc/passwd file are allowed to log in.

How do I troubleshoot NIS?

Here are three important techniques in troubleshooting NIS problems:

- Ensure the processes are running by using ps auxw
- Ensure /etc/nsswitch.conf is correctly configured
- Check system logs for configuration problems

Chapter 12

Network File System (NFS) Tips

This chapter looks at the Network File System as a means for connecting disks on a remote system to a local system and giving the appearance that they are located in the same physical site.

Note: To see available options for the commands discussed in the chapter, you need to do a man command-name command.

What is the Network File System?

Network File System is a means for connecting disks on a remote system to a local system and giving the appearance that they are located in the same physical site. It allows you to mount files from different computers over a TCP/IP network.

What is a use for NFS?

You could mount a computer with all home directories so all the users might access their home directories from any computer.

What is the core characteristic of NFS?

It is a stateless protocol. Each client and server request is unique or complete unto itself. This means NFS has a robust nature. A server can go down and the clients do not have to reboot.

What may be the weakest feature of NFS?

By its design, it is an insecure environment. If you need to share data and disk space and be secure, you need to consider an alternative to NFS.

What are the basic NFS components?

There are three basic components of an NFS:

- TCP/IP suite of protocols
- Server that uses the process known as exporting the file system
- Client that might be automatically mounted using /etc/fstab file at boot time

Is there a special requirement for mounting NFS?

You must use the syntax of hostname:/file/system/path within /etc/fstab. For example, you might use mailserver:/var/spool/mail.

What are some of the NFS commands?

domainname	sets or displays name of current domain
rpc.portmap	RPC program number to IP mapper
rpc.yppasswdd	server for modifying the password file
rpcinfo	reports RPC information
showmount	shows information about the server
ypbind	daemon lets client processes on a single node communicate with a ypserv process
ypcat	prints values in a database specified by mname
ypinit	builds and installs a database on a server
ypmatch	prints value of one or more keys from a map specified by mname
yppasswd	changes login password in network information system
yppoll	determines map version on server
yppush	forces propagation of changed server
ypset	points ypbind at a particular server

What NFS daemons do I need?

You need to have running on your server rpc.mountd and rpc.nfsd.

Note: RPC stands for Remote Procedure Call. An RPC enables procedures to be executed on a server.

How do I start these daemons?

You need two lines in a script located in /etc/rc.d/init/nfs. They are:

daemon rpc.mountd
daemon rpc.nfsd

Note: These daemons must start only after rpc.portmap is running. The NFS must be entered in the configuration file /etc/exports.

What does rpc.portmap do?

It maps calls from clients to the appropriate NFS daemon.

What does rpc.mountd do?

This daemon handles mount and unmount requests.

What does rpc.nfsd do?

This daemon translates the NFS requests to actual requests on the local filesystem server.

How does the /etc/exports file work?

It is used by rpc.mountd and rpc.nfsd to determine the files that are to be exported and their restrictions. It consists of a list of file systems, one per line. Each line consists of:

- Mount point for a local file system
- Allowable computers that might be mounted
- Mount options separated by commas

What are possible mount options for /etc/exports?

The 16 options are:

all-squash	Maps to the anonymous user all user IDs (UIDs) and group IDs (GIDs)
anongid	Sets the GID for the anonymous account
anonuid	Sets the UID for the anonymous account

insecure	Permits non-authenticated access
link_absolute	Does not convert absolute symbolic links to relative links
link_relative	Converts absolute symbolic links to relative links
map_daemon	Maps local and remote names and numeric IDs
no_root_squash	Does not do mapping from the root (default)
noaccess	Excludes subdirectories from a client
no-all-squash	Opposite of all-squash (default)
ro	Mounts the file system as read-only (default)
root-squash	Does mapping from the root
rw	Mounts the file system as read-write
secure	Requires authenticated access
squash-gids	Specifies the GIDs subject to anonymous mapping
squash-uids	Specifies the UIDs subject to anonymous mapping

What are the basic NFS mount options?

hard	Does a hard mount (default)
intr	Does an NFS interrupt
rsize=n	Specifies the datagram size in bytes for read requests (default is 1,024 bytes)
soft	Does a soft mount
timeo=n	Specifies the wait time for a request in tenths of a second (default is 0.7)
wsize=n	Specifies the datagram size in bytes for write requests (default is 1,024 bytes)

What is the difference between a hard and soft mount?

With a hard mount when a client has a major time out of 60 seconds, there is a continuous remount process until there is success. With a soft mount, the client gets an I/O error and call processing continues without trying to do a remount.

Is there is an automatic check on the integrity of NFS?

At boot time the NFS is checked to see if the pass number field of /etc/fstab has a value greater than 0 (zero).

Is there a manual way to check the integrity of NFS?

Use the fsck command. First, check the root filesystem by using the command fsck –V –a /.

Second, check all the other filesystems including NFS by using the command fsck –R –A –V –a.

This command means all filesystems should be checked except the root, there should be informational (verbose) messages, and there should not be an interactive process (repairs are automatic).

How do I check for the presence of NFS daemons?

Use the command rpcinfo – p.

This command displays all running registered RPC programs.

How do I start and stop NFS services?

To start an NFS service at the root level enter /etc/rc.d/init.d/nfs start. To stop the service, enter /etc/rc.d/init.d/nfs stop.

Is there a HOWTO for NFS?

See NFS HOWTO by Nicolai Langfeldt.

What ports do I use to firewall NFS?

The nfsd operates at port 2049, both TCP/IP and UDP protocols.

The portmapper is at port 111, both TCP/IP and UDP.

The mountd is at port 745 and 747, TCP/IP and UDP.

You should check the ports with the rpcinfo -p command.

Note: TCP/IP stands for Transmission Control Protocol/ Internet Protocol. UDP stands for User Datagram Protocol.

Is there a man page for NFS?

See man page nfs(5). In addition, see the man pages for portmap, mountd, nfsd, and exports.

What is mountd?

The NFS mount daemon is mountd. Some of the options include:

-d	verbose logging (debugging)
-f	specifies the export files
-h	short help
-n	any incoming mount request accepted
-p	puts server into a promiscuous mode (serves any network host)
-r	allows imported NFS filesystems to be exported
-v	reports current program version number

What is nfsd?

The NFS service daemon is nfsd. Its options are the same as mountd.

What does rpcinfo do?

The rpcinfo command makes an RPC call to an RPC server and reports what it finds. Its syntax is

```
rpcinfo –p [host]
rpcinfo [-n portnum] –u host program [version]
rpcinfo [-n portnum] –t host program [version]
rpcinfo –b program version
rpcinfo –d program version
```

The options being:

-b	RPC broadcast to procedure 0
-d	deletes registration for the specified RPC service
-n	uses portnum for the –t and –u options
-p	probes the port mapper for all registered RPC programs and prints a list
-t	uses TCP to make an RPC call to the specified host program

-u uses UDP to make an RPC call to the specified host program

What does showmount do?

The showmount command shows mount information for an NFS server. Some of its options include:

- -a lists the client host name and mounted directory in host:dir format
- -d lists directories of specified clients
- -e shows the NFS server's export list
- -h provides short help summary
- -v displays current program version number

What are the available RFCs on NFS?

Two Request for Comments (RFCs) are:

- RFC 1094—NFS: Network File System Protocol Specification. Sun Microsystems, Inc. (March 1989)
- RFC 1813—NFS Version 3 Protocol Specification. B Callaghan, B. Pawlowski, and P. Staubach. (June 1995)

Also, see Appendix C, "Networking Request for Comments (RFCs)."

Chapter 13

Network Administrative Tips

This chapter looks at administration tips for a network. A network is an environment where multiple types of machines, not just computers, interact with each other.

Note: To see available options for the commands discussed in the chapter, you need to use a man command-name command.

What is a network?

A network is an environment where multiple types of machines interact with each other. The machines include servers, workstations, and printers. The network's primary goal is to deliver services through a set of servers, thus the name.

What are some of the expected network services?

There are five core services common to all systems:

- File management (Chapter 3)
- Mail (Chapter 2)
- News (Chapter 5)
- Remote access (Chapter 6)
- Internet access (Chapter 4)

Note: Internet access is a recent development for the network environment, but has rapidly become an expected network service. One might include such services as bulletin boards and chat, but these services are manifested in different ways in different corporations.

What is a daemon?

A daemon is a process that handles a service. A daemon runs in the background waiting to handle a service request. In Linux the names of many daemons end in the letter **d**, such as **ftpd**, the daemon for **ftp**.

What is an intranet?

An intranet is a network that runs on Internet protocols. The basic suite of Internet protocols is called TCP/IP (Transmission Control Protocol/Internet Protocol). Since UNIX networking commands are based on TCP/IP, so is Linux.

What are some of the basic TCP/IP commands?

Here are ten of many TCP/IP networking commands and daemons:

ftpd	daemon for file transfers
gated	daemon (gateway) for table route management
host	prints host and zone information
ifconfig	configures network interface parameters
named	daemon for domain name and IP address translation
netstat	prints network status
nslookup	queries domain servers
pppd	daemon to create domain PPP serial connection
route	manages routing tables
routed	daemon to update dynamically routing tables

Note: For discussions on the above commands, see Chapter 9, "TCP/IP Tips."

What are the important command operators?

Here are eight important operators:

-	(dash) used for options
.	(period) tells the shell to execute all commands in the file that are passed as an argument
&	(ampersand) after any other command tells the computer to run the command in the background

|	(vertical bar) separates programs on the command line to "pipe" the output from one command to another
>	sends the output of a program to a file or another device
<	feeds a program the contents of a file or input from another device or source
>>	appends the output of a program onto the end of a specified file
<<	tells a program when the end of input is reached

How do I use online help?

There are at least four commands that may be used:

apropos finds all man pages for a keyword (similar to man -k keyword)

Note: No options. It uses the whatis database, which is an index of keywords contained in all man pages. To create this database, which may take overnight, run from the root level the command /etc/cron.weekly/makewhatis.cron.

info displays online help information for a specified command

-d dirname	adds a directory to the directory listing to be searched
-f infofile	specifies files to be used by info
-h	displays usage information about info

Note: The syntax is info [options] command.

man displays information about a command in the man(ual) pages

man (n)	where n is a man page section number
man -a	displays all man pages matching a specific command
man -h	displays a help message and exits
man -k	finds a man page by string
man -p path	finds a man page by path
man -s	finds a man page by system

Note: The syntax is man [options] [section] command.

whatis — searches for a complete word, similar to apropos, in the whatis database under the /usr/man directory

Note: The makewhatis command builds the whatis command database.

How can one make long commands easier?

There are three commands that let you manage command names so they are easier for you to use:

alias — lets you define a long command as an abbreviation (alias [new-name=current-name])

Note: No options. The syntax is alias [abbrev=command]. If you type only alias, you get all defined abbreviations.

type — lets you see a command's location and type

Note: No options. The syntax is type command. It tells you if the command is a built-in shell command or a separate executable command.

unalias — lets you delete a command defined by alias

Note: No options. The syntax is unalias alias-name.

What is the meaning of [] in command syntax?

The square brackets ([]) mean that part of the command is optional. The only thing that is never optional is, of course, the command.

What are some network commands to handle files?

There are at least two basic commands for file management:

chmod — lets you change file permissions

u	user
g	group
o	other
r	read
w	write
x	execute

+	adds
-	deletes
=	sets the permissions as specified
Example:	**chmod ug+rx file1** means to add read and execute permissions to user and group of file1.

Other options reflect action:

-c	lists only files whose permissions changed
-f	stops any error message displays
-v	wordy displays of permission changes
-R	recursively changes file permissions in all subdirectories

Note: The syntax is **chmod [options] permission files.**

chown lets you change file owner and group

-c	lists only files whose permissions changed
-f	stops any error messages displays
-v	wordy displays for permission changes
-R	recursively changes file permissions in all subdirectories

Note: The syntax is **chown [options] user-name.group-name files.** This command requires that you be logged in at the **root** to make changes.

How do I find files?

There are at least five important commands for file management:

find finds files based on criteria such as name, size, etc.

Note: When **find** is used without arguments, the output is a listing of all files in the current directory including the subdirectories. The syntax is **find path [options]**. To display all files that end in .gz, you would enter **find. -name "*.gz"**.

locate finds files based on a periodically updated database

Note: No options. The command **updatedb** builds the database used by the **locate** command.

13

look — searches files for a string and also is used as a dictionary command for words found in the /usr/dict directory

whereis — finds binaries, man pages, and sources for a command

- -b — searches only for binaries
- -m — searches only for man pages
- -v — searches only for sources

which — searches in the directories listed in the PATH environment variable for a command

Note: No options.

How do I archive and compress files?

There are at least eight commands for archiving and compressing files:

compress — compresses files using Lempel-Ziv compression

- -c — compresses file to standard output and retains original
- -d — decompresses the file
- -r — recursively compresses files in subdirectories
- -v — verifies by a message that each file is compressed
- -V — prints a version number and exits

Note: The syntax is compress [options] files. A .Z is appended as a suffix to the filename.

cpio — copies files to and from an archive

- -a — resets access times of input files
- -B — copies using 5,120 bytes per record (default equals 512)
- -c — reads or writes header information as ASCII
- -d — creates directories as needed
- -i — extracts files whose names match the expression
- -m — retains previous file modification time
- -o — copies to archive files whose names are provided on standard output
- -p — copies files to another directory on the same system
- -v — prints a listing of filenames

Note: The syntax is cpio [options] expression.

gunzip	uncompresses files compressed with either compress or gzip	

Note: The options are the same as for the gzip command. The file suffix can be either .gz or .Z.

gzip	compresses files better than compress	
	-c	writes file to standard output and retains the original file
	-d	uncompresses the file
	-h	displays a help message
	-l	lists contents of a compressed file
	-n	does not save original name and stamp
	-r	recursively compresses files in all subdirectories
	-v	displays wordy output
	-V	displays version number

Note: The syntax is gzip [options] files.

tar	creates an archive of files in one or more directories	
	-c	creates a new archive
	-C dir	extracts files into the specified directory
	-d	compares files in an archive with files in the current directory
	-f file	uses the specified file as the archive
	-L n	specifies capacity as n kilobytes
	-N date	archives files newer than the specified date
	-r	extends the archive with more files
	-t	displays a listing of the contents of an archive
	-T file	archives or extracts the filenames specified in file
	-v	displays wordy messages
	-x	extracts from the archive
	-z	compresses or uncompresses archive with gzip

Note: The syntax is tar [options] files_or_directories.

uncompress uncompresses files compressed with compress

-c	writes file to standard output and retains the original file
-r	recursively uncompresses files in all subdirectories
-v	displays a message as each file is uncompressed
-V	displays version number and exits

Note: The syntax is uncompress [options] files. It removes the .Z suffix.

unzip	extracts (default), lists, or tests a zipped file
zip	adds (default), lists, or tests a zipped file

What commands display processing status?

There are at least six commands for displaying processing status:

free displays amount of the system's free and used memory

-b	displays memory in bytes
-k	displays memory in kilobytes (the default)
-m	displays memory in megabytes
-s n	repeats the command every n seconds
-t	displays a total amount summary

Note: The syntax is free [options].

printenv displays the current environmental variables (no options)

ps displays a listing of currently running processes

a	displays processes of other users
f	displays family tree process
j	displays output using jobs format
l	displays process details in long format
m	displays memory usage data for each process
u	displays user name and start time
x	displays process not associated with any terminal.

Note: The syntax is ps [options]. The - (dash) prefix is not used with these options.

pstree shows parent-child relationships clearly in the form of a tree, similar to **ps**

-a	displays command line arguments
-c	displays full subtrees
-l	displays long lines
-n	sorts processes by process ID
-p	displays process IDs

Note: The syntax is **pstree [options] [process-id]**.

top displays a listing of the most processor- and memory-intensive processes

-d N	specifies the delay between updates in N seconds
-q	causes **top** to run with the highest priority (must be at the root)

Note: The syntax is **top [options]**.

uname displays system and kernel information

-a	displays all information
-m	displays the machine type
-n	displays the machine's host name
-p	displays the processor type
-r	displays the operating system release (such as 5.2.0)
-s	displays the operating system name
-v	displays the compilation date of the operating system

Note: The syntax is **uname [options]**.

What commands are available to manage processes?

There are ten basic commands for process management:

bg runs an interrupted process in the background (no options)

dmesg prints a system boot log that can be used to diagnose system problems

dump creates a backup of selected directories

13

fg	runs a process in the foreground (no options)	

Note: Used to continue a process after an interruption by a Ctrl+Z.

halt	shuts down Linux and powers down the computer	
	-f	forces a halt
	-i	shuts down all network interfaces before halting system
	-n	does not flush in-memory buffers before halting
	-r	forces the system to halt

Note: The syntax is halt [options].

kill	sends a signal, usually termination, to a process	
	-l	displays a listing of the signal names and numbers
	-sign	sends the specified signal where sign is a name or number

Note: The syntax is kill [options] process-id.

ldd	displays the shared libraries to run a program	
	-d	relocates functions and reports missing functions
	-r	relocates both data and functions and reports missing objects
	-v	prints the version number of ldd
	-V	prints the version of the dynamic linker (ld.so)

Note: The syntax is ldd [options] programs.

nice	runs a process with lower priority	
	+n	adds n to nice value (makes a higher priority)
	-n	subtracts n from nice value (makes a lower priority)

Note: The syntax is nice [options] programs.

reboot	stops Linux and restarts the computer	

-i	shuts down all network interfaces before rebooting
-f	forces halt
-n	does not flush in-memory buffers before rebooting

Note: The syntax is reboot [options].

shutdown the administrator's logoff; shuts down Linux

-c	cancels a shutdown in progress
-f	performs a fast reboot
-h	halts the system after terminating all the processes
-k	sends warning messages, but does not shut down the system
-r	reboots the system after terminating all processes
-t	specifies the time between the message and the kill signal

Note: The syntax is shutdown [options] time [messages].

What commands handle user management?

There are at least six commands for user management:

adduser adds a user and can be used only at the root level

Note: The syntax is adduser user-ID.

chsh changes the default shell that is started at login

-s shell	specifies the name of the shell executable to be used (found in /etc/shells)

Note: The syntax is chsh [-s shell] [username]. The user's default shell is found in /etc/passwd.

groups displays a listing of groups that includes a specified user (no options)

id displays the user and group ID for a specified user name

-g	displays group ID
-n	displays group name

13

-u displays user ID

Note: The syntax is id [options] [username].

passwd changes a password (no options; syntax is passwd username)

su lets one become another user or root when there is no argument

Note: The command su (switch user) requires a password if a general user tries to switch to become another user, while the root level does not require a password.

What commands handle job management?

There are at least four commands for managing jobs:

at schedules a task or job to run at a specified time

atq lists the queue of waiting jobs

atrm removes a specified job

batch runs jobs according to load average

How can I make a banner?

Enter $ banner expression.

How do I set date and time?

There are two basic commands for setting date and time:

cal gives you various views of the calendar

-j displays number of the day between 1 and 366

-y displays the calendar for all the months of the current year

Note: Without an option, cal prints a calendar of the current month. When a month number is specified, one gets a view of that month (1 = January). The syntax is cal [options] [month-number] [year].

date displays or sets date and time

-s sets the date and time

-u displays or sets time using Greenwich Mean Time

Note: The syntax is date options +format in which you can specify a display format for date and time in format of MMDDHHmm CC YY. MM is month, DD is day, HH is hour, mm is minutes, CC is century, and YY is year.

How do I power down the system?

Use halt -p.

This is when a system halt has been tried. The -p means poweroff.

What are some networking commands?

This is an abbreviated listing, but these are commands you must know to do networking administration and maintenance on a Linux system:

ifconfig	configures network interfaces (used at the root level)
irc	permits you to communicate interactively with other people on the Internet or intranet
netcfg	Red Hat Linux's network configuration tools run under XFree86
netstat	displays the status of network connections on TCP, RAW, UDP, or UNIX sockets
ping	requests packet echoes from network hosts
pppd	Point-to-Point Protocol daemon runs as a background program when connected to the Internet
pppstats	prints Point-to-Point network statistics
setfdprm	sets floppy drive parameters
setserial	configures specific serial ports and status can be reported
statserial	prints serial port status and is run at the root level
telnet	runs a telnet session
tput	changes or resets terminal settings
uptime	shows how long your system has been running
vmstat	prints virtual memory statistics
w	shows who is logged on to the system
who	prints the login name, terminal type, login time, and remote host name of each logged-on user

When should I use a HOWTO?

You should use a HOWTO when you are seeking to perform a specific task or find support. HOWTOs cover installation, administrative, and maintenance procedures. They also cover support such as listings for consultants and value-add vendors.

Where do I find HOWTOs?

The ASCII versions of HOWTOs are found in the directory /usr/doc/HOWTO. However, they are compressed with gzip. To read without uncompressing, use the command zless name-HOWTO.gz.

What is a man page?

A man page (manual page) is online documentation about the system. A man page is actually a page from a printed manual. A compilation of all the man pages would be over 1,500 pages. They are not tutorials, but precise technical documentation. Man pages are a set of directories, each containing a section of the man pages.

How do I find a man page?

To read without uncompressing a man page, use the command man command-name.

What is the syntax for the man command?

The basic syntax for man is man [options] [sections] command-name. The options are:

man — displays information about a command in the man(ual) pages

man (n)	where n is a man page section number (1-9 or n)
man -a	displays all man pages matching a specific command
man -h	displays a help message and exits
man -k	finds a man page by string

man -p path	finds a man page in the directory given by path instead of using the default
man -s	finds a man page by system
man -t	formats a man page for a PostScript printer

How do I print a man page?

With a PostScript printer use the command man -t command-name | lpr.

How do authors divide the man pages?

The basic format for man pages is:

Name
Synopsis
Description
Command-Line Options
See Also
Bugs

Note: Over time some authors have included such additional sections as Author, Sort Keys, Updating, and Notes.

How does Red Hat divide the man pages?

Red Hat divides the content of the man pages into categories, or sections. These sections are listed below in the order they are searched. This means that a command or call that is in both sections 8 and 2 would produce a search result found in 8 only. The sections are:

1	User commands
8	System administration and maintenance commands
2	System calls
3	Functions and library routines
4	Special files, device drivers, and hardware
5	Configuration files and file formats
6	Games and demos
7	Miscellaneous
9	Kernel internals
n	Tcl/Tk commands

How do I find multiple man page sections for a command or call?

The basic syntax to specify a section is man # topic. For example, if you were to enter man 1 chmod you would see the system command for changing mode. You would also see that the man page is no longer valid and that the Texinfo documentation is now the authoritative source. However, if you were to enter man 2 chmod you would get the system call man page for chmod.

Where are man pages found online?

Look in directory /usr/man. There are ten Linux manual sections:

/usr/man/man1	Commands
/usr/man/man2	System calls
/usr/man/man3	Library calls
/usr/man/man4	Special files
/usr/man/man5	File formats
/usr/man/man6	Games
/usr/man/man7	Macro packages
/usr/man/man8	System management
/usr/man/man9	Kernel routines
/usr/man/mann	Tcl/Tk commands

How can I search the man pages for a string?

First, you must run at the root level /etc/cron.weekly/ makewhatis.cron. This is an overnight process. Second, after the database is built you can use the command man -k string.

Note: Another command can be used instead of man -k string. It is apropos string, and it gives the same output.

How do I see the source of a man page?

To see, for example, the source page for chmod, the shell command, you would enter:

```
cd /usr/man/man1
more chmod.1
```

Can I write my own man page?

There are two blank directories, /usr/man/mann and /usr/man/cat, available for this purpose. The easiest method is to put your man page with its description in a text file. However, man pages are designed for the **nroff** text formatter. One can have a file mixed with text and **nroff** directives. To verify that you have created a man page, use the following: **$ nroff -m filename | more.**

What happens when I access a man page?

Besides being displayed, a copy of the formatted page is saved in the /etc/catn directory. This makes future accesses quicker.

How do I move about in a man page?

After you display a man page, the important keystrokes are:

Enter	Pages down line by line
Space	Pages down page by page
b	Pages up one page
n	Finds the next occurrence of the previous search
q	Quits and returns you to your prior location
/	Searches for a string when followed by the string and Enter

What are some keywords for searching man pages?

Some keywords and interesting possibilities for searching man pages are:

Database	Password
Directory	Printer
Emacs	Query
File (include type)	Resource
Function	Service
Graphics	Socket
MS-DOS	Strings
Netnews	System calls
Networking	Utility
Newsgroup	

How do I find out about compatible hardware?

See Hardware-HOWTO.gz. This HOWTO lists known hardware that works with Linux and how to locate drivers. It covers some 20 different types of hardware devices for Intel platforms including laptops, memory, video and sound cards, controllers, network adapters, drives, modems, printers, and scanners. The author is Patrick Reijnen (patrick@bart.nl).

What types of editors are available?

These five editors may be available to you:

ed	A line editor that works with a buffer. This means the text resides in an in-memory storage area until you explicitly store it to a file.
GNU emacs	An intimidating text editor so powerful that a separate book can be written on it. It runs either as a text-mode full-screen display or as an xterm window under X.
jed	A text editor with the initials of its author, Joe E. Davis. A unique feature is that you can edit binary files.
Joe	A text editor that does not do text formatting and uses commands similar to the Wordstar PC word processor. It is named after its author, Joseph H. Allen.
Vim	Vim was not named after its author. It stands for Vi IMproved. It is supposed to be an enhanced version of the UNIX text editor vi.

Note: It is possible that Joe and Vim might ask you for your terminal type. To see if your terminal is set, enter $ echo $TERM. If there is no answer, you can do the following: $ export TERM=name where name equals Linux, vt100, or xterm. Linux is used when you are directly logged into the system console. If you are dialed into Linux, you use vt100. If you are using a graphical user interface, you use xterm. If you are using bash, this command can be put into your .profile file.

What types of graphic programs are available?

These six graphic and image programs may be available to you:

Ghostscript A utility used for printing PostScript documents. It is almost a complete PostScript implementation. Documentation is found in /usr/doc.

Ghostview A front end to the Ghostscript interpreter. It is excellent for viewing and printing all or parts of documents.

Gnuplot A plotting utility that runs under X. It is a command-line driven program.

xfig It runs under X and generates encapsulated PostScript files that can be included in documents.

Xpaint It is a display and edit image program. It runs under X Window and has the feel of the MacPaint program.

XV This program is for viewing almost any image such as GIF, JPEG, PostScript, and Windows BMP. Documentation is found at /usr/doc/ if XV is installed.

What types of programs are available to do programming?

These four programs let you do programming in Linux:

gawk GNU awk is an enhanced version of the UNIX language awk created by Alfred V. Aho, Peter J. Weinberger, and Brian W. Kerningham. For documentation, see the /usr/doc/gawk directory.

Perl Practical Extraction and Report Language (Perl) may be one of the most popular scripting languages for the UNIX platform. It uses syntax similar to C and uses a style similar to that of UNIX shell scripting.

Python Python is an object-oriented scripting language. It may be of special interest to system administrations.

tcl/tk Tool Control Language and the Toolkit are programming environments for creating X graphical user interfaces. The official Web site for tcl/tk is http://www.scriptics.com.

What types of utilities are available?

These eight utilities may be available to you:

DOSEMU DOS emulator

GNU bc	Calculator
gzip	Compressing and expanding utility for files
ical	Calendar program
ispell	Full-screen spell checker
Midnight Commander	File manager with a text-based interface
patch	Utility for applying changes to a text file
xfm	X-based file manager

What package supports basic networking?

The net-tools package supports basic networking.

What man pages are available for networking administration?

See Appendix B for a listing of some of the man pages available. The appendix is primarily for the person who is a day-to-day system administrator. However, a user who has a workstation and has to act on occasion as system administrator can use this appendix. The appendix lists some 500 commands, users, functions, and files that relate to networking.

What package supports network debugging?

The Tcpdump package supports network debugging.

How do I load balance a router?

Router load balance requires a TCP bidirectional connection involving multiple packets. A Web site that may assist in this area is http://www.coyotepoint.com/cp_products.shtml.

How do I configure Ethernet network adapters?

See Ethernet-HOWTO.gz. This HOWTO explains how to configure and use Linux Ethernet network adapters. It covers card selection criteria, includes an FAQ, gives performance tips, and considers configuration issues. The majority of the HOWTO has vendor, manufacturer, and model specific information. The editor is Paul Gortmaker (Paul.Gortmaker@anu.edu.au).

How do I create an intranet server?

See Intranet-Server-HOWTO.gz. This HOWTO gives the information for tying together an intranet with UNIX, Novell Netware, Windows NT, and Windows 95 with a Linux server. It covers installing the HTTP server, connecting to the Linux server, setting up the intranet, and accessing the Web. The author is Pramod Karnad (karnad@indiamail.com).

How do I set up Network File System (NFS)?

See NFS-HOWTO.gz. This HOWTO tells how to configure Linux to support server and client using NFS. It also covers security and has an FAQ. The author is Nicolai Langfeldt (janl@math.uio.no). See Chapter 12.

How do I set up a Linux User Group?

See User-Group-HOWTO.gz. This HOWTO discusses how to establish a Linux User Group. It includes a description of a Linux User Group (LUG), a listing of LUGs, activities of LUGs, and legal and organizational issues. The author is Kendall Grant Clark.

Where do I find names for network devices?

They are found within the kernel so there are no files with network device names. Four important device names in the kernel are:

eth0	first Ethernet card
lo	loopback device
ppp0	first serial port for the Point-to-Point Protocol (PPP)
sl0	first serial port for the Serial Line Internet Protocol (SLIP)

What program do you use to do network configuration?

After the kernel is properly configured for TCP/IP use /usr/bin/netcfg.

Where is the host name kept?

See the HOSTNAME variable in /etc/sysconfig/network.

Where do I find network names and their IP addresses?

See /etc/networks. Red Hat Linux does not automatically install this file.

How do I check the routing status to another host?

Use the command /sbin/route and specify the host's IP address.

How do I check on a network's status?

Use the command netstat -i to display the Kernel Interface Table. This table includes interface name, maximum bytes a packet can transfer, number of received or transferred error-free packets, number of dropped packets, and any flags allowed, such as B equals broadcast.

What is a UUCP network?

A UNIX-to-UNIX CoPy network handles requests, basically e-mail and news, from remote sites over telephone lines. There are a number of varieties of UUCP. The version commonly distributed with Linux is Taylor UUCP.

What is a major disadvantage of a UUCP network?

A major disadvantage of a UUCP network is the low bandwidth. It is a dial-up system over telephone lines.

Who are the primary users of a UUCP network?

The primary group that operates UUCP networks is hobbyists. It is inexpensive and has minimal requirements.

What is a major contribution to the Internet from UUCP?

The Internet contribution by UUCP is Usenet, which got started in 1979 by some graduate students in North Carolina at Duke and the University of North Carolina.

Chapter 14

General Networking Tips

This chapter discusses general networking tips. These are tips that consider issues that cross over different network types, such as general system administration, and package and kernel upgrading.

Note: To see available options for the commands discussed in the chapter, you need to do a man command-name command.

What is a general networking tip?

A general networking tip is a tip that deals with the things that have been overlooked but critically support the networking effort. These tips include starting and shutting down the system, archiving the archives, checking the clocks, letting loose the daemons, handling the hardware, and keeping the kernel.

How do I start and stop a service?

Red Hat provides a set of scripts in the /etc/rc.d/init.d directory that start and stop services. The syntax to start a service at the root level is /etc/rc.d/init.d/daemon-name start. To stop the service, enter /etc/rc.d/init.d/daemon-name stop.

Note: For example, for an NFS server the daemon is nfs and for an Apache server it is httpd.

How can I get reports on the status of the processes?

The ps command, report process status, can give you many different views of the system processes. One option is to enter ps –aux.

where:

a	gives all process
u	displays a user-oriented format
x	gives process without controlling ttys

An abbreviated report would look similar to the following:

USER	PID	%CPU	%MEM	SIZE	RSS	TTY	STAT	START	TIME	COMMAND
root	387	0.0	0.0	0	0	?	SW	03.11	0:00	[nfsd]
root	451	0.0	3.9	2384	1220	?	S	03.11	0:00	httpd
xfs	476	0.0	3.1	1988	968	?	S	03.11	0:00	xfs
news	532	0.0	7.7	2536	804	?	S	03.11	0:00	/usr/bin/actived
root	575	0.0	3.7	2136	1152	tty1	S	03.11	0:00	login — root
root	576	0.0	1.2	1060	384	tty2	S	03.11	0:00	/sbin/mingetty tty
root	583	0.0	3.1	1708	952	tty1	S	03.14	0:00	-bash
nobody	1075	0.0	4.3	2560	1324	?	S	04.02	0:00	httpd
root	1223	0.0	3.1	2644	960	tty1	R	05.25	0:00	ps-aux

Is there a method for getting even more process information?

To get more information for a single process enter ps pid.

For example, when the pid (process identification) is entered for 1075, the next to last line of the above report, the result is:

PID	TTY	STAT	TIME	COMMAND
1075	?	S	0:00	httpd

What is the importance of rc.sysinit?

The system initialization script is rc.sysinit. It is called from /etc/inittab. Some of its functions include the following:

- Checks root filesystems for quotas
- Configures networking
- Enters the root filesystem in mtab
- Finds module dependencies
- Initializes the serial port
- Remounts the root filesystem read/write
- Sets some of the initial $PATH variables
- Sets the system clock
- Sets the system host name
- Turns on swapping

What is the default run level of the /etc/init file?

The default run level of the /etc/init file is 3—full multiuser mode. The default statement is found in the line id:3:initdefault:.

Another run level can be placed in this line (only 1, 2, or 5). The other options are:

0—halt (do not set as the default)

1—single user mode

2—multiuser without NFS

4—unused

5—X11

6—reboot (do not set as the default)

Note: The run level can be changed at the root level by entering init runlevel.

How do I display the etc/inittab file?

To display this file, enter more /etc/inittab.

How do I find more information on the inittab file?

To see online information about the inittab file, enter man inittab.

What is the importance of the rc.local script?

The rc.local script runs after rc.sysinit and gets the operating system name and the computer's architecture. This information is put in the /etc/issue file.

What are some of the archiving commands?

Some of the commands for archiving are:

cpio	create and unpack file archives
tar	copy or restore files

What are some of the essential networking daemons?

Here are 20 networking daemons:

bootpd	Internet Boot Protocol daemon
fingerd	Finger daemon
ftpd	File Transfer Protocol Daemon
identd	Identify user running TCP/IP process
imapd	IMAP mailbox server daemon
inetd	Internet services daemon
kerneld	Provides automatic kernel module loading
lpd	Printer daemon
mountd	NFS mount request server
named	Internet domain name server
nfsd	NFS daemon
pop3d	POP server
pppd	Maintains PPP connections
rdistd	Remote file distribution server
rexecd	Remote execution server
routed	Routing daemon
syslogd	System logging daemon
tcpd	TCP network daemon
update	Buffer flush daemon
ypserv	NIS server process

What are the basic commands for clock management?

Here are eight commands for managing clocks:

clock	determines CPU time
date	prints or sets the system data and time
hwclock	sets and queries the hardware clock (keeps the time when Linux is not running)
rdate	gets network date and time
setclock	sets the hardware clock from the system clock
tzset	initializes time conversion file
zdump	prints a time zone list
zic	creates time conversion information files

What are some of the commands for handling the hardware?

Here are eight commands to manage networking and system hardware:

arp	manages the kernel's Address Resolution Protocol (ARP) cache
cfdisk	maintains curses based disk partitions
fdisk	maintains disk partitions for Linux
kbdrate	manages the keyboard's repeat rate and delay time
ramsize	prints RAM disk information
rarp	manages the Reverse Address Resolution Protocol (RARP) table
setserial	gets and sets serial port information
slattach	attaches a serial line to a network interface

What are some of the basic commands for managing the kernel?

Here are eight basic commands for the kernel:

adjtimex	adjusts kernel clock
depmod	creates dependency file used with modprobe
insmod	installs a loadable kernel module
kerneld	automatically manages kernel user space
ksyms	displays exported kernel symbol information
lsmod	lists loaded kernel modules
modprobe	loads a set of modules
rmmod	removes unloadable modules

What are the basic user networking commands called?

The basic user networking commands are called TCP/IP commands because the original UNIX commands were based on this suite of protocols. See Chapter 9, "TCP/IP Tips."

How can I automate tasks?

Red Hat Linux has four directories that you can use to automate tasks:

/etc/crontab/
/etc/cron.hourly/

/etc/cron.daily/
/etc/cron/weekly/

The format is minute hour day month year command

where

minute	MM on the 24-hour clock
hour	HH on the 24-hour clock
day	DD
month	NN (1-12)
year	YY
command	* command "message"

What is an issue concerning more than one Ethernet board?

When booting the autoprobe only checks for one Ethernet device. You must explicitly tell the kernel about any additional Ethernet devices.

What is the first Ethernet device called?

The first Ethernet device is called eth0. This name is defined in the kernel, not in the /dev directory.

What are some of the network devices supported in the kernel?

At least six types of network devices are supported in the Linux kernel:

- Local loopback interface (lo)
- Ethernet cards (eth0, eth1, ...)
- DE-600 interfaces (dl0, dl1, ...)
- PLIP interfaces (plip0, plip1, ...)
- PPP interfaces (ppp0, ppp1, ...)
- SLIP interfaces (sl0, sl1, ...)

Is there a HOWTO available on Ethernet?

For more technical information on Ethernet, see the Linux Ethernet-HOWTO by Paul Gortmaker (February 1998).

What is the importance of the linuxconf tool?

The linuxconf tool can be run under X to manage your network services. Some of the functions of linuxconf include:

- A comprehensive graphic interface for system administration
- Configuration and activation tool
- Help information on services
- Method for adding new capabilities or features
- Method for saving different system configurations
- Network system maintenance tool

How do I shut down a network?

There are a number of ways to shut down a system, but most of them make the users angry. The primary command for this function is shutdown. The syntax is shutdown [-krhfnc] [-t secs] time [warning message].

The options are:

-k	warning only
-r	reboot after shutdown
-h	halt after shutdown
-f	do a "fast" reboot
-n	do a shutdown real fast
-c	can do a running shutdown
-t secs	time between warning and kill signal

The syntax for a proper immediate shutdown, but will make network users angry, is shutdown –h now.

How do I prepare for system crashes?

There are four things you need to have to prepare for a system crash:

- Backup plan
- Backups
- Emergency boot disks
- Copies of important files

What are some actions I need to take to avoid a crash?

The following five are actions you need to follow to prevent system crashes:

- Create emergency boot disks that include the kernel
- Make a backup after a clean installation
- Use an uninterruptible power supply
- Use the filesystem tools
- Use the shutdown command

What are some actions I should not do to avoid a crash?

The following five are actions you should avoid to prevent system crashes:

- Disable e2fsck in etc/rc.d/rc.sysinit
- Fill the hard drive with unnecessary software
- Forget to make backups
- Run the fsck command on mounted filesystems
- Turn off the computer when finished without using the shutdown command

How can I do a quick check of the storage space?

To check the status of free space use the df command. The following is an example report:

Filesystem	1K-blocks	Used	Available	Use%	Mounted on
/dev/hda8	257598	28898	215396	12	/
/dev/hda1	19485	2276	16203	12	/boot
/dev/hda6	1232895	3095	1166096	0	/home
/dev/hda5	1232895	322258	846933	28	/usr
/dev/hda7	259598	6808	237486	3	/usr

Note: The first line is the root that contains the kernel, device drivers, and related directories. The second is the location of the boot software. The third line is the user's personal home and contains the user directories and personal files. The fourth and fifth lines means user-installed by the system administrator software.

What are some important filesystem tools?

The following nine tools can be used as a basic filesystem toolbox:

badblocks	searches for bad blocks
debugfs	debugs an ext2 filesystem
dump	used to make filesystem backups
dumpe2fs	gives filesystem information
e2fsck	used for second extended filesystem
fsck	checks and repairs filesystems
mke2fs	creates a second Linux extended filesystem
restore	used to restore a filesystem using backups created by dump
tune2fs	adjusts tunable system parameters (only for an ext2 filesystem)

How do I use badblocks?

The badblocks command searches a device for bad blocks. Syntax is badblocks [-b block-size] [-o output-file] [-v] [-w] device block-count.

-b block-size	block size in bytes
-o output-file	write bad block list to specified file
-v	verbose mode
-w	write-test mode

How do I use debugfs?

The debugfs command examines and changes the state of an ext2 filesystem. The syntax is debugfs [[-w] device].

-w	specifies the filesystem to open in the read-write mode

How do I use dumpe2fs?

The dumpe2fs dumps ext2 filesystem information. The syntax is dumpe2fs device.

How do I use e2fsck?

The **e2fsck** command checks an ext2 filesystem. The syntax is **e2fsck** [options] device.

How do I use fsck?

The **fsck** command checks and repairs a Linux filesystem. The syntax is fsck [-ANRTV] [-s] [-t fstype] [fs-options] filesys [...].

-A	checks all filesystems in one run
-N	no execution; shows what has to be done
-R	skips the root file system
-T	no title on startup
-V	verbose mode
-s	serializes **fsck** operations
-t fstype	specifies the filesystem type to be checked

Note: A filesystem is a complete system such as Linux, while a file system, such as root, is a component.

How do I use mke2fs?

The **mke2fs** creates an ext2 filesystem. Its counterpart command is **mkfs** which builds a Linux filesystem.

How do I use tune2fs?

The **tune2fs** command adjusts tunable filesystem parameters on an ext2 filesystem.

Warning: Never use **tune2fs** to change parameters on a read-write mounted filesystem.

What does the traceroute command do?

The **traceroute** command prints the route packets take to the network host. The syntax is

traceroute [-m max_ttl] [-n] [-p prt] [-q nqueries] [-r] [-s src_addr] [-t tos] [-w waitime] host [packetsize]

The only mandatory argument is destination host or IP address.

What is the w utility?

The w utility, or command, summarizes the system's current activity as to which users are logged on and what they are doing on their machines. The syntax is w [options] [user].

-h	suppresses the heading
-i	sorts output by idle time
-n	shows network addresses as numbers
-w	interprets addresses and attempts to display them symbolically

What does perror do?

The perror command prints a system error message describing the last error encountered during a call to a library function.

What is Samba?

Samba, or Session Message Block (SMB), is a protocol that allows a Linux user to share files and printers used by Microsoft's operating systems.

What are some of the important components of Samba?

Five of the important components of Samba are:

- smbd
- smb.conf
- nmbd
- smbstatus
- testparm

What are some of the important Samba files ?

Three of the important Samba files are the following:

- /etc/smb.conf
- /var/log/samba/

- home/samba/

Where can I find more information on Samba?

There is a HOWTO and a URL. The HOWTO is SMB HOWTO by David Wood. The URL is http://us1.samba.org/samba/docs.

What is RPM?

RPM stands for Red Hat Package Manager. This utility was originally developed by Red Hat but is now found in other Linux distributions. It is an easy method for installing, upgrading, deleting, or querying a software package. RPM is a significant enhancement over the tar utility that is used to install tarballs.

Note: See the man page for RPM to see all the various options. In addition, there is the RPM-HOWTO.

What is the basic strategy for keeping a system up to date?

The basic strategy for keeping a system up to date is to keep yourself informed by checking:

- Magazines such as *Linux Journal* or *Linux Magazine*
- Web sites such as http//freshmeat.net and http://slashdot.org
- Newsgroups such as comp.os.linux.announce

Where can I get the latest kernel upgrade?

The latest kernel upgrade can be found at ftp//ftp.redhat.com/redhat/updates.

Download the desired kernel packages for your version and platform. For example at the time of this writing, you need to navigate to the /6.0/i386/ directory and download kernel-*.i386.rpm.

How do I upgrade using a stock kernel by Red Hat?

To do a kernel upgrade at the root, do the following:

```
rpm –Uvh kernel-version-architecture.rpm
cd /boot
```

ls

Next, edit the LILO configuration file. One might enter pico –w /etc/lilo.conf and change image=/boot… so that it points to the new kernel file.

Note: There are three premises in the above: You are using an Intel platform (i386), using LILO to boot your system, and using the pico editor.

What is the importance of Linux kernel 2.2.x?

The Linux kernel 2.2.0 was released on January 25, 1999. It does include many new features, performance enhancements, and additional hardware support. Red Hat Linux 6.0 includes this kernel.

Caution: Upgrading a 5.2 distribution involves a number of package upgrades. Information on doing this type of upgrade is found at ftp://ftp.redhat.com/redhat/updates/5.2/kernel-2.2.i386/

What are some important kernel 2.2 enhancements?

There are at least nine broad kernel enhancements:

- Faster processing speed
- Improved networking
- NFS daemon strengthen
- Better TCP stack support
- Flexible firewalling
- Improved cross platform support
- More powerful routing
- Sound system is modular
- Better sound card support

What is a major difference between kernel 2.2 and 2.3?

Kernel 2.3 has approximately two dozen new drivers, especially IDE.

What general networking RFCs are available?

Here are 14 Request for Comments on general networking:

1173	Responsibilities of host and network managers: A summary of the "oral tradition" of the Internet. J. Van Bokkelen. (August 1990)
1175	FYI on where to start: A bibliography of internetworking information. K.L. Bowers, T.L. LaQuey, J.K. Reynolds, K. Roubicek, M.K. Stahl, and A. Yuan. (August 1990)
1208	Glossary of networking terms. O.J. Jacobsen and D.C. Lynch. (March 1991)
1242	Benchmarking terminology for network interconnection devices. S. Bradner. (July 1991)
1302	Building a Network Information Services Infrastructure. D. Sitzler, P. Smith, and A. Marine. (February 1992)
1346	Resource Allocation, Control, and Accounting for the Use of Network Resources. P. Jones. (June 1992)
1355	Privacy and Accuracy Issues in Network Information Center Databases. J. Curran and A. Marine. (August 1992)
1441	Introduction to version 2 of the Internet-standard Network Management Framework. J. Case, K. McCloghrie, M. Rose, and S. Waldbusser. (April 1993)
1463	FYI on Introducing the Internet—A Short Bibliography of Introductory Internetworking Readings. E. Hoffman and L. Jackson. (May 1993)
1498	On the Naming and Binding of Network Destinations. J. Saltzer. (August 1993)
1527	What Should We Plan Given the Dilemma of the Network? G. Cook. (September 1993)
1925	The Twelve Networking Truths. R. Callon. (April 1996)
1944	Benchmarking Methodology for Network Interconnect Devices. S. Bradner and J. McQuaid. (May 1996)
2007	Catalogue of Network Training Materials. J. Foster, M. Isaacs, and M. Prior. (October 1996)

15

Chapter 15

Shell Tips

This chapter covers the basic utilities and operators for using a shell.

Note: To see available options for the commands discussed in the chapter, you need to do a man command-name command.

What is a shell?

A shell is a Linux interface or, more precisely, a command-line interpreter and a programming language. A shell helps you run a program easily.

What is bash?

The Red Hat default shell is bash, or Bourne Again Shell by Brian Fox and Chet Ramey. Steve Bourne wrote the Bourne Shell.

Are there other shells besides bash?

Yes. Some of the other shells are:

ash	Smallest Linux shell
ksh	Korn shell originally by Eric Gisin
tcsh	The Compatible Shell by Will Joy and many others
zsh	One of the largest Linux shells by Paul Falstad

What is sh-utils?

The GNU shell package (sh-utils) is a set of utilities that provides over 30 programs. This package includes:

basename Strips directory and suffix from filenames

chroot	Makes root (/) directory something else on the filesystem

Note: The syntax is chroot old-location new-location.

date	Displays or sets date and time
dirname	Strips non-directory suffix from filenames
echo	Echoes a string to display
env	Runs a program in a modified environment
expr	Evaluates expressions and writes the result to standard output
factor	Generates prime numbers
false	Returns a status 1
groups	Prints a user's group
hostname	Shows the host's system name
id	Prints IDs of users and groups
logname	Prints user's login name
nice	Changes the processing schedule's priorities
nohup	Runs a command immune to hang-ups
pathchk	Checks for valid filenames
printenv	Prints all or part of an environment
printf	Formats and prints data
pwd	Prints name of current directory
seq	Outputs sequences of numbers
sleep	Pauses for a specified amount of time
stty	Changes and prints terminal settings
su	Becomes root or another user with that user's password
tee	Reads from standard input and writes to standard output
test	Checks file types and compares values
true	Returns a status of 0 (zero)
tty	Prints the filename of the terminal connected to standard input.
uname	Prints all or part of the system information
uptime	Shows how long the system has been running
users	Prints a list of currently logged-in users
who	Shows who is logged on
whoami	Prints user ID
yes	Repeatedly outputs a string until killed

What are the basic shell operators?

Here are eight basic operators:

- `-` (dash) used for options
- `.` (period) tells the shell to execute all commands in the file that are passed as an argument
- `&` (ampersand) after any other command tells the computer to run the command in the background
- `|` (vertical bar) separates programs on the command line to "pipe" the output from one command to another
- `>` sends the output of a program to a file or another device
- `<` feeds a program the contents of a file or input from another device or source
- `>>` appends the output of a program onto the end of a specified file
- `<<` tells a program when end of input is reached

How can I find a shell command?

Use **$ help command-name**. If you enter **q** you will get no commands because no command begins with the letter q. Expect to find only commands that begin with the letter you enter.

What is a script?

A script is a defined process or method for executing a set of commands.

How do I run a script?

There are two ways. The first way is to run a script when you have executed permission for the script file. The second way is to enter **bash** and then the filename of the script.

Chapter 16

GNU Project Tips

16

This chapter covers questions about the Free Software Foundation and the GNU Project. There are also details on how to use the GNU file utilities.

What is the GNU Project?

In 1984, Richard Stallman founded the Free Software Foundation and created the GNU Project. GNU stands for "GNU's not UNIX." The goal is to develop a complete free UNIX and a variant is GNU/Linux. It is because of this project that the software for Linux is so rich.

Where do I find information on the GNU Project?

You can find more information about the past, present, and future of the GNU project at http://www.gnu.org. The e-mail address is gnu@gnu.org.

How do I find information about installed GNU Project distributions?

Do an info command such as # info autoconf or the man command # man ed.

What are some of the GNU Project distributions?

The following 33 GNU distributions show the broad areas that are affected by the GNU Project:

autoconf	produces shell scripts that automatically configure source code packages
automake	generates makefilein files for use with autoconf

bash	Bourne Again Shell is compatible with sh and offers many extensions found in csh and ksh (default shell for Red Hat Linux)
bc	an interactive algebraic language with arbitrary precision numbers
bison	compatible replacement for the parser generator yacc
calc	an extensible, advanced desk calculator and mathematical tool that runs as part of GNU emacs
cfengine	used to maintain site-wide configuration of a heterogeneous network using a simple high-level language
checker	a package that works with GCC to detect memory use errors in a program
cpio	copies file archives to and from disk, or to another part of the local machine
cvs	Concurrent Versions System (like RCS (Reversion Control System)) that allows you to keep old versions of files (usually source code), and a log of who, when, and why changes occurred, etc.
DejaGnu	a framework to test programs with a single front end for all tests
dld	a dynamic linker, which allows the dynamic loading of object files into a running binary
ed	standard text editor that is line-oriented and can be used interactively or in scripts
emacs	an extensible, customizable real-time display editor (Edit Macros) and computing environment that provides an interface to the X Window System
gawk	compatible with the latest POSIX specification of awk
gcal	a program for printing calendars with different styles of calendar sheets, eternal holiday lists, and fixed date warning lists
gdbm	a library of database routines for programmers
gdk	a library of graphics routines for programmers
Ghostscript	an interpreter for the PostScript and PDF graphics languages
Ghostview	provides a graphical front end to Ghostscript, allowing a PostScript or PDF file to be previewed using an X Window interface
gnus	Usenet news reading in emacs

grep	includes GNU grep, egrep, and fgrep which find lines that match entered patterns
groff	a document formatting system based on a device-independent version of troff
gzip	compresses and decompresses files
ispell	an interactive spell checker that suggests “near misses” to replace unrecognized words
mtools	a set of public domain programs to allow Linux systems to read, write, and manipulate files on an MS-DOS file system
smail	a mail transport system designed as a compatible drop-in replacement for sendmail that uses a much simpler configuration format than sendmail
GNU SQL	portable multiple user relational database management system
GNU tar	includes multi-volume support, the ability to archive sparse files, compression/decompression, remote archives, and special features that allow tar to be used for incremental and full backups
tabs	a program to set hardware terminal tab settings
tview	provides a graphical front end to Ghostscript, allowing a PostScript or PDF file to be previewed using an X Window interface
wdiff	front end to GNU diff; compares two files, finding the words deleted or added to the first to make the second
xinfo	an X windows program for reading info files

What are some general GNU utilities?

The following ten general GNU utilities demonstrate the impact of the GNU Project on Linux:

binutils	includes these programs: ar, c++filt, demangle, gas, gprof, ld, nlmconv, nm, objcopy, objdump, ranlib, size, strings, and strip
diffutils	includes GNU diff, which compares files showing line-by-line changes in several flexible formats
fileutils	includes these utilities: chgrp, chmod, chown, cp, dd, df, dir, dircolors, du, install, ln, ls, mkdir, mkfifo, mknod, mv, rm, rmdir, sync, touch, and vdir
findutils	includes find, locate, and xargs

fontutils	converts font formats, and creates fonts for use with Ghostscript, TeX, etc.
inetutils	common networking utilities and servers
shellutils	includes basename, chroot, date, dirname, echo, env, expr, factor, false, groups, hostname, id, logname, nice, nohup, pathchk, printenv, printf, pwd, seq, sleep, stty, su, tee, test, true, tty, uname, uptime, users, who, whoami, and yes
termutils	contains utilities for controlling terminals; tput is a portable way for shell scripts to use special terminal capabilities
texinfo	a set of utilities which generates printed manuals, plain ASCII text, and online hypertext documentation (called info), and can read online info documents
texutils	includes utilities such as cat, head, sort, and tail

What are some file GNU utilities?

The following 12 file GNU utilities illustrate the importance of the GNU Project on Linux server or system administration:

chgrp	changes a user's group
chmod	changes a file's access permissions
chown	changes a file's owner (user and group)
cp	copies files
df	summarizes disk free space
dir	lists contents of a directory (same as ls –C)
ls	lists contents of a directory
mkdir	makes a directory
mknod	makes special files
mv	moves files or directories
rm	removes files
rmdir	removes directories

How do I use chgrp?

The chgrp command changes the permissions of the directory or a file to a new group. The syntax is:

```
chgrp new-group directory
chgrp new-group file
```

How do I use chmod?

The chmod command lets you change file permissions. The syntax is chmod [options] permission files.

The permission options are:

u	user
g	group
o	other
r	read
w	write
x	execute
+	adds
-	deletes
=	sets the permissions as specified

Example: chmod ug+rx file1 means to add read and execute to user and group of file1.

Other options that reflect action include the following:

-c	lists only files whose permissions changed
-f	stops any error message displays
-v	wordy displays of permission changes
-R	recursively changes file permissions in all subdirectories

How do I use chown?

The chown command lets you change file owner and group. The syntax is chown [options] user-name.group-name files.

The following options are the same as chmod:

-c	lists only files whose permissions changed
-f	stops any error message displays
-v	wordy displays for permission changes
-R	recursively changes file permissions in all subdirectories

Note: This command requires that you be logged in at the root to make changes.

How do I use cp?

The cp command lets you copy a file using the syntax cp file1 file2.

The options include the following:

-a	preserves file attributes
-b	makes a backup
-d	copies only a link
-i	prompts for permission before overwriting a file
-l	creates only hard disk links
-p	preserves file ownership, permissions, and time stamp
-R	recursively copies files in all subdirectories
-s	creates only soft links
-u	copies a file if its time stamp is later than at the destination
-v	displays wordy messages as copying processes

How do I use df?

The df command summarizes free and available space for all mounted storage devices. Some of the options include the following:

-a	displays information for all filesystems
-i	displays inode information
-t type	displays information about specified types of the filesystems only
-T	prints the filesystem type
-x type	excludes specified types of filesystems from the output
-help	displays a help message

How do I use dir?

The dir command uses the same options as the ls command. The dir command without options is similar to ls –C. This option lists files in columns, sorted vertically.

How do I use ls?

The ls command lists all non-hidden files for the current directory when a directory name is omitted. Some of the options without any argument that list for the current directory are the following:

ls -a	lists all (including hidden) files
ls -c	sorts by file creation time
ls -d	lists directory like files
ls -f	lists all files as on the disk
ls -l	creates a "long" (detailed) formatted list

Note: An equivalent command is vdir.

ls -r	sorts file listing in reverse alphabetical order
ls -s	shows the file size in kilobytes
ls -t	sorts files by time stamp
ls - l	displays a one-column file listing
ls -R	recursively lists the files in all subdirectories

How do I use mkdir?

The mkdir command creates (makes) a directory. The two major options are the following:

-a mode	assigns the specified permission
-p	creates parent directories when they do not exist

How do I use mknod?

The mknod command creates a device file with specified major and minor numbers. The one option is –m mode, which sets the mode of created files to mode; it is symbolic as in chmod.

How do I use mv?

The mv command lets you move a file (limited to two arguments). Some of the options are:

-b	makes a backup
-f	removes the file without a prompt

16

-i	prompts for permission before overwriting a file
-v	displays filename before moving it

Note: This command may be used to rename or move a file, depending on syntax used.

How do I use rm?

The rm command lets you delete (remove) a file (rm * deletes all files in the current directory). Some of the options include the following:

-f	removes the file without a prompt
-i	prompts for permission before overwriting a file
-R	recursively removes files in all subdirectories and directories
-v	displays filename before removing it

How do I use rmdir?

The rmdir command deletes (removes) a directory. Some of the options are the following:

-f	removes files without prompting
-i	prompts before removing a file
-r	recursively removes files in all subdirectories and directories
-v	displays each filename before removing it

Chapter 17

Packaging Tips

This chapter covers general questions about packaging and the Red Hat Package Manager (RPM) for Red Hat Linux 6.0. The questions in this chapter are limited to ones related to general server management. For example, RPM has many functions, but the query function is detailed in this chapter because it may assist you in identifying the packages that have server information.

What is a package?

A package is a software collection written in a particular format to achieve a specific goal. It makes installation easier. Red Hat Linux has over 450 packages available of which about 270 are installed originally on the server. The packages available for Red Hat Linux Server 6.0 are listed in Appendix D and are described in *The Official Red Hat Linux Installation Guide*.

Note: Detailed package information can also be acquired online by entering rpm –qi package-name.

What does RPM stand for?

RPM stands for Red Hat Package Manager.

What is RPM?

RPM can assist you in installing, deleting, updating, finding (querying), and verifying installation of a package. It is an open packaging system, and is available for the use of anyone. It uses one-line commands to process any action.

Note: To use a graphical interface rather that the RPM command line system you might consider GnoRPM.

Where do I get more information on RPM?

There are a number of sources for getting information including:

- man rpm
- rpm help
- *Maximum RPM* by Ed Bailey (1997) may be available from either Red Hat Software or your local bookstore
- RPM-HOWTO by Donnie Barnes

How do I find a package using RPM?

Enter the command rpm -q package-name to find a specific package. For example, rpm –q cpio returns cpio-2.4.2-12.

How do I see if I have an installed package?

Use the command rpm -q package-name to display the name, version, and release number for an installed package. For example, rpm –q man returns man-1.5g-2.

How do I find all packages on my machine?

Enter rpm –qa to find all the installed packages on your computer.

How do I find detailed information on a package?

Detailed package information is found online by entering rpm –qi package-name.

How do I find filenames for an installed package?

Use the command rpm -ql package-name. For example, rpm –ql cpio returns:

```
/bin/cpio
/usr/doc/cpio-2.4.2
/usr/doc/cpio-2.4.2/NEWS
/usr/doc/cpio-2.4.2/README
/usr/info/cpio.info.gz
/usr/man/man1/cpio1
```

How do I find a package associated to a file?

Use the command rpm –qf path-to-filename. For example, rpm –qf /bin/cpio returns cpio-2.4.2-12.

How do I install a package?

The simplest installation command is rpm -i filename-version-release.architecture.rpm.

How do I uninstall a package?

Read the package installation log and check for possible dependencies. When you are confident that you have the data, enter rmp -e package-name. Do not enter the name of the original package file. This prevents dependency errors.

How do I upgrade a package?

The simplest upgrade command is rpm -U file-name.rpm.

How do I verify a package?

Use the command rpm -V package-name. Verifying compares information about the installed package against the original package. This comparison includes size, permissions, and type.

What packages support archiving?

A number of packages support archiving. The basic packages are:

cpio
ncompress
tar
zip

What package supports browsing?

The lynx package supports HTML, text formatting, forms, and tables.

What package supports chat (IRC)?

Internet Relay Chat (IRC) uses ircii.

What package supports compiling?

The binutils supports compiling.

What packages support debugging?

There are at least four debugging packages:

ElectricFence
gdb
strace
xxgdb

What packages support editing?

There are many editing packages, but you probably will use one of the emacs packages.

What package supports faxing?

The efax package supports faxing.

What packages support file management?

There are over a dozen packages that support file management. The five basic packages are:

file
fileutils
findutils
stat
which

What package supports ftp?

The ncftp package supports ftp.

What packages support GIF files?

There are three GIF packages:

libungif
libungif-devel
libungif-progs

What packages support JPEG files?

There are three packages that support JPEG files:

libjpeg
libjpeg-devel
librjpeg6a

What packages support mail?

The following packages support mail:

elm	may be the most popular terminal mode mailer
exmh	a graphical interface to the MH mail system
fetchmail	for remote mail service
fetchmailconf	a tcl/tk graphical configurator
mailx	the /bin/mail program is the basic mail program
metamail	implementation of Multipurpose Internet Mail Extensions (MIME)
mutt	a full-screen Linux mailer
nmh	mailer with a command-line interface only
pine	uses the editor pico and has text-based mail and news client

What package supports network debugging?

The tcpdump package supports network debugging.

What package supports basic networking?

The net-tools package supports basic networking.

What packages support newsgroup?

Three packages that support the Network News Transport Protocol (NNTP) are:

slrn
tin
trn

What package supports scheduling?

The ical package supports scheduling.

What packages support scripting?

Two of the scripting language packages are:

python
tcl

What package supports security?

The basic library package cracklib checks passwords for characteristics related to security.

What packages support sound?

Some packages that support sound are:

aumix
playmidi
sox

What packages support text manipulation?

Some text manipulation packages are:

diffutils
gawk
less
perl
sed

textutils
words

What packages support TIF files?

Two packages that support TIF files are:

libtiff
libtiff-devel

What package supports Usenet news?

The inews package supports Usenet news.

What packages support version control?

Two packages that support version control are:

cvs	handles collection of files
rcs	handles multiple revisions of files

Chapter 18

Apache Server Tips

This chapter provides very basic descriptive information on the Apache server as to the features it supports and the essential configuration files. For additional information, two important URLs and a short list of books on the server are given.

Note: To see available options for the commands discussed in the chapter, you need to do a man command-name command. In addition, RPM install syntax may require the architecture such as i386.

What is an Apache server?

The software (version 1.3.6-7) for an Apache Web server comes with the Red Hat Linux 6.0 distribution. This server is possibly the most popular Web server type. To check for the latest version of software, go to Red Hat's FTP server in the /pub/contrib area.

What is a Web server?

A Web server is based on the Hypertext Transfer Protocol (HTTP). It is concerned with the services of the World Wide Web (WWW) rather than with the Internet.

What features or functions does an Apache server support?

The following ten features or functions may be supported on an Apache server:

- Common Gateway Interface (CGI)
- Customized logs
- File-based configuration
- HTTP authentication

- HTTP/1.1 protocol
- Java servlets
- Perl
- Session tracking
- Status reports
- Virtual hosts

How do I install Apache RPM?

To install the package enter the following:

rpm –i latest_apache.rpm
rpm –i apache-1.3.6-7.rpm (rpm install name (apache) version (1.3.6) release (-7))

How do I upgrade the Apache RPM?

To upgrade the Apache package, enter rpm –U latest_ apache.rpm.

Note: An upgrade does not overwrite the old configuration file. The files are appended with the extension of .rpmnew.

What is httpd?

The Hypertext Transfer Protocol (HTTP) daemon or server is designed to run on a standalone machine.

What are the essential Apache configuration files?

There are four essential Apache files and they are found in the /usr/local/apache/conf/ directory:

httpd.conf	primary configuration file
access.conf	permissions file
srm.conf	resource configuration file
mime.types	Multipurpose Internet Mail Extensions

Where does the Apache RPM install files?

The Apache RPM installs files in six directories:

/etc/http/conf	configuration files
/etc/rc.d/	system startup scripts
/home/httpd	default icons and CGI scripts
/usr/doc	readme files
/usr/man	man pages
/usr/sbin	executable programs

What are the golden rules for server configuration maintenance?

The three golden rules of server configuration maintenance are:

- Server-wide configurations in httpd.conf
- Directory-specific configurations in access.conf
- Server-wide resource configurations in srm.conf

What are some of the specific types of information found in httpd.conf?

The httpd.conf file contains:

- Configuration directives that give server controls
- Logfile locations
- User ID
- Listening port

Most defaults can be kept except the ServerAdmin should be the Webmaster's address.

How can I test my server?

Here are the three steps for testing your server:

1. Specify the ServerType as standalone.
2. Specify the ServerName as localhost.
3. Access the server as http://www.localhost.

What are some of the specific types of information found in srm.conf?

The srm.conf file contains:

- Location of Web document tree
- Location of CGI program directories
- Language priority

Most defaults should be kept. The most important default is the one for DocumentRoot, which is /home/httpd/html.

What are some of the specific types of information found in access.conf?

The access.conf file contains:

- Access types
- Document availability
- Security settings

The defaults should be kept here.

What is the difference between a standalone and an inetd server?

A standalone server is ready to process a request. An inetd (Internet daemon) starts a new server upon each request to the HTTP port. It is recommended to use the standalone default because it uses considerably less overhead.

Why might I want an inetd server configuration?

An inetd server is excellent for configuration testing. The server rereads all settings upon any request. However, one can also use with the standalone server type the ServerName as localhost to do the testing.

How do I run an inetd server?

To run an inetd server in httpd.conf, change the default of the ServerType from standalone to inetd.

Is there any essential requirement of the inetd configuration?

You need to edit the **/etc/services** file. Each service requires a line of information that includes the following:

- Official service name
- Port number
- Protocol name
- Services alias (optional)

Each entry is separated by a space. For example, the **httpd** entry might look as follows:

```
http 8080/tcp httpd httpd
```

The port 8080 is used because an **inetd** server runs better on this port than the one for the standalone server, which is port 80.

How do I start a standalone server?

From the root level, you need to enter **# /sbin/httpd –f /etc/httpd/conf/httppd.conf**.

How do I start an inetd server?

You cannot start an **inetd** server. It requires a request to the designated port, 8080.

How can I stop the Apache server?

Red Hat Linux includes scripts that control the startup and shutdown of services. Enter **stop**, which gracefully stops the server, rather than **kill**, which is a bit abrupt.

What are two important URLs to find information?

Two of many sites that have information on the Apache server are as follows:

http://www.apache.org
http://www.apacheweek.com

What are some of the books written on the Apache server?

Here is a list of five books without recommendation on the Apache server:

- *Apache: The Definitive Guide* by Ben Laurie, et al. O'Reilly & Associates, 1999.
- *Apache Server: Administrator's Handbook* by Mohammed J. Kabir. IDG Books, 1999.
- *Apache Server Bible* by Mohammed J. Kabir. IDG Books, 1998.
- *Apache Server for Dummies* by Ken A.L. Coar. IDG Books, 1998.
- *Apache Web Server Installation and Administration Guide* compiled by Gordon McComb. iuniverse.com, 1999.

Chapter 19

Words and Acronyms Tips

This chapter looks at important words and acronyms that are basic to the comprehension of server technology and system administration.

What is API?

The Application Program Interface is a set of calling conventions that define how a service is invoked through a software package (application).

What is ARP?

ARP is the Address Resolution Protocol used to map IP addresses to Ethernet addresses.

What is ARPA?

The founder of the Internet is the Advanced Research Projects Agency. It created the ARPANET.

What is a backbone?

A backbone is the primary connectivity mechanism for a hierarchical distributed system.

What is BBS?

The Bulletin Board System is the early form of the dial-up mailbox system and possibly the most popular mailing environment in the world.

What is BGP?

The Border Gateway Protocol exchanges routing information between autonomous systems.

What is a bridge?

A bridge is a device that connects two or more physical networks and forwards packets between them.

What is CSLIP?

Compressed Serial Line Internet Protocol exchanges IP packets over a serial line. It uses the header compression of most TCP/IP datagrams.

What is a daemon?

A daemon is more than a variation on the word demon. It is software that waits to handle a request. It is an "attending spirit," not a monster.

What is dip?

The Dial-up IP Protocol Driver (dip) handles Serial Line Interface Protocol (SLIP) and Point-to-Point (PPP) connections for IP addresses.

What is DNS?

The Domain Name Service is a distributed Internet database used for mapping of host names to IP addresses.

What is a domain?

A domain is a collection of sites with a common dominator. It can be location, purpose, or interest.

What is EGP?

The External Gateway Protocol exchanges routing information between autonomous systems.

What is electronic mail?

Electronic mail, known as e-mail or email, is the service that permits you to exchange messages with another user on a remote host without requiring you to know how to access that host.

What is Ethernet?

Ethernet is a networking method that handles traffic using a single shared bus.

What is a file?

A file is an object in a path that has no further branching. It is also known as a filename. A file is a collection of bytes.

What is file management?

It is the process of managing and controlling file services on a server, that is, giving permission to users on a network to read, write, delete, and copy files.

What is a filesystem?

A filesystem, as distinctive from file system, is a method for handling information in a unique way, usually identified as an operating system such as Linux, UNIX, or Microsoft Windows 9X.

What is a firewall?

A firewall is a controlled entry point to the internal network from an external network such as the Internet. The opposite of a firewall is a gateway. It uses a set of rules to determine what is allowed and what is barred. It protects as well as monitors traffic.

What is FTP?

The File Transfer Protocol is a file transfer service. It is used for transferring files using TCP/IP connections.

What is a gateway?

A gateway is a combination of hardware and software that connects two different types of networks. It can be a device such as a router or a computer. A gateway that connects an internal network to the Internet is sometimes called a firewall.

What is the GNU Project?

In 1984 Richard Stallman founded the Free Software Foundation and created the GNU Project. GNU stands for "GNU's not UNIX." The goal is to develop a complete free UNIX and a variant is GNU/Linux. It is because of this project that the software for Linux is so rich.

What is a host?

A host is a network node that can receive and transmit messages.

What is ICMP?

The Internet Control Message Protocol is used by TCP/IP to return error information.

What is an internet (small i)?

An internet is a collection of networks interconnected by a set of routers that allow the networks to operate as a single, large virtual network.

What is the Internet?

The Internet is a series of different networks providing multiple services based on a TCP/IP backbone. Its origins are in ARPANET.

What is IP?

The Internet Protocol is a suite of networking protocols and is associated with Transmission Control Protocol (TCP).

What is an IP address?

An IP address is a method for identifying the network interfaces on individual computer systems. The format is nnn.nnn.nnn.nnn. The range for each block is 0 to 255.

What is IRC?

Internet Relay Chat is a server-based application that permits groups of people to communicate "simultaneously" in a text-based mode.

What is a kernel?

A kernel is an operating system's core.

What is a LAN?

A LAN is a Local Area Network that is limited by a parameter of less than a mile.

What is a library?

A library is a set of common routines used in programs or applications.

What is a man page?

A man page is an online document (manual) that was originally developed for UNIX, but now plays a significant role in Linux online documentation.

What is masquerading?

It is the presenting of one IP address to the world while having multiple internal addresses.

What is MIME?

Multipurpose Internet Mail Extensions is an e-mail system that permits the attaching of binary files such as images, executable programs, and sound files.

What is a module?

A module is a collection of routines. They are usually bound to the kernel and found in a library.

What is NFS?

The Network File System is a standard networking protocol suite for transparent remote accessing.

What is NIS?

The Network Information System is a Remote Procedure Call (RPC) based application that permits the sharing of configuration files. NIS was originally known as Yellow Pages but because of a trademark issue, it was changed to its present name. Many associated files begin with the letters yp.

What is NNTP?

The Network News Transfer Protocol is used to transfer news of a TCP/IP network connection.

What is a package?

A package is a software collection written in a particular format to achieve a specific goal. It makes installation easier. Red Hat Linux has over 450 packages available, of which about 270 are installed originally on the server. The packages available for Red Hat Linux Server 6.0 are listed in Appendix D and are described in *The Official Red Hat Linux Installation Guide*.

What is PLIP?

PLIP stands for Parallel Line Internet Protocol. It permits TCP/IP connections on a computer's parallel port.

What is a port?

A port is an Internet transport protocol abstraction used to distinguish among multiple simultaneous connections to a single destination host.

What is PPP?

The Point-to-Point Protocol is link-layer protocol used in association with the Internet Protocol.

What is a printer?

A printer is a set of printer capabilities defined in /etc/printcap. A given physical printer can be defined a number of times in /etc/printcap as to how it handles fonts (type or size) and paper size.

What is a proxy?

A proxy is a server that acts for another server. This server is used in network security solutions.

What is quota?

Quota may be the most valuable word in a system or network administrator's vocabulary. It is a system-imposed limit. It can be anything from the amount of disk space to the number of e-mail messages that can be kept online.

What is RARP?

The Reverse Address Resolution Protocol allows hosts to find their IP address at boot time.

What is a resolver?

A resolver is a library that maps host names to IP addresses and IP addresses to host names.

What is an RFC?

A Request for Comments is one of the document steps in establishing an Internet standard.

What is RIP?

The Routing Information Protocol dynamically adjusts routes inside a LAN.

What is a route?

A route is the sequence of hosts a request or message travels from originating host to destination host.

What is routing?

Routing is the process of controlling and moving traffic between physical network nodes.

What is RPC?

The Remote Procedure Call protocol executes procedures within a process on a remote host.

What is RPM?

RPM stands for Red Hat Package Manager. It can assist you in installing, deleting, updating, finding (querying), and verifying installation of a package. It is an open packaging system, and is available for the use of anyone. It uses one-line commands to process any action.

What is sendmail?

It is a very powerful and complex mailing program. Its configuration file is sendmail.cf.

What is a server?

A server is a computer that is the centerpiece of a network (intranet) that can process one or more network services.

What is a service?

A service is a process that implements a function for other processes.

What is SLIP?

The Serial Line Internet Protocol exchanges IP packets over a serial line.

What is SMTP?

The Simple Mail Transfer Protocol transports mail on TCP connections. It can also handle mail batches on a UUCP link.

What is spool?

Spool stands for Simultaneous Peripheral Operation Off Line. It allows for offline printing so the computer is not tied up with a long print.

What is TCP?

The Transmission Control Protocol is one part of the TCP/IP suite of protocols.

What is TCP/IP?

It is a suite of over 100 protocols to make a "standard" networking architecture for the Internet.

What is TFTP?

Trivial File Transfer Protocol is a system-independent means of file transfer between TCP/IP connections. It does not ensure correct file transfers, only the potential use of the shortest route.

What is URL?

Uniform Resource Locator is the method for specifying the protocol, format, login (usually for FTP rather than HTTP), and location of materials on the Internet.

What is Usenet?

It is the largest electronic bulletin board in the world. It is a message storing and forwarding network.

What is UUCP?

The UNIX-to-UNIX CoPy protocol is a suite of network transport commands for a dial-up network.

What is WWW?

The World Wide Web is a collection of servers that use a common protocol, Hypertext Transfer Protocol (HTTP).

Chapter 20

System Call Tips

This chapter summarizes the basic functions of approximately 100 of the 200-plus Linux system calls.

Note: To see available options for the commands discussed in the chapter, you need to do a man command-name command.

What is a system call?

A system call directly invokes the system that is the kernel.

20

What is the first step in creating a new system call?

The first step in creating a new system call is defining a prototype.

What do I need to create a prototype?

You need three things to create a prototype:

- Function return type
- Types of arguments
- Number of arguments

Is there a simple method for creating a prototype?

Six macros can be used in union to easily create a system call prototype. The form is syscallX(type, name, typeN, argN, ...)

where

X	0-5 (macros) for number of system call arguments
type	system call return type
name	system call name

typeN	Nth argument type
argN	Nth argument name

Note: The _syscall() macros do not produce a prototype.

What are some of the system calls for file management?

The following 20 system calls are for file management:

chmod	changes file access permissions
chown	changes file ownership
fchmod	changes file permissions
fchown	changes file ownership
fcntl	manipulates file descriptor
flock	applies or removes an advisory lock on an open file
fstat	gets file status
link	makes a new name for a file
lstat	gets file link status
mknod	makes block or character special files
mmap	maps files or devices into memory
msync	synchronizes a file with a memory map
munmap	unmaps files or devices out of memory
readlink	reads a symbolic link's value
rename	changes a file's name or location
stat	gets file status
symlink	makes a new name for a file
truncate	truncates a file to a specified length
umask	sets a file-creation mask
unlink	deletes a name and possibly the referred file

What are some of the system calls for directory management?

The following seven system calls are for directory management:

chdir	changes the current directory to the specified path
chroot	changes root directory
fchdir	changes the current directory as an open file descriptor
getdents	gets directory entries
mkdir	creates a directory

readdir	reads directory entry
rmdir	removes an empty directory

What are some of the system calls for call processing management?

The following 16 system calls are for call processing management:

exit	terminates the current process immediately
acct	switches process accounting on and off
execve	executes specified program
getpgid	gets process group identifier
getpriority	gets program scheduling priority
getsid	gets session identifier of the process
kill	terminates a process
killpg	terminates a process group
msgget	gets a message queue identifier
msgop	completes message operations
nanosleep	pauses execution for a specified time
open	opens a file or a device
ptrace	traces a process
setpriority	sets program scheduling priority
times	gets process times
wait	suspends the execution of the current process

What are some of the system calls for managing sockets?

The following 11 system calls are for managing sockets:

accept	accepts a connection on a socket
bind	binds a name to a socket
connect	initiates a connection on a socket
getsockname	gets socket name
getsockopt	gets socket options
listen	listens for connections on a socket
sendto	sends a message to a socket
sendmsg	sends a message to a socket
setsockopt	sets socket options
socket	creates an end point for communications

socketpair	creates a pair of connected sockets

What are some of the system calls for timers?

The following seven system calls are for timers:

adjtimex	tunes kernel clock
alarm	sets an alarm clock for delivery of a signal
getitimer	gets an interval timer's value
gettimeofday	gets time of day
setitimer	sets an interval timer's value
settimeofday	sets time of day
time	gets time in seconds

What are some of the system calls for filesystem management?

The following 20 system calls are for filesystem management:

fstatfs	gets filesystem statistics
gethostid	gets the current host's unique identifier
gethostname	gets the current host's name
getpeername	gets the name of the connected peer
getrlimit	gets resource limits
getrusage	gets resource usage
halt	stops the system
mount	mounts a filesystem
mremap	remaps a virtual memory address
quotactl	manipulates disk quotas
reboot	reboots the system
sethostid	sets the current host's unique identifier
sethostname	sets the current host's name
setrlimit	sets resource limits
statfs	gets mounted filesystem statistics
sysctl	reads or write system (kernel) parameters
sysfs	gets filesystem type information present in the kernel
sysinfo	gets overall system statistics
umount	unmounts a filesystem
ustat	gets filesystem statistics

What are some of the system calls for access management?

The following five system calls are for access management:

access	checks user permissions for a file
fchmod	changes file permissions
fchown	changes file ownership
flock	applies or removes an advisory lock on an open file
iopl	changes input and output privilege level

What are some of the system calls for user management?

The following six system calls are for user management:

geteuid	gets effective user identifier
getuid	gets real user identifier
seteuid	sets effective user identifier
setfsuid	sets user identifier used by filesystem checks
setreuid	sets real and effective user identifiers
setuid	sets real user identifier

What are some of the system calls for group management?

The following nine system calls are for group management:

getegid	gets the effective group identifier
getgid	gets the real group identifier
getgroups	gets supplementary group identifiers
setegid	sets the effective group identifier
setfsgid	sets group identifier used by filesystem checks
setgid	sets group identifier
setgroups	sets supplementary group identifiers
setpgid	sets process group identifier
setregid	sets real group identifier

What are some of the system calls to handle domains?

The following two system calls are for handling domains:

getdomainname	gets the domain name
setdomainname	sets the domain name

Chapter 21

Server/System Administration Tips

This chapter looks at server and system administrative tasks. A Linux system can become complex with many different types of servers, services, applications, utilities, and functions.

This is a very brief overview in general terms of the important subject of system administration and management. This book has been directed towards the essential requirement of any system administrator, knowledge of the filesystem and system (network) structures.

What is a system administrator?

A system administrator is a person responsible for the direct control and management of all aspects of a network. It can be an individual with a standalone workstation to an individual responsible for a corporate network with Internet connection, hundreds of terminals, dozens of printers, and hundreds or thousands of workstations. The difference between the two individuals is the degree of responsibility.

Note: The author has written a 600-page book, *IS Project Management Handbook*, that outlines the requirements of just managing and controlling an IS project, which is one component of being a system administrator.

What are the broad requirements of a system administrator?

There are seven broad requirements for a system administrator to be effective and efficient:

- Be able to communicate, communicate, and communicate
- Be able to logically plan processes
- Be able to make changes without major impacts on the system
- Be able to test all changes

- Have support plans
- Know how hardware and software work
- Know the location of system components, hardware, and software

What are some of the specific tasks of a system administrator?

The following ten specific tasks express some of the day-to-day operational functions of a system administration in the context of this book on servers:

- Account management
- Customer service
- Security integrity management
- Server configuration and management
- Server data backup and restoration
- Server hardware and software updates
- Server performance analysis
- Server problem determination
- System startup and shutdown
- Traffic management

Where in the filesystem does a system administrator manage?

The system administrator manages as a special user called **root**. A system administrator is also referred to as a superuser.

Caution: A standalone workstation administrator should have a user account and only work at the root level when necessary because changes at the **root** change the system. A quick and catastrophic method for deleting your entire system is entering rm –r / at the root.

What is a major security risk for the root?

A Linux system can be booted from a floppy and its root password changed. The process is simple:

1. Using a boot disk, boot the system
2. Mount the root partition

3. Remove any root password by editing **/etc/psswd**
4. Reboot from the hard disk
5. Set a new root password

Note: An inconvenience, but one could disable the floppy disk drive.

What is account management?

Account management is setting user IDs, groups, and permissions for directories and files. In addition, this includes managing with the command **quota** and its associated commands.

What is customer service?

Customer service is the essential reason for a corporate system administrator. A corporate network is not a plaything, but a tool critical to the success of any corporation. It is a fundamental requirement to answer customer requirements first, then technical requirements. All major tasks of a system administrator revolve around customer service:

- Problem resolution
- Communication
- Incremental system change
- Process planning
- Knowing how things work

What is the planning process?

The planning process includes the following steps:

- Know why you are going to make the change (install, delete, or update)
- Know the steps to be taken
- Determine resources (skills, time, money, and materials)
- Communicate to applicable customers important information on effects such as a new interface, date of change, etc.
- Document plan for a complex project
- Make changes incremental when possible
- Plan to return original process when there is a major obstacle for success without significant system downtime

- Test, test, and more testing

What types of communication tools are available?

For quick communication to the users, there are at least six commands available to a system administrator to notify users of a system problem:

- echo
- mesg
- motd
- talk
- wall
- write

Note: The above commands require the user to be currently logged on to the system. In addition, some of these are one-way forms of communication. Probably the best form of communication is e-mail.

How do I get assistance to be a system administrator?

This book points you to a number of sources that can assist you in being a better system administrator. Some of the major sources are the following:

- Man pages (Appendices B and E)
- HOWTOs (Appendix A)
- Request for Comments (RFCs) (Appendix C)
- Newsgroups (Chapter 5)
- Mailing lists
- Web sites on Red Hat Linux and system administration (http://www.redhat.com)

Note: Appendix B lists man pages with brief descriptions associated with networking, while Appendix E lists approximately 1,800 man pages without descriptions.

What is a major tool for solving problems?

The major tool for solving problems is reading and analyzing any logs associated with the problem.

What might be the most important task of a system administrator?

One might think immediately of system maintenance, however, one would be incorrect. Probably the most important task of a system administrator, other than customer service, is the managing and controlling of permissions.

How do I add a user to the system?

There are two ways to add a user to the system, manually or with a configuration tool. The following is the six-step manual process:

1. Edit /etc/passwd
2. Edit /etc/group
3. Create a home directory
4. Copy files from /etc/skel to the new home
5. Change ownerships and permissions
6. Set the password

How do I edit /etc/passwd?

The first action in editing /etc/passwd is making a backup. Add the user with a distinctive username, user ID number, and password. There are seven fields or segments per line in /etc/passwd delimited by colons (:). When a field is left blank, a colon has to be entered so that you might have a line with two or more colons in sequence. The seven fields are as follows:

username	unique identifier for user
password	should be unique to the user
user ID (UID)	unique system identifier for the user
group ID (GID)	group identifier for the user
comment	usually the user's name
home directory	user's login directory
login command	command executed when the user logs in, usually a shell

How do I edit /etc/group?

The first action in editing /etc/group is making a backup. There are four fields or segments per line in /etc/group delimited by colons (:). When a field is left blank, a colon has to be entered so that you might have a line with two or more colons in sequence. A group can be based on any association, department, function, or even a system device. The four fields are as follows:

group name	unique identifier for the group
password	usually left blank or an *, but a password can be assigned
group ID (GID)	unique number that identifies the group
users	lists of all user IDs in the group (separated by commas)

Note: While a user may belong to more than one group, a user can only be active in one group at a time.

How do I create a home directory?

The example used here implies that the location for grouping home directories is /home/user and the /etc/shells file is used for executing the login command. Do the following:

```
shell:/home/user$ cd /home
shell:/home/user$ mkdir jdoe
```

How do I copy files from /etc/skel to the new home?

Based on the above example include the following step:

```
shell:/home/user$ cp /etc/skel/*  /home/jdoe
```

How do I change ownerships and permissions?

The following is an example using the user jdoe:

```
cd /home/jdoe
chown –R jdoe.user
chmod –R go=u, go-w
```

Note: This example changes the directory to that of jdoe. The chown command recursively changes ownership of directories and their contents to jdoe. The chmod recursively changes permissions so users in the file's group and other users in the file's group can read and write to files.

How do I set the password?

The straightforward method is to issue the passwd command at the root. Next, set the password for the user. The syntax is passwd UID password.

Chapter 22

Red Hat Package Manager Tips

This chapter looks at the Red Hat Package Manager (RPM). This utility, while developed by Red Hat, has become a common package with variations in other Linux distributions. It has become a replacement for the tar.gz method. This utility is a basic tool for managing and controlling servers and their associated services because the software is continually being updated or a service has to be added to the filesystem.

What is a package?

A package is a collection or archive of files that includes information on the package name, version number, and description.

What are the fundamental features of RPM?

To go with the common options there are four fundamental features or advantages in using RPM:

- A new package can be installed with loss of customized files
- An installed package with files in multiple can be removed cleanly
- A package can be verified to be installed properly
- A package can be queried to ensure dependency files are available

What are the basic modes for using RPM?

There are the five expected functions or modes that any packaging utility should have:

Add	Install (rpm –i)
Delete	Uninstall (rpm –e)
Update	Upgrade (rpm –U)
Search	Query (rpm –q)
Validate	Verify (rpm –V)

How do I get the version number of RPM?

To get the version number of the RPM you are using, enter **rpm - -version**. This command would display, for example:

RPM version 3.0

How can I get online help about RPM?

To get online help you would enter **rpm - -help**. Since it is long, you might want to enter **rpm - -help | less**. This give you the opportunity to scroll down or up through the help file.

Note: If you enter **rpm** you will get an abbreviated help file. In addition, it is two dashes(- -), not one.

What are the basic steps in building any RPM?

There is a five-step process in building any RPM. The steps are as follows:

1. Ensure the /etc/rpmc file is set up
2. Get the source code for the RPM
3. Make a patch if any source was changed
4. Ensure all the components are properly located
5. Build the package

Note: For detailed information on these steps, see the RPM-HOWTO. A copy can be found at the URL http://metalab.unc.edu/mdw/HOWTO/RPM-HOWTO-6.html.

How do I find a list of all RPMs?

To find a listing of all possible RPMs, over 41,000, go to the URL http://sunsite.auc.dk/linux/RPM/index.html.

This site includes all versions and distributions. There are indices by:

- Category
- Date of creation beginning with those less than a week old
- Name
- Maintainer
- Distribution

How do I find just RPMs for Red Hat Linux?

To find a listing of Red Hat Software's RPMs, over 18,000, go to the URL http://sunsite.auc.dk/linux/RPM/Red Hat Software.html.

How do I find Red Hat documentation on RPM?

The Red Hat Linux 6.0 manual is found on the Web. For the RPM chapter, see http://www.redhat.com/corp/support/manuals/RHL-6.0-Manual/installguide/manual/doc072.html.

How do I install a package?

The basic syntax for installing a package at the root level is rpm –i packagename-version-release.i386.rpm or rpm –i pkg-1.0-2.i386.rpm, where -386 is the architecture (Intel chip), -2 is the release number, 1.0 is the version number, and pkg is the package name.

Note: The general syntax for install is rpm –i [options] [packages].

What are the options for rpm -i?

There are 11 options that can be used with the install command. They are the following:

-v	verifies what RPM is doing by displaying the process
-h or - -hash	prints 50 hash marks (#) as the package is installed for sort purpose
- -excludedocs	excludes the installation of any files marked as documentation
- -force	forces a package to be installed
- -includesdocs	includes the installation of any files marked as documentation (default)
- -nodeps	does not check for dependency prior to installation
- -oldpackage	allows for an older package to replace a newer package
- -percent	prints amount of extraction for the package
- -replacefiles	replaces installed files with new files
- -replacepkgs	replaces installed packages with new packages

- -test tests to see if the package can be installed properly

Note: The general syntax for the first two listed options can be either rpm –i –v –h [packages] or rpm –ivh [packages].

How can I install a package from an FTP site?

The general syntax for installing a package from an FTP site is rpm –i ftp URL/package.

How can I reinstall a package that is corrupt?

To reinstall a package that might be corrupt, include in the command line the option - -replacepkgs.

How can I install files already installed by another package?

To install conflicting files, include the option - -replacefiles in the command line.

How do I uninstall a package?

Uninstalling a package is simpler than installing. The syntax is rpm –e package. Package version, etc., is not required.

How do I handle the "... break dependencies" error?

When you get the "removing these packages would break dependencies" error message when you are installing, enter on the command line the option - -nodeps.

How do I update a package?

The upgrading process is very similar to the install process. Instead of using the –i option, you use the –U option. Notice that it is a capital U.

How do I use RPM to query about a package?

The simplest query is rpm –q package.

The general syntax is rpm –q [options] [packages].

The simplest query could be rpm –q elm.

The results would be:

elm-2.5.0-0.2pre8

What are the options for query?

There are five options for querying packages that can be in the form of rpm –q –[option] or rpm –q[option].

A summary of the options is as follows:

Option	Description
-c	lists configuration files
-d	lists documentation files
-i	lists complete package information
-l	lists all package files
-s	lists package file states

What kind of information do I get when I enter rpm –qi?

For example, if you entered rpm –qi ftp you would get information similar to that below:

```
Name        : ftp                          Relocations: (not relocatable)
Version     : 0.10                         Vendor: Red Hat Software
Release     : 22                           Build Date: Sun Mar 21 16:16:22 1999
Install date : Mon Jun 28 08:59:38 1999    Build Host: porky.devel.redhat.com
Group       : Applications/Internet        Source RPM: ftp-0.10-22.src.rpm
Size        : 91471                        License: BSD
Packager    : Red Hat Software <http://developer.redhat.com/bugzilla/>
Summary     : The standard UNIX FTP (file transfer protocol) client
Description :
The ftp package provides the standard UNIX command-line FTP client.
FTP is the file transfer protocol, which is widely used Internet protocol
for transferring files and for archiving files.

If your system is on a network, you should install ftp in order to do
file transfers.
```

How do I use RPM to verify a package is installed properly?

The general syntax for verifying a package is rpm –V [package].

If the package is verified correctly, there is no output. If there is a difference between the installed package and the database record, then you get an output consisting of an 8-character string. When there is no specific error, there is a period (.). The eight tests and the characters that represent them are as follows:

5	MD5 sum
S	File size
L	Symlink
T	Mtime
D	Device
U	User
G	Group
M	Mode (permissions and file type)

A file that failed every tests would have this output:

5SLTDUGM

Chapter 23

Red Hat Tools Tips

This chapter looks at some of the rich inventory of tools available from the Red Hat Linux distribution. The major configuration tool is linuxconf.

Note: To see available options for the commands discussed in the chapter, you need to do a man command-name command.

What tools can I find in the control panel?

In the control panel, you can find eight tools. They are the following:

- helptool
- kernelcfg
- linuxconf
- modemtool
- netcfg
- printtool
- thsysv
- timetool

Note: Linuxconf can handle most of the functions of the control panel.

23

What can I do with helptool?

The basic function of helptool is to search the man pages and other types of documentation for a specified string. It is available to all users. You click the control panel button to get its main dialog box.

What can I do with kernelcfg?

The kernelcfg command is a graphical interface to the kerneld daemon. In addition, it serves as an interface to such commands as init, lsmod, and rmmod.

What can I do with linuxconf?

The linuxconf utility handles a broad range of tasks and programs for system configuration. For the latest information on linuxconf, see the URL http://www.solucorp.qc.ca/linuxconf.

Linuxconf was developed because most people do not use administrative tools frequently. This is also true of system administrators. Some tools are used frequently, some are rarely used.

What can I do with modemtool?

The basic function of modemtool is to create a symbolic link, /dev/modem, that points to a modem serial point.

What can I do with netcfg?

The basic purpose of netcfg is to assist in managing important network information. The information includes configuring the Point-to-Point Protocol (Chapter 10) and DNS (Chapter 4).

What can I do with printtool?

The basic function of printtool is to install or configure printers on the system.

What can I do with thsysv?

The basic function of thsysv is to configure the system for the services that are to start or stop during each Linux runlevel.

Note: There are seven runlevels that are specified in /etc/inittab. To display this file, enter more /etc/inittab.

What can I do with timetool?

The basic function of timetool is to set the system's date and time. Do not confuse this command with the timeconfig command, which is used to set time zones for the system.

What other tools are available besides those in the control panel?

This listing is some of the tools available beyond those tools in the control panel:

- ab
- apxs
- comanche
- fetchmailconf
- glint
- installit
- kbdconfig
- makehistory
- mouseconfig
- newsrequeue
- ntsysv
- readprofile
- scsi_info
- setup
- swat
- timeconfig
- usermount
- userpasswd
- Xconfigurator

What does ab do?

The ab tool is for benchmarking the Apache Web server. In particular it checks for performance, that is, requests per time.

23

What does apxs do?

The basic function of apxs is for installing and building extension modules for the Apache Web server.

What does comanche do?

The basic function of comanche is to configure the Apache Web server. For details on the Apache Web server, see Chapter 18.

What does fetchmailconf do?

The basic function of fetchmailconf is to assist in configuring the system for e-mail retrieval.

What does glint do?

The basic function of glint is to interface with RPM. It is accessed from an X11 terminal window.

What does installit do?

The basic function of installit is to put a source copy into a specified destination.

What does kbdconfig do?

The kbdconfig tool is for configuring a keyboard. The information is found in /etc/sysconfig/keyboard.

What does makehistory do?

The basic function of makehistory is to recover a Usenet history database. It rebuilds a database as well as restores articles.

What does mouseconfig do?

The basic function of mouseconfig is configuring a mouse. The impacted files are /etc/sysconf/mouse and /dev/mouse.

What does newsrequeue do?

The basic function of newsrequeue is to rewrite batchfiles after a system crash.

What does ntsysv do?

The basic function of ntsysv is to configure runlevel services. See the thsysv tool earlier in this chapter.

What does readprofile do?

The readprofile tool reads the kernel profile information found in /proc/profile.

What does scsi_info do?

The basic function of scsi_info is to retrieve SCSI address parameters found in /proc/scsi/scsi. This tool automatically converts arbitrary device assignments to the user-configured addresses.

What does setup do?

The basic purpose of setup is to call up initialization functions for devices and filesystems found in linux/init/main.c. In addition, it mounts the root.

What does swat do?

The basic function of swat (Samba Web Administration Tool) is to configure the smb.conf file. It is run from inetd.

What does timeconfig do?

The timeconfig tool is used to configure system time parameters found in /etc/sysconfig/clock and /etc/localtime. It is compatible to Red Hat's startup scripts.

What does usermount do?

The usermount tool allows users to manage removable media such as floppy disks. It uses /etc/fstab.

What does userpasswd do?

The basic function of userpasswd is a graphical interface that allows a user to easily change a password.

What does Xconfigurator do?

The basic function of Xconfigurator is to configure the XFree86 server and display. It sets up the required file links to use XFree86 on Red Hat Linux.

Chapter 24

Hardware Tips

This chapter focuses on the hardware devices in a network that assist the user or the general functionality of the network. This chapter broadly looks at processors (computers), keyboards, the mouse, CD-ROM and disk drives, modems, and printers. This chapter includes pointers to associated documentation.

Note: To see available options for the commands discussed in the chapter, you need to do a man command-name command.

What is important to know about hardware?

There are seven broad requirements, two directly involving hardware, for a system administrator to be effective and efficient:

- Be able to communicate, communicate, and communicate
- Be able to logically plan processes
- Be able to make changes without major impacts on the system
- Be able to test all changes
- Have support plans
- Know how hardware and software work
- Know the location of system components, hardware, and software

How do I find out about compatible hardware?

See Hardware-HOWTO.gz. This HOWTO lists known hardware that works with Linux and how to locate drivers. It covers some 20 different types of hardware devices for Intel platforms including laptops, memory, video and sound cards, controllers, network adapters, drives, modems, printers, and scanners. The author is Patrick Reijnen (patrick@bart.nl).

What type of processors will Linux run on?

Linux was designed to run originally on an 80386 system. However, for efficiency reasons it is recommended to use a variant of the 80486 or Pentium chipset. Linux also runs on other processors such as those from Motorola, Sun, and Hewlett-Packard.

What is the /proc file?

It is a data structure collection in memory that appears as a set of directories and files. It is managed by the kernel and is the process file system of the kernel. To see the contents, enter **ls –l /proc | less**.

Note: The piped **less** permits you to scroll through this file up and down. It gives the processes run on the system.

What is the /proc/cpuinfo file?

This file contains information about your cpu (chip or microprocessor) as known by the kernel. It can contain nearly two dozen characteristics including processor, vendor_id, cpu family, model, stepping, cpu MHz, fdiv_bug, and flags. To see the contents of this file, enter **cat /proc/cpuinfo**.

What is the /proc/pci file?

If you have a Pentium chipset, this file gives information about a PCI motherboard. To see this file, enter **cat /proc/pci | less**.

What other types of information are available through /proc?

There are three other /proc files for information on IRQ, DMA, and IO address. They are:

- /proc/interrupts — IRQ (interrupt requests) address information
- /proc/dma — DMA (Direct Memory Access) channel information
- /proc/ioports — IO port address information

What types of information are found in /proc/interrupts?

The information displayed will include interrupts for timer, keyboard, cascade, rtc, and mouse. To see the file's content, enter **cat /proc/interrupts**.

What types of information are found in /proc/ioports?

The file can contain more than a dozen IO addresses. These IO addresses include the ones for the Direct Memory Access (DMA) controller, keyboard, timer, real-time clock (rtc), video controller, and floppy drive. To see the file's content, enter **cat /proc/ioports**.

What are some of the network devices supported in the kernel?

There are at least six types of network devices supported in the Linux kernel:

- Local loopback interface (lo)
- Ethernet cards (eth0, eth1, ...)
- DE-600 interfaces (dl0, dl1, ...)
- PLIP interfaces (plip0, plip1, ...)
- PPP interfaces (ppp0, ppp1, ...)
- SLIP interfaces (sl0, sl1, ...)

What is /dev?

It is the directory for device special files.

What are some of the files found in the /dev directory?

Some of the device files found in the /dev directory include:

- xdaN (1 – 8)
- xdbN (1 – 8)
- zqftN (0 – 3)
- MAKEDEV
- mouse
- cdrom

What is /dev/null?

This is commonly called the bit bucket, the place for non-required output.

What is /etc/fstab?

This file contains a list of all devices that can be mounted automatically by the filesystem. The file contains the device name, where the device is to be mounted, type of filesystem, and options.

How do I determine keyboard rate?

To determine a keyboard's typematic rate (term's origin is from IBM on its earlier PCs) in characters per second (cps) and repeat delay in milliseconds (ms), enter kbdrate. The result should be similar to the following:

```
Typematic Rate set to 10.9 cps (delay = 250 mS)
```

How can I determine if the kernel identifies my mouse?

To determine if the kernel identifies your mouse you can look at boot messages in two locations by entering either dmesg | less or less /var/log/messages.

How is a generic mouse linked?

A generic mouse device /dev/mouse has a symbolic link. On a system with a PS/2 Auxiliary Device interface you would get the following results if you entered:

```
ls –l /dev/mouse
lrexrwxrwx   l root    root          5 Sep 23 06:22 /dev/mouse -> psaux
```

What is /dev/printer?

Local print requests socket.

Where is an entry on a physical printer kept?

A physical printer is a device, so information on it is kept in the /dev directory.

What are essential files for the printer?

The essential associated files and directories are:

/dev/lp*	line printer devices
/dev/printer	local request socket
/etc/hosts.equiv	lists machine names allowed for printer access
/etc/hosts.lpd	lists machine names allowed for printer access, but under another administrator
/etc/printcap	printer description file
/var/spool/*	spool directories
/var/spool/*/minfree	minimum free space to leave

What is the /etc/printcap file?

This file contains the specifications, perhaps too extensive for one's taste, for each named printer in the system. This text file can be edited with your editor of choice. It should be in the root and have the permissions –rw-r- -r- -. Some of the data kept in /etc/printcap include the following:

- Print device name
- Spool directory name
- Error file
- Remote printing host
- Remote printer name

Note: The permissions entry translates as owner with read and write, the group with read, and all others none.

How do I define a printer using printtool?

The printtool program detects parallel printer devices. If /dev/lp0, /dev/lp1, or /dev/lp2 is not displayed, either your printer is not turned on or you do not have printing support. If there is no support, click the OK button. Next, give your printer a unique name that is not lpr. Follow the configuration instructions. Finally, do an ASCII or PostScript test from the Tests menu.

How do I set up serial communication devices?

See **Serial-HOWTO.gz**. This HOWTO explains how to set up serial communication devices. It covers supported serial hardware, serial port names, some interesting programs, dialing out and in with your modem, setting up a terminal connection, communication programs and utilities, tips, and troubleshooting. The author is Greg Hankins (**gregh@cc.gatech.edu**).

See **Serial-Programming-HOWTO.gz**. This HOWTO explains how to program the serial port. It covers getting started and some program examples. The author is Peter H. Baumann (**Peter.Baumann@dlr.de**).

What is a rule about modems?

The basic rule on the modem is do not use a WinModem because it is primarily software driven and is compatible to the operating systems of Microsoft.

How do I check that the CD-ROM driver is in the kernel?

To determine if the CD-ROM driver is in the kernel, enter **cat /proc/devices**.

There are two sections, character devices and block devices. Look in the block devices section, probably at the end of the file, and check for **22 ide1** if you have an IDE interface.

What is an issue with more than one Ethernet board?

When booting, the autoprobe only checks for one Ethernet device. You must explicitly tell the kernel about any additional Ethernet devices.

What is the first Ethernet device called?

The first Ethernet device is called **eth0**. This name is defined in the kernel, not in the **/dev** directory.

Is there a HOWTO available on Ethernet?

For more technical information on Ethernet, see the Linux Ethernet-HOWTO by Paul Gortmaker (February 1998).

What are some of the commands for handling the hardware?

Here are eight commands to manage networking and system hardware:

arp	manages the kernel's Address Resolution Protocol (ARP) cache
cfdisk	maintains curses based disk partitions
fdisk	maintains disk partitions for Linux
kbdrate	manages the keyboard's repeat rate and delay time
ramsize	prints RAM disk information
rarp	manages the Reverse Address Resolution Protocol (RARP) table
setserial	gets and sets serial port information
slattach	attaches a serial line to a network interface

How do I find storage device space data?

The df command summarizes free and available space for all mounted storage devices. Some of the options include the following:

-a	displays information for all filesystems
-i	displays inode information
-t type	displays information about specified types of filesystems only
-T	prints the filesystem type
-x type	excludes specified types of filesystems from the output
-help	displays a help message

What are the purposes of mmap and munmap?

These two system calls are used for device memory mapping:

mmap	maps files or devices into memory
munmap	unmaps files or devices out of memory

What does scsi_info do?

The basic function of scsi_info is to retrieve SCSI address parameters found in /proc/scsi/scsi. This tool automatically converts arbitrary device assignments to the user-configured addresses.

What does setup do?

The basic feature of setup is to call up initialization functions for devices and filesystems found in linux/init/main.c. In addition, it mounts the root.

Are there any newsgroups on hardware for Linux?

There is one newsgroup especially for hardware and Linux; it is comp.os.linux.hardware.

What RFCs are available on hardware devices?

While there are a number of RFCs on hardware devices, they are more appropriate for general networking concerns rather than Linux specific.

Are there any HOWTOs on hardware devices?

The following list is some of the HOWTOs related to hardware:

- 3 Button Serial Mouse (mini)
- Brief Introduction to Alpha Systems and Processors
- Clock (mini)
- Firewall and Proxy Server
- Hardware Compatibility
- Linux Busmouse
- Linux CD-ROM
- Linux CD-Writing
- Linux Ethernet
- Linux I/O Port Programming (mini)
- Linux Keyboard and Console
- Linux PCI
- Linux Printing
- Linux SCSI

- Linux Serial
- Linux Sound
- Multi Disk System Tuning
- XFree86 Video Timings

Note: Most HOWTOs have some information on hardware.

Are there any man pages on hardware devices?

The following list of 62 man pages is from /usr/man/man4.

aha152x_cs	charsets	console
console_codes	console_ioctl	console_ioctls
ddp	dummy_cs	english
fd	fmvj18x_cs	ftl_cs
full	hd	i82365
ibmtr_cs	icmp	initrd
intro	ip	ipfw
ispell	kmen	lp
magic	mailcap	mem
memory_cb	memory_cs	mouse
netdevice	netlink	netwave_cs
null	packet	pcmcia_core
pcnet_cs	port	ram
random	raw	rtnetlink
sd	serial_cs	socket
st	tc574_cs	tc575_ch
tc589_cs	tcic	tcp
tty	ttys	udp
unix	vcs	vcsa
wavelan	wavelan_cs	x25
xirc2ps_cs	zero	

Chapter 25

Filesystem Structure Tips

This chapter uses the list (ls) command to determine the filesystem structure for the Red Hat Linux distribution in its original installation. This chapter shows how the ls command can assist a server or system administrator in locating directories and files. Red Hat Linux is large with the root directory and at least 13 directories, excluding any user directories. One of the major requirements of any system administrator is to comprehend the filesystem's organization or structure. The usual documentation just lists the options and arguments for the use of the ls command, but it is the combination of options and the use of the directory wildcard argument that gives this command its power.

Note: A smart system administrator knows how to find information, not necessarily remembering everything.

The ls command has over 80 options; many are display-format options. Its associated commands are dir and vdir. This chapter looks at how to use certain syntax so you can locate all directories on your filesystems and their associated directories and files. In addition, example results are given.

Note: To see available options for the commands discussed in the chapter, you need to do a man command-name command.

How do I use ls?

The ls command has many option and argument variants; however, the simplest effective one is ls [options] [directory].

25

The power of the ls command is the combination of options and the use of /* for the directory argument. Some of the options without any argument that list for the current directory are the following:

ls -a lists all (including hidden) files

ls -c	sorts by file creation time
ls -d	lists directory like files
ls -f	lists all files as on the disk
ls -l	creates a "long" (detailed) formatted list
ls -m	lists files horizontally and separated by commas
ls -x	lists files in columns, sorted horizontally

What are the original directories in the Red Hat distribution?

Using the syntax **ls –d /*** you get the following result:

```
/bin    /dev   /home   /lost+found   /proc   /sbin   /usr
/boot   /etc   /lib    /mnt          /root   /tmp    /var
```

Using the syntax **ls –d | less** you get the following result:

```
/bin
/boot
/dev
/etc
/home
/lib
/lost+found
/mnt
/proc
/root
/sbin
/tmp
/usr
/var
```

Note: The piped **less** command was used in case the result is more than one screen. The **less** command permits you to scroll up or down the screen.

How do I display the basic contents of the filesystem?

To find the basic contents of all the directories in the filesystem with one single command, enter **ls –ax /* | less**.

This syntax displays each directory's basic contents in horizontal columns beginning with the /bin directory and ending with the /var directory. In addition, you can scroll up or down the screen.

Note: To print the results you would enter ls –ax /* | lpr.

How do I display the contents of the filesystem?

To find the comprehensive contents of all the directories in the filesystem with one single command, enter ls –ax /*/*/* | less. This syntax displays each directory's contents in horizontal columns beginning with the /bin directory and ending with the /var directory. In addition, you can scroll up or down the screen. It is very, very long.

Note: This argument is too long: ls –ax /*/*/*/*.

What are the basic contents of the /bin directory?

This directory contains essential system files. These are executable binary files. The name of the directory is short for binary.

If you enter ls –ax /bin | less the results should be similar to the following:

.	..	arch	ash	ash.static	awk
basename	bash	bsh	cat	chgrp	chmod
chown	consolechars	cp	cpio	csh	date
dd	df	dmesg	dnsdomainname	doexec	domainname
echo	ed	egrep	ex	false	fgrep
fsconf	gawk	gawk-3.0.3	grep	gunzip	gzip
hostname	igawk	ipcalc	kill	linuxconf	ln
loadkeys	login	lpdconf	ls	mail	mkdir
mknod	mktemp	more	mount	mt	mv
netconf	netstat	nice	nisdomainname	ping	ps
pwd	red	remadmin	rm	rmdir	rpm
rvi	rview	sed	setserial	sh	sleep
sort	stty	su	sync	tar	tcsh
touch	true	unmount	uname	userconf	useleep
vi	view	xconf	ypdominname	zcat	

To list only those beginning with the letter b, enter ls –ax /bin/b* | less. The result is:

25

/bin/basename /bin/bash /bin/bsh

Note: The piped less is used throughout even if not required for a given directory in case your screen is not large enough for a given listing. The –a option lists all files including those that begin with a period (.).

What are the basic contents of the /boot directory?

This directory contains the information required for booting.

If you enter ls –ax /boot | less the results should be similar to the following:

.	..	System.map	System.map-2.2.5-15
boot.3000	boot.b	chain.b	lost+found
map	module-info-2.2.5-15	os2_d.b	vmlinux-2.2.5-15
vmlinuz	vmlinuz-2.2.5-15		

What are the basic contents of the /dev directory?

This directory contains device files. These files are used to access the various types of hardware connected to the filesystem. For example, the file for the mouse is /dev/mouse. The files are grouped logically. As shown, it is a very large directory.

If you enter ls –ax /dev | less the results should be similar to the following:

.	..	MAKEDEV	apm_bios	atibm	audio
audio1	aztcd	bpcd	capi20	capi20.00	capi20.01
capi20.02	capi20.03	capi20.04	capi20.05	capi20.06	capi20.07
capi20.08	capi20.09	capi20.10	capi20.11	capi20.12	capi20.13
capi20.14	capi20.15	capi20.16	capi20.17	capi20.18	capi20.19
cdrom	cdu31a	cdu535	cm206cd	console	cua0
cua1	cua2	cua3	cui0	cui1	cui10
cui11	cui12	cui13	cui14	cui15	cui16
cui17	cui18	cui19	cui2	cui20	cui21
cui22	cui23	cui24	cui25	cui26	cui27
cui28	cui29	cui3	cui30	cui31	cui32
cui33	cui34	cui35	cui36	cui37	cui38
cui39	cui4	cui40	cui41	cui42	cui43

cui44	cui45	cui46	cui47	cui48	cui49
cui5	cui50	cui51	cui52	cui53	cui54
cui55	cui56	cui57	cui58	cui59	cui6
cui60	cui61	cui62	cui63	cui7	cui8
cui9	cum0	cum1	cum2	cum3	cum4
cum5	cum6	cum7	cum8	cum9	cuma
cumb	cumc	cumd	cume	cumf	dcbri0
dcbri1	dcbri2	dcbri3	dcxx0	dcxx1	dsp
dsp1	enskip	fb	fb0	fb1	fb2
fb3	fb4	fb5	fb6	fb7	fd
fd0	fd0D360	fd0D720	fd0H1440	fd0H360	fd0H720
fd0d360	fd0h1200	fd0h360	fd0h720	fd1	fd1D360
fd1D720	fd1H1440	fd1H360	fd1H720	fd1d360	fd1h1200
fd1h360	fd1h720	ftape	full	gpmct1	gscd
hda	hda1	had10	hda11	hda12	hda13
hda14	hda15	hda16	hda2	hda3	hda4
hda5	hda6	hda7	hda8	hda9	hdb
hdb1	hbd10	hdb11	hdb12	hdb13	hdb14
hdb15	hdb16	hdb2	hdb3	hdb4	hdb5
hdb6	hdb7	hdb8	hdb9	hdc	hdc1
hdc10	hdc11	hdc12	hdc13	hdc14	hdc15
hdc16	hdc2	hdc3	hdc4	hdc5	hdc6
hdc7	hdc8	hdc9	hdd	hdd1	hdd10
hdd11	hdd12	hdd13	hdd14	hdd15	hdd16
hdd2	hdd3	hdd4	hdd5	hdd6	hdd7
hdd8	hdd9	hde	hde1	hed10	hde11
hde12	hde13	hde14	hde15	hde16	hde2
hde3	hde4	hde5	hde6	hde7	hde8
hde9	hdf	hdf1	hfd10	hdf11	hdf12
hdf13	hdf14	hdf15	hdf16	hdf2	hdf3
hdf4	hdf5	hdf6	hdf7	hdf8	hdf9
hdg	hdg1	hgd10	hdg11	hdg12	hdg13
hdg14	hdg15	hdg16	hdg2	hdg3	hdg4
hdg5	hdg6	hdg7	hdg8	hdg9	hdh
hdh1	hhd10	hdh11	hdh12	hdh13	hdh14
hdh15	hdh16	hdh2	hdh3	hdh4	hdh5
hdh6	hdh7	hdh8	hdh9	ht0	i2c0
i2c1	ida	initctl	inportbm	ipauth	ipl

ipnat	ippp0	ippp1	ippp10	ippp11	ippp12
ippp13	ippp14	ippp15	ippp16	ippp17	ippp18
ippp19	ippp2	ippp20	ippp21	ippp22	ippp23
ippp24	ippp25	ippp26	ippp27	ippp28	ippp29
ippp3	ippp30	ippp31	ippp32	ippp33	ippp34
ippp35	ippp36	ippp37	ippp38	ippp39	ippp4
ippp40	ippp41	ippp42	ippp43	ippp44	ippp45
ippp46	ippp47	ippp48	ippp49	ippp5	ippp50
ippp51	ippp52	ippp53	ippp54	ippp55	ippp56
ippp57	ippp58	ippp59	ippp6	ippp60	ippp61
ippp62	ippp63	ippp7	ippp8	ippp9	ipstate
iscc0	iscc1	isccctl0	isccctl1	isct1	isdn0
isdn1	isdn10	isdn11	isdn12	isdn13	isdn14
isdn15	isdn16	isdn17	isdn18	isdn19	isdn2
isdn20	isdn21	isdn22	isdn23	isdn24	isdn25
isdn26	isdn27	isdn28	isdn29	isdn3	isdn30
isdn31	isdn32	isdn33	isdn34	isdn35	isdn36
isdn37	isdn38	isdn39	isdn4	isdn40	isdn41
isdn42	isdn43	isdn44	isdn45	isdn46	isdn47
isdn48	isdn49	isdn5	isdn50	isdn55	isdn52
isdn53	isdn54	isdn55	isdn56	isdn57	isdn58
isdn59	isdn6	isdn60	isdn61	isdn62	isdn63
isdn7	isdn8	isdn9	isdnctrl	isdnctrl0	isdnctrl1
isdnctrl10	isdnctrl11	isdnctrl12	isdnctrl13	isdnctrl14	isdnctrl15
isdnctrl16	isdnctrl17	isdnctrl18	isdnctrl19	isdnctrl2	isdnctrl20
isdnctrl21	isdnctrl22	isdnctrl23	isdnctrl24	isdnctrl25	isdnctrl26
isdnctrl27	isdnctrl28	isdnctrl29	isdnctrl3	isdnctrl30	isdnctrl31
isdnctrl32	isdnctrl33	isdnctrl34	isdnctrl35	isdnctrl36	isdnctrl37
isdnctrl38	isdnctrl39	isdnctrl4	isdnctrl40	isdnctrl41	isdnctrl42
isdnctrl43	isdnctrl44	isdnctrl45	isdnctrl46	isdnctrl47	isdnctrl48
isdnctrl49	isdnctrl5	isdnctrl50	isdnctrl51	isdnctrl52	isdnctrl53
isdnctrl54	isdnctrl55	isdnctrl56	isdnctrl57	isdnctrl58	isdnctrl59
isdnctrl6	isdnctrl60	isdnctrl61	isdnctrl62	isdnctrl63	isdnctrl7
isdnctrl8	isdnctrl9	isdninfo	js0	js1	js2
js3	kmem	log	logibm	loop0	loop1
loop2	loop3	loop4	loop5	loop6	loop7
lp0	lp1	lp2	mcd	mem	midi0
midi00	midi01	midi02	midi03	midi1	midi2

midi3	mixer	mixer1	mmetfgrap	mouse	mpu401data
mpu401stat	nb0	nb1	nb10	nb100	nb101
nb102	nb103	nb104	nb105	nb106	nb107
nb108	nb109	nb11	nb110	nb111	nb112
nb113	nb114	nb115	nb116	nb117	nb118
nb119	nb12	nb120	nb121	nb122	nb123
nb124	nb125	nb126	nb127	nb13	nb14
nb15	nb16	nb17	nb18	nb19	nb2
nb20	nb21	nn22	nb23	nb24	nb25
nb26	nb27	nb28	nb29	nb3	nb30
nb31	nn32	nb33	nb34	nb35	nb36
nb37	nb38	nb39	nb4	nb40	nb41
nn42	nb43	nb44	nb45	nb46	nb47
nb48	nb49	nb5	nb50	nb51	nn52
nb53	nb54	nb55	nb56	nb57	nb58
nb59	nb6	nb60	nb61	nn62	nb63
nb64	nb65	nb66	nb67	nb68	nb69
nb7	nb70	nb71	nn72	nb73	nb74
nb75	nb76	nb77	nb78	nb79	nb8
nb80	nb81	nn82	nb83	nb84	nb85
nb86	nb87	nb88	nb89	nb9	nb90
nb91	nn92	nb93	nb94	nb95	nb96
nb97	nb98	nb99	nftape	nht0	nqft0
nqft1	nqft2	nqft3	nrawqft0	nrawqft1	nrawqft2
nrawqft3	nrft0	nrft1	nrft2	nrft3	nst0
nst1	nst2	nst3	nst4	nst5	nst6
nst7	ntpqic11	ntpqic120	ntpqic150	ntpqic24	null
nzqft0	nzqft1	nzqft2	nzqft3	optcd	par0
par1	par2	parport0	parport1	parport2	pcd0
pcd1	pcd2	pcd3	pda	pda1	pda2
pda3	pda4	pdb	pdb1	pdb2	pdb3
pdb4	pdc	pdc1	pdc2	pdc3	pdc4
pdd	pdd1	pdd2	pdd3	pdd4	pf0
pf1	pf2	pf3	pg0	pg1	pg2
pg3	port	printer	psaux	pt0	pt1
pt2	pt3	ptmx	pts	ptya0	ptya1
ptya2	ptya3	ptya4	ptya5	ptya6	ptya7
ptya8	ptya9	ptyaa	ptyab	ptyac	ptyad

ptyae ptyaf ptyb0 ptyb1 ptyb2 ptyb3
ptyb4 ptyb5 ptyb6 ptyb7 ptyb8 ptyb9
ptyba ptybb ptybc ptybd ptybe ptybf
ptyc0 ptyc1 ptyc2 ptyc3 ptyc4 ptyc5
ptyc6 ptyc7 ptyc8 ptyc9 ptyca ptycb
ptycc ptycd ptyce ptycf ptyd0 ptyd1
ptyd2 ptyd3 ptyd4 ptyd5 ptyd6 ptyd7
ptyd8 ptyd9 ptyda ptydb ptydc ptydd
ptyde ptydf ptye0 ptye1 ptye2 ptye3
ptye4 ptye5 ptye6 ptye7 ptye8 ptye9
ptyea ptyeb ptyec ptyed ptyee ptyef
ptyp0 ptyp1 ptyp2 ptyp3 ptyp4 ptyp5
ptyp6 ptyp7 ptyp8 ptyp9 ptypa ptypb
ptypc ptypd ptype ptypf ptyq0 ptyq1
ptyq2 ptyq3 ptyq4 ptyq5 ptyq6 ptyq7
ptyq8 ptyq9 ptyqa ptyqb ptyqc ptyqd
ptyqe ptyqf ptyr0 ptyr1 ptyr2 ptyr3
ptyr4 ptyr5 ptyr6 ptyr7 ptyr8 ptyr9
ptyra ptyrb ptyrc ptyrd ptyre ptyrf
ptys0 ptys1 ptys2 ptys3 ptys4 ptys5
ptys6 ptys7 ptys8 ptys9 ptysa ptysb
ptysc ptysd ptyse ptysf ptyt0 ptyt1
ptyt2 ptyt3 ptyt4 ptyt5 ptyt6 ptyt7
ptyt8 ptyt9 ptyta ptytb ptytc ptytd
ptyte ptytf ptyu0 ptyu1 ptyu2 ptyu3
ptyu4 ptyu5 ptyu6 ptyu7 ptyu8 ptyu9
ptyua ptyub ptyuc ptyud ptyue ptyuf
ptyv0 ptyv1 ptyv2 ptyv3 ptyv4 ptyv5
ptyv6 ptyv7 ptyv8 ptyv9 ptyva ptyvb
ptyvc ptyvd ptyve ptyvf ptyw0 ptyw1
ptyw2 ptyw3 ptyw4 ptyw5 ptyw6 ptyw7
ptyw8 ptyw9 ptywa ptywb ptywc ptywd
ptywe ptywf ptyx0 ptyx1 ptyx2 ptyx3
ptyx4 ptyx5 ptyx6 ptyx7 ptyx8 ptyx9
ptyxa ptyxb ptyxc ptyxd ptyxe ptyxf
ptyy0 ptyy1 ptyy2 ptyy3 ptyy4 ptyy5
ptyy6 ptyy7 ptyy8 ptyy9 ptyya ptyyb
ptyyc ptyyd ptyye ptyyf ptyz0 ptyz1

ptyz2	ptyz3	ptyz4	ptyz5	ptyz6	ptyz7
ptyz8	ptyz9	ptyza	ptyzb	ptyzc	ptyzd
ptyze	ptyzf	qft0	qft1	qft2	qft3
qng	ram	ram0	ram1	ram11	ram12
ram13	ram14	ram15	ram19	ram2	ram3
ram4	ram5	ram6	ram7	ram8	ram9
ramdisk	random	rawqft0	rawqft1	rawqft2	rawqft3
rd	rft0	rft1	rft2	rft3	rmidi0
rmidi1	rmidi2	rmidi3	rmt16	rmt8	rtc
sbpcd	sbpcd0	sbpcd1	sbpcd2	sbpcd3	scd0
scd1	scd2	scd3	scd4	scd5	scd6
scd7	sda	sda1	sda10	sda11	sda12
sda13	sda14	sda15	sda2	sda3	sda4
sda5	sda6	sda7	sda8	sda9	sdb
sdb1	sdb10	sdb11	sdb12	sdb13	sdb14
sdb15	sdb2	sdb3	sdb4	sdb5	sdb6
sdb7	sdb8	sdb9	sdc	sdc1	sdc10
sdc11	sdc12	sdc13	sdc14	sdc15	sdc2
sdc3	sdc4	sdc5	sdc6	sdc7	sdc8
sdc9	sdd	sdd1	sdd10	sdd11	sdd12
sdd13	sdd14	sdd15	sdd2	sdd3	sdd4
sdd5	sdd6	sdd7	sdd8	sdd9	sde
sde1	sde10	sde11	sde12	sde13	sde14
sde15	sde2	sde3	sde4	sde5	sde6
sde7	sde8	sde9	sdf	sdf1	sdf10
sdf11	sdf12	sdf13	sdf14	sdf15	sdf2
sdf3	sdf4	sdf5	sdf6	sdf7	sdf8
sdf9	sdg	sdg1	sdg10	sdg11	sdg12
sdg13	sdg14	sdg15	sdg2	sdg3	sdg4
sdg5	sdg6	sdg7	sdg8	sdg9	sdh
sdh1	sdh10	sdh11	sdh12	sdh13	sdh14
sdh15	sdh2	sdh3	sdh4	sdh5	sdh6
sdh7	sdh8	sdh9	sdi	sdi1	sdi10
sdi11	sdi12	sdi13	sdi14	sdi15	sdi2
sdi3	sdi4	sdi5	sdi6	sdi7	sdi8
sdi9	sdj	sdj1	sdj10	sdj11	sdj12
sdj13	sdj14	sdj15	sdj2	sdj3	sdj4
sdj5	sdj6	sdj7	sdj8	sdj9	sdk

sdk1	sdk10	sdk11	sdk12	sdk13	sdk14
sdk15	sdk2	sdk3	sdk4	sdk5	sdk6
sdk7	sdk8	sdk9	sdl	sdl1	sdl10
sdl11	sdl12	sdl13	sdl14	sdl15	sdl2
sdl3	sdl4	sdl5	sdl6	sdl7	sdl8
sdl9	sdm	sdm1	sdm10	sdm11	sdm12
sdm13	sdm14	sdm15	sdm2	sdm3	sdm4
sdm5	sdm6	sdm7	sdm8	sdm9	sdn
sdn1	sdn10	sdn11	sdn12	sdn13	sdn14
sdn15	sdn2	sdn3	sdn4	sdn5	sdn6
sdn7	sdn8	sdn9	sdo	sdo1	sdo10
sdo11	sdo12	sdo13	sdo14	sdo15	sdo2
sdo3	sdo4	sdo5	sdo6	sdo7	sdo8
sdo9	sdp	sdp1	sdp10	sdp11	sdp12
sdp13	sdp14	sdp15	sdp2	sdp3	sdp4
sdp5	sdp6	sdp7	sdp8	sdp9	sequencer
sg0	sg1	sg2	sg3	sg4	sg5
sg6	sg7	sga	sgb	sgc	sgd
sge	sgf	sgg	sgh	sjcd	smtpe0
smtpe1	smtpe2	smtpe3	sndstat	sonycd	srnd0
srnd1	st0	st1	st2	st3	st4
st5	st6	st7	staliomem0	staliomem1	staliomem2
staliomem3	stderr	stdin	stdout	sunmouse	systty
tape-d	tape-reset	tlk0	tlk1	tlk2	tlk3
tpqic11	tpqic120	tpqic150	tpqic24	tty	tty0
tty1	tty10	tty11	tty12	tty2	tty3
tty4	tty5	tty6	tty7	tty8	tty9
ttyD0	ttyD1	ttyD10	ttyD11	ttyD12	ttyD13
ttyD14	ttyD15	ttyD16	ttyD17	ttyD18	ttyD19
ttyD2	ttyD3	ttyD4	ttyD5	ttyD6	ttyD7
ttyD8	ttyD9	ttyE0	ttyE1	ttyE10	ttyE100
ttyE101	ttyE102	ttyE103	ttyE104	ttyE105	ttyE106
ttyE107	ttyE108	ttyE109	ttyE11	ttyE110	ttyE111
ttyE112	ttyE113	ttyE114	ttyE115	ttyE116	ttyE117
ttyE118	ttyE119	ttyE12	ttyE120	ttyE121	ttyE122
ttyE123	ttyE124	ttyE125	ttyE126	ttyE127	ttyE128
ttyE129	ttyE13	ttyE130	ttyE131	ttyE132	ttyE133
ttyE134	ttyE135	ttyE136	ttyE137	ttyE138	ttyE139

ttyE14 ttyE140 ttyE141 ttyE142 ttyE143 ttyE144
ttyE145 ttyE146 ttyE147 ttyE148 ttyE149 ttyE15
ttyE150 ttyE151 ttyE152 ttyE153 ttyE154 ttyE155
ttyE156 ttyE157 ttyE158 ttyE159 ttyE16 ttyE160
ttyE161 ttyE162 ttyE163 ttyE164 ttyE165 ttyE166
ttyE167 ttyE168 ttyE169 ttyE17 ttyE170 ttyE171
ttyE172 ttyE173 ttyE174 ttyE175 ttyE176 ttyE177
ttyE178 ttyE179 ttyE18 ttyE180 ttyE181 ttyE182
ttyE183 ttyE184 ttyE185 ttyE186 ttyE187 ttyE188
ttyE189 ttyE19 ttyE190 ttyE191 ttyE192 ttyE193
ttyE194 ttyE195 ttyE196 ttyE197 ttyE198 ttyE199
ttyE2 ttyE20 ttyE200 ttyE201 ttyE202 ttyE203
ttyE204 ttyE205 ttyE206 ttyE207 ttyE208 ttyE209
ttyE21 ttyE210 ttyE211 ttyE212 ttyE213 ttyE214
ttyE215 ttyE216 ttyE217 ttyE218 ttyE219 ttyE22
ttyE220 ttyE221 ttyE222 ttyE223 ttyE224 ttyE225
ttyE226 ttyE227 ttyE228 ttyE229 ttyE23 ttyE230
ttyE231 ttyE232 ttyE233 ttyE234 ttyE235 ttyE236
ttyE237 ttyE238 ttyE239 ttyE24 ttyE240 ttyE241
ttyE242 ttyE243 ttyE244 ttyE245 ttyE246 ttyE247
ttyE248 ttyE249 ttyE25 ttyE250 ttyE251 ttyE252
ttyE253 ttyE254 ttyE255 tttyE256 ttyE26 ttyE27
ttyE28 ttyE29 ttyE3 ttyE30 ttyE31 ttyE32
ttyE33 ttyE34 ttyE35 ttyE36 ttyE37 ttyE38
ttyE39 ttyE4 ttyE40 ttyE41 ttyE42 ttyE43
ttyE44 ttyE45 ttyE46 ttyE47 ttyE48 ttyE49
ttyE5 ttyE50 ttyE51 ttyE52 ttyE53 ttyE54
ttyE55 ttyE56 ttyE57 ttyE58 ttyE59 ttyE6
ttyE60 ttyE61 ttyE62 ttyE63 ttyE64 ttyE65
ttyE66 ttyE67 ttyE68 ttyE69 ttyE7 ttyE70
ttyE71 ttyE72 ttyE73 ttyE74 ttyE75 ttyE76
ttyE77 ttyE78 ttyE79 ttyE8 ttyE80 ttyE81
ttyE82 ttyE83 ttyE84 ttyE85 ttyE86 ttyE87
ttyE88 ttyE89 ttyE9 ttyE90 ttyE91 ttyE92
ttyE93 ttyE94 ttyE95 ttyE96 ttyE97 ttyE98
ttyE99 ttyI0 ttyI1 ttyI10 ttyI11 ttyI12
ttyI13 ttyI14 ttyI15 ttyI16 ttyI17 ttyI18
ttyI19 ttyI2 ttyI20 ttyI21 ttyI22 ttyI23

ttyI24	ttyI25	ttyI26	ttyI27	ttyI28	ttyI29
ttyI3	ttyI30	ttyI31	ttyI32	ttyI33	ttyI34
ttyI35	ttyI36	ttyI37	ttyI38	ttyI39	ttyI4
ttyI40	ttyI41	ttyI42	ttyI43	ttyI44	ttyI45
ttyI46	ttyI47	ttyI48	ttyI49	ttyI5	ttyI50
ttyI51	ttyI52	ttyI53	ttyI54	ttyI55	ttyI56
ttyI57	ttyI58	ttyI59	ttyI6	ttyI60	ttyI61
ttyI62	ttyI63	ttyI7	ttyI8	ttyI9	ttyM0
ttyM1	ttyM2	ttyM3	ttyM4	ttyM5	ttyM6
ttyM7	ttyM8	ttyM9	ttyMa	ttyMb	ttyMc
ttyMd	ttyMe	ttyMf	ttyP0	ttyP1	ttyP2
ttyP3	ttyP4	ttyR0	ttyR1	ttyR10	ttyR11
ttyR12	ttyR13	ttyR14	ttyR15	ttyR16	ttyR17
ttyR18	ttyR19	ttyR2	ttyR20	ttyR21	ttyR22
ttyR23	ttyR24	ttyR25	ttyR26	ttyR27	ttyR28
ttyR29	ttyR3	ttyR30	ttyR31	ttyR32	ttyR33
ttyR34	ttyR35	ttyR36	ttyR37	ttyR38	ttyR39
ttyR4	ttyR40	ttyR41	ttyR42	ttyR43	ttyR44
ttyR45	ttyR46	ttyR47	ttyR48	ttyR49	ttyR5
ttyR50	ttyR51	ttyR52	ttyR53	ttyR54	ttyR55
ttyR56	ttyR57	ttyR58	ttyR59	ttyR6	ttyR60
ttyR61	ttyR62	ttyR63	ttyR64	ttyR7	ttyR8
ttyR9	ttyS0	ttyS1	ttyS2	ttyS3	ttya0
ttya1	ttya2	ttya3	ttya4	ttya5	ttya6
ttya7	ttya8	ttya9	ttyaa	ttyab	ttyac
ttyad	ttyae	ttyaf	ttyb0	ttyb1	ttyb2
ttyb3	ttyb4	ttyb5	ttyb6	ttyb7	ttyb8
ttyb9	ttyba	ttybb	ttybc	ttybd	ttybe
ttybf	ttyc0	ttyc1	ttyc2	ttyc3	ttyc4
ttyc5	ttyc6	ttyc7	ttyc8	ttyc9	ttyca
ttycb	ttycc	ttycd	ttyce	ttycf	ttyd0
ttyd1	ttyd2	ttyd3	ttyd4	ttyd5	ttyd6
ttyd7	ttyd8	ttyd9	ttyda	ttydb	ttydc
ttydd	ttyde	ttydf	ttye0	ttye1	ttye2
ttye3	ttye4	ttye5	ttye6	ttye7	ttye8
ttye9	ttyea	ttyeb	ttyec	ttyed	ttyee
ttyef	ttyp0	ttyp1	ttyp2	ttyp3	ttyp4
ttyp5	ttyp6	ttyp7	ttyp8	ttyp9	ttypa

ttypb	ttypc	ttypd	ttype	ttypf	ttyq0
ttyq1	ttyq2	ttyq3	ttyq4	ttyq5	ttyq6
ttyq7	ttyq8	ttyq9	ttyqa	ttyqb	ttyqc
ttyqd	ttyqe	ttyqf	ttyr0	ttyr1	ttyr2
ttyr3	ttyr4	ttyr5	ttyr6	ttyr7	ttyr8
ttyr9	ttyra	ttyrb	ttyrc	ttyrd	ttyre
ttyrf	ttys0	ttys1	ttys2	ttys3	ttys4
ttys5	ttys6	ttys7	ttys8	ttys9	ttysa
ttysb	ttysc	ttysd	ttyse	ttysf	ttyt0
ttyt1	ttyt2	ttyt3	ttyt4	ttyt5	ttyt6
ttyt7	ttyt8	ttyt9	ttyta	ttytb	ttytc
ttytd	ttyte	ttytf	ttyu0	ttyu1	ttyu2
ttyu3	ttyu4	ttyu5	ttyu6	ttyu7	ttyu8
ttyu9	ttyua	ttyub	ttyuc	ttyud	ttyue
ttyuf	ttyv0	ttyv1	ttyv2	ttyv3	ttyv4
ttyv5	ttyv6	ttyv7	ttyv8	ttyv9	ttyva
ttyvb	ttyvc	ttyvd	ttyve	ttyvf	ttyw0
ttyw1	ttyw2	ttyw3	ttyw4	ttyw5	ttyw6
ttyw7	ttyw8	ttyw9	ttywa	ttywb	ttywc
ttywd	ttywe	ttywf	ttyx0	ttyx1	ttyx2
ttyx3	ttyx4	ttyx5	ttyx6	ttyx7	ttyx8
ttyx9	ttyxa	ttyxb	ttyxc	ttyxd	ttyxe
ttyxf	ttyy0	ttyy1	ttyy2	ttyy3	ttyy4
ttyy5	ttyy6	ttyy7	ttyy8	ttyy9	ttyya
ttyyb	ttyyc	ttyyd	ttyye	ttyyf	ttyz0
ttyz1	ttyz2	ttyz3	ttyz4	ttyz5	ttyz6
ttyz7	ttyz8	ttyz9	ttyza	ttyzb	ttyzc
ttyzd	ttyze	ttyzf	urandom	vcs0	vcs1
vcs10	vcs11	vcs12	vcs13	vcs14	vcs15
vcs16	vcs17	vcs18	vcs19	vcs2	vcs20
vcs21	vcs22	vcs23	vcs24	vcs25	vcs26
vcs27	vcs28	vcs29	vcs3	vcs30	vcs31
vcs32	vcs33	vcs34	vcs35	vcs36	vcs37
vcs38	vcs39	vcs4	vcs40	vcs41	vcs42
vcs43	vcs44	vcs45	vcs46	vcs47	vcs48
vcs49	vcs5	vcs50	vcs51	vcs52	vcs53
vcs54	vcs55	vcs56	vcs57	vcs58	vcs59
vcs6	vcs60	vcs61	vcs62	vcs63	vcs7

vcs8	vcs9	vcsa0	vcsa1	vcsa10	vcsa11
vcsa12	vcsa13	vcsa14	vcsa15	vcsa16	vcsa17
vcsa18	vcsa19	vcsa2	vcsa20	vcsa21	vcsa22
vcsa23	vcsa24	vcsa25	vcsa26	vcsa27	vcsa28
vcsa29	vcsa3	vcsa30	vcsa31	vcsa32	vcsa33
vcsa34	vcsa35	vcsa36	vcsa37	vcsa38	vcsa39
vcsa4	vcsa40	vcsa41	vcsa42	vcsa43	vcsa44
vcsa45	vcsa46	vcsa47	vcsa48	vcsa49	vcsa5
vcsa50	vcsa51	vcsa52	vcsa53	vcsa54	vcsa55
vcsa56	vcsa57	vcsa58	vcsa59	vcsa6	vcsa60
vcsa61	vcsa62	vcsa63	vcsa7	vcsa8	vcsa9
wvisfgrab	xda	xda1	xda2	xda3	xda4
xda5	xda6	xda7	xda8	xdb	xdb1
xdb2	xdb3	xdb4	xdb5	xdb6	xdb7
xdb8	zero	zqft0	zqft1	zqft2	zqft3

What are the basic contents of the /etc directory?

This directory contains many of the configuration files. Notice below in the displayed directory how many times "conf" appears. The password, **passwd**, is located in this directory.

If you enter **ls –dx /etc | less** the results should be similar to the following:

.	..	.pwd.lock	.resolv.conf.swp
DIR_COLORS	HOSTNAME	MUttrc	X11
adjtime	aliases	aliases.db	at.deny
bashrc	charsets	codepages	conf.linuxconf
conf.modules	cron.d	cron.daily	cron.hourly
cron.monthly	cron.weekly	crontab	csh.cshrc
default	exports	fdprm	fstab
ftpaccess	ftpconversions	ftpgroups	ftphosts
ftpusers	gettydefs	gpm-root.conf	group
group-	gtk	host.conf	hosts
hosts.allow	hosts.deny	httpd	im_pallette-small.pal
info-dir	inittab	inputrc	ioctl.save
isapnp.gone	issue	issue.net	ld.so.cache
ld.so.conf	lilo.conf	lmhosts	localtime
login.defs	logrotate.conf	logrotate.d	lynx.cfg

mail	mail.rc	mailcap	mailcap.vga
man.config	mime-magic	mime-magic.dat	mime.types
minicom.users	motd	mtab	named.boot
named.conf	news	nmh	nsswitch.conf
nwserv.conf	nwserv.stations	pam.d	paper.config
passwd	passwd-	pcmcia	pine.conf
pine.conf.fixed	ppp	printcap	profile
profile.d	protocols	pwdb.conf	rc.d
redhat-release	rmt	rpc	securetty
security	sendmail.cf	sendmail.cw	sendmail.mc
services	shells	skel	smb.conf
smbusers	smrsh	snmp	sound
sysconfig	syslog.conf	sys.conf.inn	termcap
uucp	yp.conf		

What are the basic contents of the /home directory?

This directory is the base directory for users. In a large organization the system administrator might need to create a number of subdirectories such as **/home/mgt, /home/mktg,** and **/home/workers** with individual users under each.

If you enter **ls –ax /home | less** the results should be similar to the following:

. .. ftp httpd lost+found samba

If you enter **ls –am /home | less** the results should be similar to the following:

., .., ftp, httpd, lost+found, samba

If you enter **ls –al /home | less** the results should be similar to the following:

```
drwxr-xr-x   6   root   root   1024   Sep   23   06:19
.
drwxr-xr-x   16  root   root   1024   Sep   23   06:19
..
drwxr-xr-x   6   root   root   1024   Sep   23   06:19
ftp
```

If you enter **ls –ax /home/* | less** the results should be similar to the following:

```
/home/ftp:
. .. bin etc lib pub

/home/httpd:
. .. cgi-bin html icons

/home/lost+found:
. ..

/home/samba:
. ..
```

If you enter **ls –ax /home/*/* | less** the results should be similar to the following:

```
/home/ftp/bin:
. .. compress cpio gzip ls tar zcat

/home/ftp/etc:
. .. group ld.so.cache passwd

/home/ftp/lib:

.                         ..                   ld-2.1.1.so       ld-linux.so.2
libc-2.1.1.so             libc.so.6            libnsl1-2.1.1.so  libnsl.so.1
libnss_files-2.1.1.so     libnss_files.so.2

/home/ftp/pub:
. ..

/home/httpd/cgi-bin:
. ..

/home/htpd/html:
. .. index.html manual poweredby.gif

/home/httpd/icons:
. .. README a.gif
(followed by 57 GIF files)
```

What are the basic contents of the /lib directory?

This directory contains the shared libraries used by any program when it runs. The directory permits programs to be smaller than they would be if each had all the software components required for running.

If you enter **s –ax /lib | less** the results should be similar to the following:

.	..	cpp
ld-2.1.1.so	ld-linux.so.1	ld-linux.so.1.9.5
ld-linux.so.2	ld.so	ld.so.1.9.5
libBrokenLocale-2.1.1.so	libBrokenLocale.so.1	libNoVersion-2.1.1.so
linVersion.so.1	libSegFault.so	libc-2.1.1.so
libc.so.6	libcom_err.so.2	libcom_err.so.2.0
libcrypt-2.1.1.so	libcrypt.so.1	libdb-2.1.1.so
libdb.so.2	libdb.so.3	libdb1-2.1.1.so
libdb1.so.2	libdl-2.1,1.so	libdl.so.1
libdl.so.1.9.5	libdl.so.2	libe2p.so.2
libe2p.so.2.3	libext2fs.so.2	libextefs.so.2.4
libm-2.1.1.so	libm.so.6	libncp.so
libncp.so.2	libncp.so.2.2.0	libnsl-2.1.1.so
libnsl.so.1	libnss1_compat-2.1.1.so	libnss1_compat.so.1
libnss1_db-2.1.1.so	libnss1_db.so.1	libnss1_dns-2.1.1.so
libnss1_dns.so.1	libnss1_files-2.1.1.so	libnss1_files.so.1
libnss1_nis-2.1.1.so	libnss1_nis.so.1	libnss_compat-2.1.1.so
libnss_compat.so.1	libnss_compat.so.2	libnss_db-2.1.1.so
libnss_db.so.1	libnss_db.so.2	libnss_dns-2.1.1.so
libnss_dns.so.1	libnss_dns.so.2	libnss_files-2.1.1.so
libnss_files.so.1	libnss_files.so.2	libnss_hesiod-2.1.1.so
libnss_hesiod.so.2	libnss_nis-2.1.1.so	libnss_nis.so.1
libnss_nis.so.2	libnss_nisplus-2.1.1.so	libnss_nisplus.so.2
libpam.so	libpam.so.0	libpam.so.0.66
libpam_misc.a	libpam_misc.so	libpam_misc.so.0
libpam_misc.so.0.066	libroc.so.2.0.0	libpthread-0.8.so
libpthread.so.0	libpwdb.a	libpwdb.so
libpwdb.so.0	libpwdb.so.0.0.58	libresolv-2.1.1.so
libresolv.so.2	librt-2.1.1.so	librt.so.1
libss.so.2	libss.so.2.0	libtermcap.so,2
libtermcap.so.2.0.8	libutil-2.1.1.so	libutil.so.1

libuuid.so.1	libuuid.so.1.2	modules
security		

What are the basic contents of the /lost+found directory?

This directory is allocated space for use by **fsck**.

If you enter **ls –ax /lost+found | less** the results should be similar to the following:

. ..

What are the basic contents of the /mnt directory?

This directory contains the mount points for removable media such as CD-ROMs.

If you enter **ls –ax /mnt | less** the results should be similar to the following:

. .. cdrom floppy

What are the basic contents of the /proc directory?

It is a data structure collection in memory that appears as a set of directories and files. It is managed by the kernel and is the process file system of the kernel.

If you enter **ls –ax /proc | less** the results should be similar to the following:

.	..	1	103	192	2	239	250
264	278	296	3	310	324	341	352
363	378	379	380	381	382	383	384
385	386	387	4	422	437	451	454
455	456	458	459	460	461	462	463
464	476	5	531	532	575	576	577
578	579	580	582	623	704	705	apm
bus	cmdline	cpuinfo	devices	dma	fb	filesystems	fs
ide	interrupts	ioports	kcore	kmsg	ksyms	loadavg	locks
pci	rtc	scsi	self	slabinfo	stat	swaps	sys
tty	uptime	version					

What are the basic contents of the /root directory?

This is the filesystem's top directory. It should be used only for system administration tasks.

If you enter **ls –ax /root | less** the results should be similar to the following:

.	..	.Xdefaults	.bash_history	.bash_logout	.bash_profile
.bashrc	.cshrc	.tcshrc			

What are the basic contents of the /sbin directory?

This directory contains the essential maintenance programs such as **lilo** and **shutdown**. Most of the programs in this directory are only root executable.

If you enter **ls –ax /sbin | less** the results should be similar to the following:

.	..	arp	askrunlevel	badblocks
cardctl	cardmgr	cfdisk	chkconfig	clock
ctrlaltdel	debugfs	depmod	dnsconf	dumpe2fs
e2fsck	e2label	fdisk	fixperm	fsck
fsk.ext2	fsck.minix	ftl_check	ftl_format	genksyms
getty	halt	hdparm	hwclock	ifconfig
ifdown	ifport	ifup	ifuser	init
initlog	insmod	insmod.static	install-info	installkernel
ipchains	ipchains-restore	ipchains-save	ipfwadm-wrapper	ipmaddr
iptunnel	ipx_configure	ip_internal_net	isapnp	kbdrate
kerneld	killall5	ksyms	ldconfig	lilo
loglevel	losetup	lsmod	mailconf	mingetty
minilogd	mkbootdisk	mke2fs	mkfs	mkfs.ext2
mkfs.minix	mkinitrd	mkswap	modinfo	modprobe
mount.ncp	mount.ncpfs	mount.smb	mount.smbfs	netreport
nwmsg	pam_filter	pcinitrd	pidof	plipconfig
pnpdump	portmap	poweroff	probe	pump
pwdb_chkpwd	quotacheck	quotaoff	quotaon	rarp
reboot	rmmod	rmmod.static	rmt	route
rpcdebug	runlevel	sash	scsi_info	service
setsysfont	sfdisk	shitdown	slattach	sln

stinit	sulogin	swapoff	swapon	telinit
tune2fs	update	uugetty	ypbind	

What are the basic contents of the /tmp directory?

This directory contains temporary files created by a program that is running. Be careful of programs that create large numbers of temporary files. The solution is to mount /tmp as a separate filesystem.

If you enter ls –ax /tmp | less the results should be similar to the following:

. .. .X11-unix .font-unix install.log

What are the basic contents of the /usr directory?

The subdirectories contain large software packages installed by the user. It should be mounted as a separate filesystem.

If you enter ls –ax /usr | less the results should be similar to the following:

.	..	X11R6	bin	dict	doc	etc
games	i386-redhat-linux	i486-linux-libc5	include	info	lib	libexec
local	lost+found	man	sbin	share	src	tmp

What are the basic contents of the /var directory?

This directory contains various system logs. In addition, it handles temporary information such as that in /var/spool.

If you enter ls –ax /var | less the results should be similar to the following:

.	..	cache	catman	db	lib	local	lock
log	lost+found						
mars_new	named	nis	preserve	run	spool	tmp	yp

Appendix A

HOWTOs Table of Contents

This appendix tries to demonstrate the breadth of knowledge required of a Linux system or server administrator. This appendix gives the table of contents for 41 HOWTOs; many are referred to in this book.

Linux Benchmarking HOWTO

Andrew D. Balsa, andrewbalsa@usa.net
<mailto:andrew-balsa@usa.net>

v 0.12, August 1997

This HOWTO discusses some issues associated with the benchmarking of Linux systems and presents a basic benchmarking toolkit.

1. Introduction
 1.1 Why is benchmarking so important?
 1.2 Invalid benchmarking considerations
2. Benchmarking procedures and interpretation of results
 2.1 Understanding benchmarking choices
  2.1.1 Synthetic vs. applications benchmarks
  2.1.2 High-level vs. low-level benchmarks
 2.2 Standard benchmarks available for Linux
 2.3 Links and references
3. The Linux Benchmarking Toolkit (LBT)
 3.1 Rationale
 3.2 Benchmark selection
 3.3 Test duration
 3.4 Comments
  3.4.1 Kernel 2.0.0 compilation:
  3.4.2 Whetstone:
  3.4.3 Xbench-0.2:
  3.4.4 UnixBench version 4.01:
  3.4.5 BYTE Magazine's BYTEmark benchmarks:
 3.5 Possible improvements

3.6 LBT Report Form
3.7 Network performance tests
3.8 SMP tests
4. Example run and results
5. Pitfalls and caveats of benchmarking
5.1 Comparing apples and oranges
5.2 Incomplete information
5.3 Proprietary hardware/software
5.4 Relevance
6. FAQ
7. Copyright, acknowledgments, and miscellaneous
7.1 How this document was produced
7.2 Copyright
7.3 New versions of this document
7.4 Feedback
7.5 Acknowledgments
7.6 Disclaimer
7.7 Trademarks

The Linux Busmouse HOWTO

Chris Bagwell, cbagwell@sprynet.com

v 1.91, June 1998

This HOWTO describes how to install, configure, and use a bus mouse under Linux.

1. Introduction
1.1 Disclaimer
1.2 Feedback
1.3 Acknowledgements
2. Determining your mouse type
2.1 Mouse interfaces
2.2 Inport mice
2.3 Logitech mice
2.4 PS/2 mice
2.5 ATI combo video/mice
2.6 Mouse protocols
3. Getting your mouse working
3.1 AID CDATA interrupt
3.2 Inport and Logitech mice
3.3 ATI-XL mice
3.4 PS/2 mice

3.5 Configuring the kernel
3.5.1 Compiling the kernel
3.5.2 selection
3.5.3 Changing interrupts with newer kernels
3.6 The mouse devices
4. Using your mouse
4.1 gpm
4.2 XFree86
4.3 XFree86 and gpm
5. Still can't get your mouse going?

The Linux CD-ROM HOWTO

Jeff Tranter, tranter@pobox.com

v 1.14, March 1999

This HOWTO describes how to install, configure, and use CD-ROM drives under Linux. It lists supported hardware and answers a number of frequently asked questions.

1. Introduction
1.1 Acknowledgments
1.2 New Versions of This Document
1.3 Feedback
1.4 Distribution Policy
2. CD-ROM Technology
3. Supported Hardware
3.1 ATAPI CD-ROM Drives
3.2 SCSI CD-ROM Drives
3.3 Proprietary CD-ROM Drives
3.4 Parallel Port Drives
3.5 Alternate Drivers
4. Installation
4.1 Installing the Hardware
4.2 Configuring and Building the Kernel
4.3 Creating Device Files and Setting Boot Time Parameters
4.3.1 Sbpcd Driver
4.3.2 Sonycdu535 Driver
4.3.3 Cdu31a Driver
4.3.4 Aztcd Driver
4.3.5 Gscd Driver
4.3.6 Mcd Driver
4.3.7 Mcdx Driver

A

- 4.3.8 Cm206 Driver
- 4.3.9 Optcd Driver
- 4.3.10 Sjcd Driver
- 4.3.11 Paride Driver
- 4.3.12 SCSI Driver
- 4.3.13 IDECD Driver
- 4.4 Booting the Linux Kernel
- 4.5 Mounting, Unmounting, and Ejecting Devices
- 4.6 Troubleshooting
  - 4.6.1 Step 1: Make sure you are really running the kernel you compiled
  - 4.6.2 Step 2: Make sure the proper kernel drivers are compiled in
  - 4.6.3 Step 3: Did the kernel detect your drive during booting?
  - 4.6.4 Step 4: Can you read data from the drive?
  - 4.6.5 Step 5: Can you mount the drive?
  - 4.6.6 Debugging Audio Problems
  - 4.6.7 When All Else Fails

5. Applications
   - 5.1 Audio CD Players
   - 5.2 PhotoCD
   - 5.3 Mkisofs
   - 5.4 ISO-9660 Utilities
6. Answers to Frequently Asked Questions
   - 6.1 How can a non-root user mount and unmount discs?
   - 6.2 Why do I get device is busy when unmounting a CD-ROM?
   - 6.3 How do I export a CD-ROM to other hosts over NFS?
   - 6.4 Can I boot Linux from a CD-ROM?
   - 6.5 How can I read digital data from audio CDs?
   - 6.6 Why doesn't the find command work properly?
   - 6.7 Does Linux support any recordable CD-ROM drives?
   - 6.8 Why do I get mount: Read-only file system when mounting a CD-ROM?
   - 6.9 Why does the disc tray open when I shut down the system?
   - 6.10 I have a "special" CD that can't be mounted
   - 6.11 Do multi-platter CD-ROM drives work with Linux?
   - 6.12 I get "/cdrom: Permission denied" errors
   - 6.13 How do I interpret IDE CD kernel error messages?
   - 6.14 How can I tell what speed CD-ROM I have?
   - 6.15 My CD-ROM stopped working after Linux was installed
   - 6.16 There are "hidden" files on a CD which I can't read
   - 6.17 Where is the CD-ROM API documented?
   - 6.18 Why don't I see long filenames on this Windows CD-ROM?

6.19 Is Microsoft's Joliet filesystem supported?
6.20 Does Linux support "enhanced" CDs?
6.21 Does Linux support DVD-ROM?
6.22 Does Linux support CD-RW?
7. References

Configuration HOWTO

Guido Gonzato, <guido@ibogeo.df.unibo.it>

v 1.3.7, September 1999

This HOWTO focuses on the fine tuning of a newly installed Linux box. It includes a set of configurations for the most common applications and services.

1. Introduction
    1.1 Why This HOWTO
    1.2 What We Will Be Configuring
2. General System Setup
    2.1 A Few Words about Security
    2.2 Start the Logbook!
    2.3 Keyboard
    2.4 Boot and Rescue Floppy
    2.5 Kernel Matters
    2.6 Sendmail Lock
    2.7 Hard Disk Performance
    2.8 Parallel Port Zip Drive
    2.9 Device Drivers
    2.10 Sound Card
    2.11 Login Messages
    2.12 host name
    2.13 Mouse
    2.14 Mount Points
    2.15 lilo(8) and LOADLIN.EXE
        2.15.1 Security Tip
    2.16 Mail Capabilities
    2.17 Printer Configuration
    2.18 SVGATextMode
3. Common Administration Tasks
    3.1 Network configuration
    3.2 Sharing the Internet
    3.3 Restricting Network Access
    3.4 NFS Exports

3.5 Name Server

4. Software Configuration
   4.1 bash(1)
   4.2 ls(1)
   4.3 less(1)
   4.4 emacs(1)
   4.5 joe(1)
   4.6 jed(1)
   4.7 pine(1)
   4.8 minicom(1)
   4.9 efax(1)
   4.10 Ghostscript
   4.11 TeX and Friends
   4.12 Avoid PPProblems!
      4.12.1 A Quick Start with eznet
      4.12.2 A Quick Start with wvdial
   4.13 POP Client
   4.14 X Window System (XFree86)
      4.14.1 Setting Up the X Server
      4.14.2 Keypad
      4.14.3 Graphical Login with xdm
      4.14.4 Window Manager
      4.14.5 Defaults for X11 Apps
   4.15 Users' Configurations
   4.16 Making .rpms
   4.17 Upgrading
5. Configuration Software
6. The End
   6.1 Copyright
   6.2 Feedback
   6.3 Disclaimer

DNS HOWTO

Nicolai Langfeldt, janl@math.uio.no

v 2.2, February 1999

This HOWTO documents how to define DNS (Domain Name System) mappings using a Linux system. DNS converts machine names to the IP addresses that all machines on the net have. It maps from name to address and from address to name.

1. Preamble

1.1 Legal stuff
1.2 Credits and request for help
1.3 Dedication
2. Introduction
3. A caching only name server
3.1 Starting named
3.2 Making it even better
3.3 Congratulations
4. A simple domain
4.1 But first some dry theory
4.2 Our own domain
4.3 The reverse zone
4.4 Words of caution
4.5 Why reverse lookups don't work
4.5.1 The reverse zone isn't delegated
4.5.2 You've got a classless subnet
5. A real domain example
5.1 /etc/named.conf (or /var/named/named.conf)
5.2 /var/named/root.hints
5.3 /var/named/zone/127.0.0
5.4 /var/named/zone/land-5.com
5.5 /var/named/zone/206.6.177
6. Maintenance
7. Converting from version 4 to version 8
8. Questions and Answers
9. How to become a bigger time DNS admin.

Linux Ethernet-HOWTO

Paul Gortmaker

2.7, May 1999

This HOWTO is a compilation of information about Ethernet devices that can be used for Linux and how to set them up. This HOWTO focuses on the hardware and low level driver aspect of the Ethernet cards.

1. Introduction
1.1 New Versions of this Document
1.2 Using the Ethernet-Howto
1.3 HELP - It doesn't work!
2. What card should I buy for Linux?
2.1 So What Drivers are Stable?
2.2 Eight bit vs 16 bit Cards

A

- 2.3 32 Bit (VLB/EISA/PCI) Ethernet Cards
- 2.4 Available 100Mbs Cards and Drivers
- 2.5 100VG versus 100BaseT
- 2.6 Type of cable that your card should support

3. Frequently Asked Questions
   - 3.1 Alpha Drivers—Getting and Using them
   - 3.2 Using more than one Ethernet Card per Machine
   - 3.3 The ether-thing didn't do anything for me. Why?
   - 3.4 Problems with NE1000/NE2000 cards (and clones)
   - 3.5 Problems with SMC Ultra/EtherEZ and WD80*3 cards
   - 3.6 Problems with 3Com cards
   - 3.7 FAQs Not Specific to Any Card
     - 3.7.1 Linux and ISA Plug and Play Ethernet Cards
     - 3.7.2 Ethercard is not detected at Boot.
     - 3.7.3 ifconfig reports the wrong I/O address for the card
     - 3.7.4 PCI machine detects card but driver fails probe
     - 3.7.5 Shared Memory ISA cards in PCI Machine do not work
     - 3.7.6 Card seems to send data but never receives anything
     - 3.7.7 Asynchronous Transfer Mode (ATM) Support
     - 3.7.8 Gigabyte Ethernet Support
     - 3.7.9 FDDI Support
     - 3.7.10 Full Duplex Support
     - 3.7.11 Ethernet Cards for Linux on SMP Machines
     - 3.7.12 Ethernet Cards for Linux on Alpha/AXP PCI Boards
     - 3.7.13 Ethernet for Linux on SUN/Sparc Hardware
     - 3.7.14 Ethernet for Linux on Other Hardware
     - 3.7.15 Linking 10 or 100 BaseT without a Hub
     - 3.7.16 SIOCSIFxxx: No such device
     - 3.7.17 SIOCSFFLAGS: Try again
     - 3.7.18 Using 'ifconfig' and Link UNSPEC with HW-addr of 00:00:00:00:00:00
     - 3.7.19 Huge Number of RX and TX Errors
     - 3.7.20 Entries in
     - 3.7.21 Linux and "trailers"
     - 3.7.22 Access to the raw Ethernet Device
4. Performance Tips
   - 4.1 General Concepts
   - 4.2 ISA Cards and ISA Bus Speed
   - 4.3 Setting the TCP Rx Window
   - 4.4 Increasing NFS performance
5. Vendor/Manufacturer/Model Specific Information
   - 5.1 3Com
     - 5.1.1 3c501

5.1.2 EtherLink II, 3c503, 3c503/16
5.1.3 Etherlink Plus 3c505
5.1.4 Etherlink-16 3c507
5.1.5 Etherlink III, 3c509/3c509B
5.1.6 3c515
5.1.7 3c523
5.1.8 3c527
5.1.9 3c529
5.1.10 3c562
5.1.11 3c575
5.1.12 3c579
5.1.13 3c589/3c589B
5.1.14 3c590/3c595
5.1.15 3c592/3c597
5.1.16 3c900/3c905/3c905B
5.1.17 3c985
5.2 Accton
5.2.1 Accton MPX
5.2.2 Accton EN1203, EN1207, EtherDuo-PCI
5.2.3 Accton EN2209 Parallel Port Adaptor (EtherPocket)
5.2.4 Accton EN2212 PCMCIA Card
5.3 Allied Telesyn/Telesis
5.3.1 AT1500
5.3.2 AT1700
5.3.3 AT2450
5.3.4 AT2500
5.3.5 AT2540FX
5.4 AMD/Advanced Micro Devices
5.4.1 AMD LANCE (7990, 79C960/961/961A, PCnet-ISA)
5.4.2 AMD 79C965 (PCnet-32)
5.4.3 AMD 79C970/970A (PCnet-PCI)
5.4.4 AMD 79C971 (PCnet-FAST)
5.4.5 AMD 79C972 (PCnet-FAST+)
5.4.6 AMD 79C974 (PCnet-SCSI)
5.5 Ansel Communications
5.5.1 AC3200 EISA
5.6 Apricot
5.6.1 Apricot Xen-II On Board Ethernet
5.7 Arcnet
5.8 AT&T
5.8.1 AT&T T7231 (LanPACER+)
5.9 Boca Research
5.9.1 Boca BEN (ISA, VLB, PCI)

A

5.10 Cabletron
  5.10.1 E10**, E10**-x, E20**, E20**-x
  5.10.2 E2100
  5.10.3 E22**
5.11 Cogent
  5.11.1 EM100-ISA/EISA
  5.11.2 Cogent eMASTER+, EM100-PCI, EM400, EM960, EM964
5.12 Compaq
  5.12.1 Compaq Deskpro/Compaq XL (Embedded AMD Chip)
  5.12.2 Compaq Nettelligent/NetFlex (Embedded ThunderLAN Chip)
5.13 Danpex
  5.13.1 Danpex EN9400
5.14 D-Link
  5.14.1 DE-100, DE-200, DE-220-T, DE-250
  5.14.2 DE-520
  5.14.3 DE-528
  5.14.4 DE-530
  5.14.5 DE-600
  5.14.6 DE-620
  5.14.7 DE-650
5.15 DFI
  5.15.1 DFINET-300 and DFINET-400
5.16 Digital/DEC
  5.16.1 DEPCA, DE100/1, DE200/1/2, DE210, DE422
  5.16.2 Digital EtherWorks 3 (DE203, DE204, DE205)
  5.16.3 DE425 EISA, DE434, DE435, DE500
  5.16.4 DEC 21040, 21041, 2114x, Tulip
5.17 Farallon
  5.17.1 Farallon Etherwave
5.18 Fujitsu
  5.18.1 Fujitsu FMV-181/182/183/184
5.19 Hewlett Packard
  5.19.1 27245A
  5.19.2 HP EtherTwist, PC Lan+ (27247, 27252A)
  5.19.3 HP-J2405A
  5.19.4 HP-Vectra On Board Ethernet
  5.19.5 HP 10/100 VG Any Lan Cards (27248B, J2573, J2577, J2585, J970, J973)
  5.19.6 HP NetServer 10/100TX PCI (D5013A)
5.20 IBM/International Business Machines
  5.20.1 IBM Thinkpad 300

5.20.2 IBM Credit Card Adaptor for Ethernet
5.20.3 IBM Token Ring
5.21 ICL Ethernet Cards
5.21.1 ICL EtherTeam 16i/32
5.22 Intel Ethernet Cards
5.22.1 Ether Express
5.22.2 Ether Express PRO/10
5.22.3 Ether Express PRO/10 PCI (EISA)
5.22.4 Ether Express PRO 10/100B
5.23 Kingston
5.24 LinkSys
5.24.1 LinkSys Etherfast 10/100 Cards.
5.24.2 LinkSys Pocket Ethernet Adapter Plus (PEAEPP)
5.24.3 LinkSys PCMCIA Adaptor
5.25 Microdyne
5.25.1 Microdyne Exos 205T
5.26 Mylex
5.26.1 Mylex LNE390A, LNE390B
5.26.2 Mylex LNP101
5.26.3 Mylex LNP104
5.27 Novell Ethernet, NExxxx and associated clones.
5.27.1 NE1000, NE2000
5.27.2 NE2000-PCI (RealTek/Winbond/Compex)
5.27.3 NE-10/100
5.27.4 NE1500, NE2100
5.27.5 NE/2 MCA
5.27.6 NE3200
5.27.7 NE3210
5.27.8 NE5500
5.28 Proteon
5.28.1 Proteon P1370-EA
5.28.2 Proteon P1670-EA
5.29 Pure Data
5.29.1 PDUC8028, PDI8023
5.30 Racal-Interlan
5.30.1 ES3210
5.30.2 NI5010
5.30.3 NI5210
5.30.4 NI6510 (not EB)
5.30.5 EtherBlaster (aka NI6510EB)
5.31 RealTek
5.31.1 RealTek RTL8002/8012 (AT-Lan-Tec) Pocket adapter
5.31.2 RealTek 8009

A

- 5.31.3 RealTek 8019
- 5.31.4 RealTek 8029
- 5.31.5 RealTek 8129/8139

5.32 Sager
- 5.32.1 Sager NP943

5.33 Schneider and Koch
- 5.33.1 SK G16

5.34 SEEQ
- 5.34.1 SEEQ 8005

5.35 SMC (Standard Microsystems Corp.)
- 5.35.1 WD8003, SMC Elite
- 5.35.2 WD8013, SMC Elite16
- 5.35.3 SMC Elite Ultra
- 5.35.4 SMC Elite Ultra32 EISA
- 5.35.5 SMC EtherEZ (8416)
- 5.35.6 SMC EtherPower PCI (8432)
- 5.35.7 SMC EtherPower II PCI (9432)
- 5.35.8 SMC 3008
- 5.35.9 SMC 3016
- 5.35.10 SMC-9000/SMC 91c92/4
- 5.35.11 SMC 91c100

5.36 Texas Instruments
- 5.36.1 ThunderLAN

5.37 Thomas Conrad
- 5.37.1 Thomas Conrad TC-5048

5.38 VIA
- 5.38.1 VIA 86C926 Amazon
- 5.38.2 VIA 86C100A Rhine II (and 3043 Rhine I)

5.39 Western Digital

5.40 Winbond
- 5.40.1 Winbond 89c840
- 5.40.2 Winbond 89c940

5.41 Xircom
- 5.41.1 Xircom PE1, PE2, PE3-10B*
- 5.41.2 Xircom PCMCIA Cards

5.42 Zenith
- 5.42.1 Z-Note

5.43 Znyx
- 5.43.1 Znyx ZX342 (DEC 21040 based)

5.44 Identifying an Unknown Card
- 5.44.1 Identifying the Network Interface Controller
- 5.44.2 Identifying the Ethernet Address
- 5.44.3 Tips on Trying to Use an Unknown Card

- 5.45 Drivers for Non-Ethernet Devices
- 6. Cables, Coax, Twisted Pair
  - 6.1 Thin Ethernet (thinnet)
  - 6.2 Twisted Pair
  - 6.3 Thick Ethernet
- 7. Software Configuration and Card Diagnostics
  - 7.1 Configuration Programs for Ethernet Cards
    - 7.1.1 WD80x3 Cards
    - 7.1.2 Digital/DEC Cards
    - 7.1.3 NE2000+ or AT/LANTIC Cards
    - 7.1.4 3Com Cards
  - 7.2 Diagnostic Programs for Ethernet Cards
- 8. Technical Information
  - 8.1 Programmed I/O vs. Shared Memory vs. DMA
    - 8.1.1 Programmed I/O (e.g., NE2000, 3c509)
    - 8.1.2 Shared memory (e.g., WD80x3, SMC-Ultra, 3c503)
    - 8.1.3 Slave (normal) Direct Memory Access (e.g., none for Linux!)
    - 8.1.4 Bus Master Direct Memory Access (e.g., LANCE, DEC 21040)
  - 8.2 Writing a Driver
  - 8.3 Driver interface to the kernel
    - 8.3.1 Probe
    - 8.3.2 Interrupt handler
    - 8.3.3 Transmit function
    - 8.3.4 Receive function
    - 8.3.5 Open function
    - 8.3.6 Close function (optional)
    - 8.3.7 Miscellaneous functions
  - 8.4 Technical information from 3Com
  - 8.5 Notes on AMD PCnet/LANCE Based cards
  - 8.6 Multicast and Promiscuous Mode
  - 8.7 The Berkeley Packet Filter (BPF)
- 9. Networking with a Laptop/Notebook Computer
  - 9.1 Using SLIP
  - 9.2 PCMCIA Support
  - 9.3 ISA Ethercard in the Docking Station
  - 9.4 Pocket/parallel port adapters.
- 10. Miscellaneous
  - 10.1 Passing Ethernet Arguments to the Kernel
    - 10.1.1 The
    - 10.1.2 The
  - 10.2 Using the Ethernet Drivers as Modules

A

10.3 Related Documentation
10.4 Disclaimer and Copyright
10.5 Closing

Firewall and Proxy Server HOWTO

Mark Grennan, mark@grenna.com

v 0.65, September 1999

This HOWTO discusses the basics of firewall systems and gives some detail on setting up both a filtering and proxy firewall on a Linux based PC.

1. Introduction
  1.1 Feedback
  1.2 Disclaimer
  1.3 Copyright
  1.4 My Reasons for writing this
  1.5 Further Readings
2. Understanding Firewalls
  2.1 Firewall Politics
  2.2 Types of Firewalls
    2.2.1 Packet Filtering Firewalls
    2.2.2 Proxy Servers
    2.2.3 Application Proxy
    2.2.4 SOCKS Proxy
3. Firewall Architecture
4. Setting up the Linux Filtering Firewall
  4.1 Hardware requirements
5. Software requirements
  5.1 Available packages
6. Preparing the Linux system
  6.1 Compiling the Kernel
  6.2 Configuring two network cards
  6.3 Configuring the Network Addresses
  6.4 Testing your network
  6.5 Securing the Firewall
7. IP filtering setup (IPFWADM)
8. IP filtering setup (IPCHAINS)
9. Making it easier
10. Installing a Transparent SQUID proxy
11. Installing the TIS Proxy server
  11.1 Getting the software

11.2 Compiling the TIS FWTK
11.3 Installing the TIS FWTK
11.4 Configuring the TIS FWTK
11.4.1 The netperm-table file
11.4.2 The /etc/services file
12. The SOCKS Proxy Server
12.1 Setting up the Proxy Server
12.2 Configuring the Proxy Server
12.2.1 The Access File
12.2.2 The Routing File
12.3 Working With a Proxy Server
12.3.1 Unix
12.3.2 MS Windows with Trumpet Winsock
12.3.3 Getting the Proxy Server to work with UDP Packets
12.4 Drawbacks with Proxy Servers
13. Advanced Configurations
13.1 A large network with emphasis on security
13.1.1 The Network Setup
13.1.2 The Proxy Setup
14. Making Management Easy
15. Defeating a Proxy Firewall

Linux Hardware Compatibility HOWTO

Patrick Reijnen, hardware_howto@.reijnen.nl.com

v 99.2, March 1999

This HOWTO lists most of the hardware supported by Linux and assists in locating any necessary drivers.

1. Introduction
1.1 Welcome
1.2 Copyright
1.3 System architectures
2. Computers/Motherboards/BIOS
2.1 Specific system/motherboard/BIOS
2.2 Unsupported
3. Laptops
3.1 Specific laptops
3.2 PCMCIA
4. CPU/FPU
5. Memory
6. Video cards

A

- 6.1 Diamond video cards
- 6.2 SVGALIB (graphics for console)
- 6.3 XFree86 3.3.2
  - 6.3.1 Accelerated
  - 6.3.2 Unaccelerated
  - 6.3.3 Monochrome
  - 6.3.4 Alpha, Beta drivers
- 6.4 S.u.S.E. X-Server
- 6.5 Commercial X servers
  - 6.5.1 Xi Graphics, Inc
  - 6.5.2 Metro-X 4.3.0

7. Controllers (hard drive)
   - 7.1 Alpha, Beta drivers
8. Controllers (hard drive RAID)
9. Controllers (SCSI)
   - 9.1 Supported
   - 9.2 Alpha, Beta drivers
   - 9.3 Unsupported
10. Controllers (I/O)
11. Controllers (multiport)
    - 11.1 Non-intelligent cards
      - 11.1.1 Supported
    - 11.2 Intelligent cards
      - 11.2.1 Supported
      - 11.2.2 Alpha, Beta drivers
12. Network adapters
    - 12.1 Supported
      - 12.1.1 Ethernet
      - 12.1.2 ISDN
      - 12.1.3 Frame Relay
      - 12.1.4 Wireless
      - 12.1.5 X25
      - 12.1.6 Pocket and portable adapters
      - 12.1.7 Slotless
      - 12.1.8 ARCnet
      - 12.1.9 TokenRing
      - 12.1.10 FDDI
      - 12.1.11 Amateur radio (AX.25)
      - 12.1.12 PCMCIA cards
    - 12.2 Alpha, Beta drivers
      - 12.2.1 Ethernet
      - 12.2.2 ISDN
      - 12.2.3 ATM

12.2.4 Frame Relay
12.2.5 Wireless
12.3 Unsupported
13. Sound cards
13.1 Supported
13.2 Alpha, Beta drivers
13.3 Unsupported
14. Hard drives
14.1 Unsupported
15. Tape drives
15.1 Supported
15.2 Alpha, Beta drivers
15.3 Unsupported
16. CD-ROM drives
16.1 Supported
16.2 Alpha, Beta drivers
16.3 Notes
17. CD-Writers
18. Removable drives
19. Mice
19.1 Supported
19.2 Alpha, Beta drivers
19.3 Notes
20. Modems
21. Printers/Plotters
21.1 Ghostscript
21.1.1 Ghostscript 5.1 supported printers
21.1.2 Alpha, Beta drivers
22. Scanners
22.1 Supported
22.2 Alpha, Beta drivers
22.3 Unsupported
23. Other hardware
23.1 Amateur Radio
23.2 VESA Power Savings Protocol (DPMS) monitors
23.3 Touch screens
23.4 Terminals on serial port
23.5 Joysticks
23.6 Video capture boards/Frame Grabbers/TV tuner
23.7 Digital Camera
23.7.1 Supported
23.7.2 Unsupported
23.8 UPS

A

- 23.9 Multifunction boards
- 23.10 Data acquisition
- 23.11 Watchdog timer interfaces
- 23.12 Miscellaneous

24. Related sources of information
25. Acknowledgments
26. Appendix A. S3 cards supported by XFree86 3.3.x
27. Appendix B. Supported PCMCIA cards
    - 27.1 Ethernet cards
    - 27.2 Fast Ethernet (10/100baseT) adapters
    - 27.3 Token-ring adapters
    - 27.4 Wireless network adapters
    - 27.5 ISDN
    - 27.6 Modem and serial cards
    - 27.7 Memory cards
    - 27.8 SCSI adapters
    - 27.9 ATA/IDE CD-ROM adapters
    - 27.10 Multifunction cards
    - 27.11 ATA/IDE card drives
    - 27.12 Miscellaneous cards
    - 27.13 Cards with separately distributed drivers
    - 27.14 Working on ...
    - 27.15 Unsupported
28. Appendix C. Supported Parallel Port devices
    - 28.1 Ethernet
    - 28.2 Hard drives
    - 28.3 Tape drives
    - 28.4 CD-ROM drives
    - 28.5 Removable drives
    - 28.6 IDE Adapter
    - 28.7 SCSI Adapters
    - 28.8 Digital Camera
29. Appendix D. Plug and Play devices
30. Appendix E. Linux incompatible Hardware
31. Glossary

The Linux Intranet Server HOWTO

Pramod Karnad, karnad@indiamail.com

v 2.11, August 1997

This HOWTO describes how to setup an Intranet using Linux as the server which binds Unix, Netware, NT, and Windows together. Hence, by just establishing the connection to the Linux box you are provided transparent access to all the various platforms.

1. Introduction
    1.1 What is required
    1.2 New versions of this document
    1.3 Feedback
2. Install the HTTP server
    2.1 Preparation before downloading
        2.1.1 The Operating System
        2.1.2 Process type (ServerType)
        2.1.3 Binding Port (Port)
        2.1.4 Server user identity (User)
        2.1.5 Server group identity (Group)
        2.1.6 Server administrator email address (ServerAdmin)
        2.1.7 Location of server directory (ServerRoot)
        2.1.8 Location of HTML files (DocumentRoot)
    2.2 Compiling HTTPd
3. Testing HTTPd
4. Connecting to the Linux Server
    4.1 Setup the Linux server
    4.2 Setup the Netware server
    4.3 Setup the Netware Client
        4.3.1 Windows 3.x
        4.3.2 Windows 95
    4.4 Setup Microsoft Client
        4.4.1 Windows for Workgroups
        4.4.2 Windows 95
        4.4.3 Windows NT
    4.5 Setup TCP/IP on Macintosh
        4.5.1 MacTCP
5. Setting up the Intranet
    5.1 NCPFS
        5.1.1 Installation
        5.1.2 Mounting NCPFS
    5.2 SMBFS
        5.2.1 Installation
        5.2.2 Mounting SMBFS
    5.3 NFS
6. Accessing the Web
    6.1 Accessing the mounted filesystems
    6.2 Connecting to the Internet

- 6.3 Other uses
- 7. More things to do
- 8. Credits and Legalities
  - 8.1 Thanks
  - 8.2 Copyright information

Linux IPCHAINS-HOWTO

Paul Russell, ipchains@rustcorp.com

v 1.0.7, March 1999

This HOWTO describes how to obtain, install, and configure the enhanced IP firewalling chains software for Linux.

1. Introduction
   - 1.1 What?
   - 1.2 Why?
   - 1.3 How?
   - 1.4 Where?
2. Packet Filtering Basics
   - 2.1 What?
   - 2.2 Why?
   - 2.3 How?
     - 2.3.1 A Kernel with Packet Filtering
     - 2.3.2 ipchains
     - 2.3.3 Making Rules Permanent
3. I'm confused! Routing, masquerading, portforwarding, ipautofw...
   - 3.1 Rusty's Three-Line Guide to Masquerading
   - 3.2 Gratuitous Promotion: WatchGuard Rules
   - 3.3 Common Firewall-like Setups
     - 3.3.1 Private Network: Traditional Proxies
     - 3.3.2 Private Network: Transparent Proxies
     - 3.3.3 Private Network: Masquerading
     - 3.3.4 Public Network
     - 3.3.5 Limited Internal Services
   - 3.4 More Information on Masquerading (See also the IP Masquerade HOWTO by David Ranch and Ambrose Au.)
4. IP Firewalling Chains
   - 4.1 How Packets Traverse the Filters
     - 4.1.1 Using ipchains
     - 4.1.2 Operations on a Single Rule
     - 4.1.3 Filtering Specifications

4.1.3.1 Specifying Source and Destination IP Addresses
4.1.3.2 Specifying Inversion
4.1.3.3 Specifying Protocol
4.1.3.3.1 Specifying UDP and TCP Ports
4.1.3.3.2 Specifying ICMP Type and Code
4.1.3.4 Specifying an Interface
4.1.3.5 Specifying TCP SYN Packets Only
4.1.3.6 Handling Fragments
4.1.4 Filtering Side Effects
4.1.4.1 Specifying a Target
4.1.4.2 Logging Packets
4.1.4.3 Manipulating the Type Of Service
4.1.4.4 Marking a Packet
4.1.4.5 Operations on an Entire Chain
4.1.4.6 Creating a New Chain
4.1.4.7 Deleting a Chain
4.1.4.8 Flushing a Chain
4.1.4.9 Listing a Chain
4.1.4.10 Resetting (Zeroing) Counters
4.1.4.11 Setting Policy
4.1.5 Operations on Masquerading
4.1.6 Checking a Packet
4.1.7 Multiple Rules at Once and Watching What Happens
4.2 Useful Examples
4.2.1 Using ipchains-save
4.2.2 Using ipchains-restore
5. Miscellaneous
5.1 How to Organize Your Firewall Rules
5.2 What Not To Filter Out
5.2.1 ICMP packets
5.2.2 TCP Connections to DNS (nameservers)
5.2.3 FTP Nightmares
5.3 Filtering out Ping of Death
5.4 Filtering out Teardrop and Bonk
5.5 Filtering out Fragment Bombs
5.6 Changing Firewall Rules
5.7 How Do I Set Up IP Spoof Protection?
5.8 Advanced Projects
5.8.1 SPF: Stateful Packet Filtering
5.8.2 Michael Hasenstein's ftp-data hack
5.9 Future Enhancements
6. Common Problems
6.1 ipchains -L Freezes!

6.2 Masquerading/Forwarding Doesn't Work!
6.3 -j REDIR doesn't work!
6.4 Wildcard Interfaces Don't Work!
6.5 TOS Doesn't Work!
6.6 ipautofw and ipportfw Don't Work!
6.7 xosview is Broken!
6.8 Segmentation Fault With '-j REDIRECT'!
6.9 I Can't Set Masquerading Timeouts!
6.10 I Want to Firewall IPX!

7. A Serious Example
7.1 The Arrangement
7.2 Goals
7.3 Before Packet Filtering
7.4 Packet Filtering for Through Packets
7.4.1 Set Up Jumps from forward Chain
7.4.2 Define the icmp-acc Chain
7.4.3 Good (Internal) to DMZ (Servers)
7.4.4 Bad (external) to DMZ (servers)
7.4.5 Good (internal) to Bad (external)
7.4.6 DMZ to Good (internal)
7.4.7 DMZ to bad (external)
7.4.8 Bad (external) to Good (internal)
7.4.9 Packet Filtering for the Linux Box Itself
7.4.9.1 Bad (external) interface
7.4.9.2 DMZ interface.
7.4.9.3 Good (internal) interface
7.5 Finally

8. Appendix: Differences between ipchains and ipfwadm.
8.1 Quick-Reference table
8.2 Examples of translated ipfwadm commands

9. Appendix: Using the ipfwadm-wrapper script.

10. Appendix: Thanks.

Linux IPX-HOWTO

Kevin Thorpe, kevin@pricetrak.com

v 2.3, May 1998

This HOWTO describes how to obtain, install and configure various tools available for the Linux operating system that use the Linux kernel IPX protocol support.

1. Introduction

- 1.1 Changes from the previous release
- 1.2 Introduction

2. Disclaimer
3. Related Documentation
   - 3.1 New versions of this document
   - 3.2 Feedback
   - 3.3 Mailing list support
4. Some of the terms used in this document
5. A brief discussion of IPX network topology
6. The IPX related files
7. Greg Pages IPX tools
   - 7.1 The IPX tools in more detail
8. Configuring your Linux machine as an IPX router
   - 8.1 Do I need to configure an internal network?
9. Configuring your Linux machine as an NCP client
   - 9.1 Obtaining ncpfs
   - 9.2 Building ncpfs for kernel 1.2.13
   - 9.3 Building ncpfs for kernels 1.3.7/++/2.0*
   - 9.4 Configuring and using ncpfs
10. Configuring your Linux machine as an NCP server
    - 10.1 The mars_nwe package
      - 10.1.1 Capability of mars_nwe
      - 10.1.2 Obtaining mars_nwe
      - 10.1.3 Building the mars_nwe package
    - 10.2 The lwared package
      - 10.2.1 Capability of lwared
      - 10.2.2 Obtaining lwared
      - 10.2.3 Building lwared
      - 10.2.4 Configuring and using lwared
11. Configuring your Linux machine as a Novell Print Client
12. Configuring your Linux machine as a Novell Print Server
    - 12.1 Prerequisites
    - 12.2 Configuration
13. An overview of the ncpfs user and administration commands
    - 13.1 User commands
    - 13.2 Administration tools
14. Configuring PPP for IPX support
    - 14.1 Configuring an IPX/PPP server
      - 14.1.1 First steps
      - 14.1.2 Design
      - 14.1.3 Configure
      - 14.1.4 Test the server configuration
    - 14.2 Configuring an IPX/PPP client

14.2.1 Configuring
14.2.2 Testing the IPX/PPP client
15. IPX tunnel over IP
15.1 Obtaining ipxtunnel
15.2 Building ipxtunnel
15.3 Configuring ipxtunnel
15.4 Testing and using ipxtunnel
16. Commercial IPX support for Linux
16.1 Caldera's Network Desktop
17. Some Frequently Asked Questions
18. Copyright Message
19. Miscellaneous and Acknowledgements

ISP-Hookup-HOWTO

Egil Kvaleberg, egil@kvaleberg.no

v 1.26, March 1998

This HOWTO describes how to use Linux to connect to an Internet Service Provider using a dial-up modem TCP/IP connection. In addition, the basic dial-up procedure and IP establishment, e-mail and news handling are covered.

1. Introduction
1.1 Copyright
1.2 Disclaimer
1.3 Translations
1.4 New versions of this document
1.5 Feedback
2. How do I connect to the rest of the world?
2.1 The basic configuration
3. How do I surf?
4. How do I send and receive e-mail?
5. News
5.1 How do I set up an online newsreader?
5.2 How do I set up an offline newsreader?
5.3 How do I set up C News?
5.4 How do I set up Leafnode?
6. How do I automate the connection procedure?
7. Final words
7.1 Other things I should know about?
8. ISP specific information
8.1 How do I learn more?

8.2 Thanks to

The Linux Keyboard and Console HOWTO

Andries Brouwer, aeb@cwi.nl

v 2.8, February 1998

This HOWTO contains some information about the Linux keyboard and console, and the use of non-ASCII characters. It describes Linux 2.0.

1. Useful programs
2. Keyboard generalities
3. Console generalities
4. Resetting your terminal
    4.1 Keyboard hardware reset
5. Delete and Backspace
    5.1 How to tell Unix what character you want to use to delete the last typed character
        5.1.1 'Getty used to do the right thing with DEL and BS but is broken now?'
        5.1.2 'Login behaves differently at the first and second login attempts?'
    5.2 How to tell Linux what code to generate when a key is pressed
        5.2.1 'Why doesn't the Backspace key generate BackSpace by default?'
    5.3 How to tell X to interchange Delete and Backspace
    5.4 How to tell emacs what to do when it receives a Delete or Backspace
    5.5 How to tell emacs to interchange Delete and Backspace
    5.6 How to tell kermit to interchange Delete and Backspace
    5.7 How to tell xterm about your favourite tty modes
    5.8 How to tell xmosaic that the Backspace key generates a DEL
    5.9 A better solution for Motif-using programs, like netscape
    5.10 What about termcap and terminfo?
6. The console character sets
7. Console switching
    7.1 Changing the number of Virtual Consoles
8. Ctrl-Alt-Del and other special key combinations
    8.1 Ctrl-Alt-Del (Boot)
    8.2 Other combinations
    8.3 X Combinations
    8.4 Dosemu Combinations
    8.5 Composing symbols

A

8.6 The SysRq key
9. How to get out of raw mode
10. The keyboard LEDs
11. The TERM variable
11.1 Terminfo
12. How to make other programs work with non-ASCII chars
13. What precisely does XFree86-2.1 do when it initializes its keymap?
14. Unusual keys and keyboards
15. Examples of use of loadkeys and xmodmap
15.1 'I can use only one finger to type with'
16. Changing the video mode
16.1 Instructions for the use of resizecons
17. Changing the keyboard repeat rate
18. Scrolling
19. Screensaving
20. Screen dumps
21. Some properties of the VT100 - application key mode
22. Hardware incompatibility
23. Copyright

Red Hat Linux KickStart HOWTO

Martin Hamilton, martinh@gnu.org

v 0.2, January 1999

This HOWTO briefly describes how to use the Red Hat Linux KickStart system to rapidly install large numbers of identical Linux boxes. For advanced users, it describes how to modify the KickStart installation procedure to do customization, and gives a quick guide to building RPM packages.

1. Copyright
2. Homepage
3. Introduction
4. Prerequisites
5. Setting up a boot floppy
6. The KickStart config file
6.1 System info
6.2 Packages to install
6.3 Post-installation shell commands
7. Installation itself
8. Mounting the boot/supp disks
9. Modifying the Red Hat installer

10. FAQs/Wish list
11. Credits
12. Appendix A - Configuring BOOTP/DHCP and NFS
13. Appendix B - Making your own RPMs
14. Appendix C - Munging your own RPMs into the distribution

The Linux Electronic Mail Administrator HOWTO

Guylhem Aznar, guylhem@oeil.qc.ca

v 3.1, July 1999

This HOWTO describes the setup and maintenance of Electronic Mail (e-mail) under Linux. It is primarily intended for administrators, rather than users. See the Mail-User's-HOWTO for information on user issues and user agents.

1. Introduction, copyright and standard disclaimer
    1.1 Email and spamming
    1.2 Goals
    1.3 New versions
    1.4 Feedback
    1.5 Copyright
    1.6 Limited warranty
2. Other sources of information
    2.1 Mail User's HOWTO
    2.2 USENET
    2.3 Mailing Lists
    2.4 Other documents from LDP
    2.5 Books
3. How Electronic Mail Works
    3.1 Mail between full-time Internet machines
    3.2 Notifiers
    3.3 Mail to part-time Internet machines
    3.4 Remote mail and remote-mail protocols
    3.5 Mailbox formats
4. Requirements
    4.1 Hardware
5. Choosing a Mail Transport Agent
    5.1 sendmail
    5.2 smail v3.2
    5.3 qmail
    5.4 exim
6. Installing Transport Software

A

6.1 Qmail v1.03
6.1.1 Getting qmail
6.1.2 Uncompressing sources
6.1.3 Preparing for compilation
6.1.4 Configuring qmail
6.1.4.1 defaultdomain, me, plusdomain
6.1.4.2 locals, rcpthosts
6.1.4.3 virtualdomains
6.1.5 Testing qmail
6.1.6 Removing your other MTA
6.1.7 That's all, folks!
6.2 Smail v3.1
6.2.1 Configuring smail
6.2.1.1 "config" file
6.2.1.2 "directors" file
6.3 "fidopaths" file
6.3.1 "routers" file
6.3.1.1 "transports" file
6.3.1.2 "maps/" directory
6.3.2 Other good examples
6.4 Restarting inetd
6.5 Smail with smtp
6.6 OUTDATED SECTION: Sendmail+IDA
6.6.1 Source installation
6.6.2 The sendmail.m4 file
6.6.3 Defining a local mailer
6.6.4 The sendmail+IDA dbm tables
6.6.5 So which entries are really required?
6.7 Sendmail 8.x
6.7.1 A sample 8.7.x mc file
6.8 Sendmail v8 tidbits
6.9 Local Delivery Agents
7. User Agent Administration
7.1 Mutt
7.2 Elm
7.3 Mailx
8. Handling remote mail
8.1 History
8.2 Getting mail
8.3 Sending mail
8.4 Reading mail
8.5 Testing
8.6 Using

9. Acknowledgements

The Linux Mail User HOWTO

Eric S. Raymond, esr@thyrsus.com

v 2.2, May 1999

This HOWTO is an introduction to the world of electronic mail (e-mail) under Linux. It focuses on user-level issues and typical configurations for Linux home and small-business machines connected to the net using an ISP. For information on configuring and administering mail, see the Mail Administrator HOWTO.

1. Introduction
  1.1 New versions of this document
  1.2 Hardware requirements for email programs
  1.3 Software sources for email programs
2. Mail User Agents
  2.1 Setting your mail editor
  2.2 mutt
  2.3 elm
  2.4 pine
  2.5 Netscape
  2.6 Emacs rmail/smail and vm
  2.7 BSD mail
  2.8 Other user agents
3. Advanced topics
  3.1 Aliases
  3.2 Forwarding
  3.3 Auto-answering
  3.4 Mailing lists
  3.5 Mail filters
  3.6 Coping with spam
4. Other sources of information
  4.1 USENET
  4.2 Books
  4.3 Periodic USENET Postings
  4.4 Where
5. Administrivia
  5.1 Feedback
  5.2 Copyright Information
  5.3 Standard Disclaimer
  5.4 Acknowledgements

A

The Linux Modem-HOWTO

David S. Lawyer, <mailto:bf347@lafn.org>

v 0.04, August 1999

This HOWTO helps with selecting, connecting, configuring, trouble-shooting, and understanding PC modems.

1. Introduction
   - 1.1 Copyright, Disclaimer, Trademarks, and Credits
     - 1.1.1 Copyright
     - 1.1.2 Disclaimer
     - 1.1.3 Trademarks
     - 1.1.4 Credits
   - 1.2 Future Plans, You Can Help
   - 1.3 New Versions of this HOWTO
   - 1.4 What is a Modem?
   - 1.5 Quick Install
     - 1.5.1 External Modem Install
     - 1.5.2 Internal Modems (on ISA bus)
     - 1.5.3 All Modems
2. Modem and Serial Port Basics
   - 2.1 Modem Converts Digital to Analog (and conversely)
   - 2.2 What is a Serial Port?
     - 2.2.1 Intro to Serial
     - 2.2.2 Pins and Wires
     - 2.2.3 Internal Modem Contains Serial Port
   - 2.3 IO Address and IRQ
   - 2.4 Names: ttyS0, ttyS1, etc.
   - 2.5 Interrupts
   - 2.6 Data Compression (by the Modem)
   - 2.7 Error Correction
   - 2.8 Data Flow (Speeds)
   - 2.9 Flow Control
     - 2.9.1 Example of Flow Control
     - 2.9.2 Hardware vs. Software Flow Control
     - 2.9.3 Symptoms of No Flow Control
     - 2.9.4 Modem-to-Modem Flow Control
   - 2.10 Data Flow Path; Buffers
   - 2.11 Modem Commands
   - 2.12 Serial Software: Device Driver Module
3. Configuring Modems (including the serial port)
   - 3.1 Configuring Overview
4. Configuring the Serial Port

- 4.1 Configuring Overview
- 4.2 Common mistakes made re low-level configuring
- 4.3 I/O Address and IRQ: Boot-time messages
- 4.4 What is the current IO address and IRQ of my Serial Port?
    - 4.4.1 What does the device driver think?
    - 4.4.2 What is set in my serial port hardware?
    - 4.4.3 What is set in my PnP serial port hardware?
- 4.5 Choosing Serial IRQs
    - 4.5.1 IRQ 0 is not an IRQ
    - 4.5.2 Interrupt sharing and Kernels 2.2+
    - 4.5.3 What IRQs to choose?
- 4.6 Choosing Addresses—Video card conflict with ttyS3
- 4.7 Set IO Address and IRQ in the hardware (mostly for PnP)
    - 4.7.1 Using a PnP BIOS to IO-IRQ Configure
- 4.8 Giving the IRQ and IO Address to Setserial
- 4.9 Other Configuring
    - 4.9.1 Configuring Hardware Flow Control (RTS/CTS)

5. Modem Configuration (excluding serial port)
    - 5.1 AT Commands
    - 5.2 Init Strings: Saving and Recalling
    - 5.3 Other Modem Commands
6. Modems for a Linux PC
    - 6.1 External vs. Internal
    - 6.2 External Modems
        - 6.2.1 PnP External Modems
        - 6.2.2 Cabling and Installation
        - 6.2.3 What the Lights (LED's) Mean
    - 6.3 Internal Modems
    - 6.4 Internal Modems You Must Avoid (WinModems, etc.)
    - 6.5 Which Internal Modems are Best to Avoid?
        - 6.5.1 MWave and DSP Modems
        - 6.5.2 Rockwell (RPI) Drivers
        - 6.5.3 PCI Modems
7. Serial Port Devices /dev/ttyS2, etc.
    - 7.1 Serial Port Device Names and Numbers
    - 7.2 Link ttySN to /dev/modem?
    - 7.3 The cua Device
8. Interesting Programs You Should Know About
    - 8.1 What is setserial?
        - 8.1.1 Introduction
        - 8.1.2 Probing
        - 8.1.3 Can Linux Configure The Serial Devices Automatically?
        - 8.1.4 Boot-time Configuration

A

8.1.4.1 New configuration method using /etc/serial.conf
8.1.4.2 Old configuration method: edit a script
8.1.5 IRQs
8.1.6 Where to Run Setserial?
8.1.6.1 Prior to version 2.15
8.1.6.2 Version 2.15 and later
8.2 What is isapnp?
8.3 What is wvdialconf?
8.4 What is stty?
9. Trying Out Your Modem (Dialing Out)
9.1 Are You Ready to Dial Out?
9.2 Dialing Out with Minicom
9.3 Dialing Out with Kermit
10. Dial-In
10.1 Overview
10.2 Getty
10.2.1 About mgetty
10.2.2 About uugetty
10.2.3 About getty_em
10.2.4 About agetty and mingetty
10.3 What Happens when Someone Dials In?
10.4 Why Manual Answer is Best
10.5 Callback
10.6 Voice Mail
11. Uugetty for Dial-In (from the old Serial-HOWTO)
11.1 Installing getty_ps
11.2 Setting up uugetty
11.2.1 Modern Modems
11.2.2 Old slow modems
11.2.3 Login Banner
11.3 Customizing uugetty
12. What Speed Should I Use with My Modem?
12.1 Speed and Data Compression
12.2 Where do I Set Speed?
12.3 Can't Set a High Enough Speed
12.3.1 How speed is set in hardware: the divisor and baud_base
12.3.2 Work-arounds for setting speed
12.3.3 Crystal frequency is not baud_base
12.4 Speed Table
13. Communications Programs and Utilities
13.1 Minicom vs. Kermit
13.2 Lists of Programs

13.2.1 Least Popular Dialout
13.2.2 Most Popular Dialout
13.2.3 Fax
13.2.4 Voicemail Software
13.2.5 Dial-in (uses getty)
13.2.6 Other
13.3 SLiRP and term
14. What Are UARTs? How Do They Affect Performance?
14.1 Introduction to UARTS
14.2 Two Types of UARTs
14.3 FIFOs
14.4 UART Model Numbers
15. Troubleshooting
15.1 I can't get 56K on my 56K modem
15.2 Uploading (downloading) files is broken/slow
15.3 For Dial-in I Keep Getting "line NNN of inittab invalid"
15.4 When I Try To Dial Out, It Says "/dev/ttySN: Device or resource busy"
15.5 I Keep Getting: "Id 'S3' respawning too fast: disabled for 5 minutes"
15.6 My Modem is Hosed after Someone Hangs Up, or uugetty doesn't respawn
15.7 uugetty Still Doesn't Work
15.8 My Modem is Physically There but Can't be Found
15.9 The following subsections are in both the Serial and Modem HOWTOs:
15.10 My Serial Port is Physically There but Can't be Found
15.11 Slow: Text appears on the screen slowly after long delays
15.12 The Startup Screen Show Wrong IRQs for the Serial Ports
15.13 "Cannot open /dev/ttyS?: Permission denied"
15.14 "Operation not supported by device" (error message) for ttySx
15.15 "Cannot create lockfile. Sorry" (error message)
15.16 Software which may help
16. Flash Upgrades
17. Other Sources of Information
17.1 Misc
17.2 Books
17.3 HOWTOs
17.4 Usenet newsgroups
17.5 Web Sites
18. Appendix A: How Modems Work (technical) (unfinished)
18.1 Modulation Details

A

18.1.1 Intro to Modulation
18.1.2 Frequency Modulation
18.1.3 Amplitude Modulation
18.1.4 Phase Modulation
18.1.5 Combination Modulation
18.1.6 56k Modems (v.90)
19. Appendix B: "baud" vs. "bps"
19.1 A simple example
19.2 Real examples
20. Appendix C: Terminal Server Connection
21. Appendix D: Other Types of Modems
21.1 Digital-to-Digital "Modems"
21.2 ISDN "Modems"
21.3 Digital Subscriber Line (DSL)

The Linux MP3 HOWTO

Philip Kerr, phil@websentric.com

v 1.10, September 1999

This HOWTO describes the hardware, software, and procedures needed to encode and play MP3 sound files under Linux.

1. Introduction
2. Copyright of this document
3. Where to get this document
4. Acknowledgments
5. Disclaimer
6. Hardware Requirements and Performance Issues
7. Software Requirements
8. Setting up your system
8.1 Setting up for Analogue Audio Capture
8.2 Setting up for CD-ROM Audio Capture
8.3 Additional Setting up
9. Encoding from Audio
10. Encoding from CD-ROM
11. Playing MP3's
12. Feedback

Multicast over TCP/IP HOWTO

Juan-Mariano de Goyeneche, <jmseyas@dit.upm.es>

v 1.0, March 1998

This HOWTO tries to cover most aspects related to multicast over TCP/IP networks. At the time of writing, many of the "standards" were in draft format.

1. Introduction
    1.1 What is Multicast
    1.2 The problem with Unicast
2. Multicast Explained
    2.1 Multicast addresses
    2.2 Levels of conformance
    2.3 Sending Multicast Datagrams
        2.3.1 TTL
        2.3.2 Loopback
        2.3.3 Interface selection
    2.4 Receiving Multicast Datagrams
        2.4.1 Joining a Multicast Group
        2.4.2 Leaving a Multicast Group
        2.4.3 Mapping of IP Multicast Addresses to Ethernet/FDDI addresses
3. Kernel requirements and configuration
4. The MBone
5. Multicast applications
6. Multicast programming
    6.1 IP_MULTICAST_LOOP
    6.2 IP_MULTICAST_TTL
    6.3 IP_MULTICAST_IF
    6.4 IP_ADD_MEMBERSHIP
    6.5 IP_DROP_MEMBERSHIP
7. The internals
    7.1 IGMP
        7.1.1 IGMP version 1
        7.1.2 IGMP version 2
    7.2 Kernel corner
8. Routing Policies and Forwarding Techniques
9. Multicast Transport Protocols
10. References
    10.1 RFCs
    10.2 Internet Drafts
    10.3 Web pages
    10.4 Books
11. Copyright and Disclaimer
12. Acknowledgements

HOWTO: Multi Disk System Tuning

Stein Gjoen, sgjoen@nyx.net

v 0.22i, May 1999

This document describes how best to use multiple disks and partitions for a Linux system.

1. Introduction
   - 1.1 Copyright
   - 1.2 Disclaimer
   - 1.3 News
   - 1.4 Credits

2. Structure
   - 2.1 Logical structure
   - 2.2 Document structure
   - 2.3 Reading plan

3. Drive technologies
   - 3.1 Drives
   - 3.2 Geometry
   - 3.3 Media
     - 3.3.1 Magnetic Drives
     - 3.3.2 Optical Drives
     - 3.3.3 Solid State Drives
   - 3.4 Interfaces
     - 3.4.1 MFM and RLL
     - 3.4.2 ESDI
     - 3.4.3 IDE and ATA
     - 3.4.4 EIDE, Fast-ATA and ATA-2
     - 3.4.5 Ultra-ATA
     - 3.4.6 ATAPI
     - 3.4.7 SCSI
   - 3.5 Cabling
   - 3.6 Host Adapters
   - 3.7 Multi Channel Systems
   - 3.8 Multi Board Systems
   - 3.9 Speed Comparison
     - 3.9.1 Controllers
     - 3.9.2 Bus Types
   - 3.10 Benchmarking
   - 3.11 Comparisons
   - 3.12 Future Development
   - 3.13 Recommendations

4. File System Structure

- 4.1 File System Features
  - 4.1.1 Swap
  - 4.1.2 Temporary Storage
  - 4.1.3 Spool Areas
  - 4.1.4 Home Directories
  - 4.1.5 Main Binaries
  - 4.1.6 Libraries
  - 4.1.7 Boot
  - 4.1.8 Root
  - 4.1.9 DOS etc.
- 4.2 Explanation of Terms
  - 4.2.1 Speed
  - 4.2.2 Reliability
  - 4.2.3 Files

5. File Systems
   - 5.1 General Purpose File Systems
   - 5.2 Microsoft File Systems
   - 5.3 Logging and Journaling File Systems
   - 5.4 Read-only File Systems
   - 5.5 Networking File Systems
   - 5.6 Special File Systems
   - 5.7 File System Recommendations
6. Technologies
   - 6.1 RAID
     - 6.1.1 SCSI-to-SCSI
     - 6.1.2 PCI-to-SCSI
     - 6.1.3 Software RAID
     - 6.1.4 RAID Levels
   - 6.2 Volume Management
   - 6.3 Linux
   - 6.4 Compression
   - 6.5 ACL
   - 6.6 cachefs
   - 6.7 Translucent or Inheriting File Systems
   - 6.8 Physical Track Positioning
     - 6.8.1 Disk Speed Values
   - 6.9 Stacking
   - 6.10 Recommendations
7. Other Operating Systems
   - 7.1 DOS
   - 7.2 Windows
   - 7.3 OS/2
   - 7.4 NT

7.5 Sun OS
7.5.1 Sun OS 4
7.5.2 Sun OS 5 (aka Solaris)
7.5.3 BeOS
8. Clusters
9. Mount Points
10. Considerations and Dimensioning
10.1 Home Systems
10.2 Servers
10.2.1 Home Directories
10.2.2 Anonymous FTP
10.2.3 WWW
10.2.4 Mail
10.2.5 News
10.2.6 Others
10.2.7 Server Recommendations
10.3 Pitfalls
11. Disk Layout
11.1 Selection for Partitioning
11.2 Mapping Partitions to Drives
11.3 Sorting Partitions on Drives
11.4 Optimizing
11.4.1 Optimizing by Characteristics
11.4.2 Optimizing by Drive Paralleling
11.5 Compromises
12. Implementation
12.1 Drives and Partitions
12.2 Partitioning
12.3 Repartitioning
12.4 Microsoft Partition Bug
12.5 Multiple Devices
12.6 Formatting
12.7 Mounting
12.8 fstab
12.9 Recommendations
13. Maintenance
13.1 Backup
13.2 Defragmentation
13.3 Deletions
13.4 Upgrades
13.5 Recovery
14. Advanced Issues
14.1 Hard Disk Tuning

- 14.2 File System Tuning
- 14.3 Spindle Synchronizing
15. Further Information
    - 15.1 News groups
    - 15.2 Mailing Lists
    - 15.3 HOWTO
    - 15.4 Mini-HOWTO
    - 15.5 Local Resources
    - 15.6 Web Pages
    - 15.7 Search Engines
16. Getting Help
17. Concluding Remarks
    - 17.1 Coming Soon
    - 17.2 Request for Information
    - 17.3 Suggested Project Work
18. Questions and Answers
19. Bits and Pieces
    - 19.1 Swap Partition: to Use or Not to Use
    - 19.2 Mount Point and /mnt
    - 19.3 Power and Heating
    - 19.4 Dejanews
20. Appendix A: Partitioning Layout Table: Mounting and Linking
21. Appendix B: Partitioning Layout Table: Numbering and Sizing
22. Appendix C: Partitioning Layout Table: Partition Placement
23. Appendix D: Example: Multipurpose Server
24. Appendix E: Example: Mounting and Linking
25. Appendix F: Example: Numbering and Sizing
26. Appendix G: Example: Partition Placement
27. Appendix H: Example II
28. Appendix I: Example III: SPARC Solaris
29. Appendix J: Example IV: Server with 4 Drives
30. Appendix K: Example V: Dual Drive System
31. Appendix L: Example VI: Single Drive System

Linux Networking-HOWTO (Previously the Net-3 HOWTO)

Current Author: {Poet} poet@linuxports.com

v 1.5, August 1999

Original Authors: Terry Dawson (main author), VK2KTJ; Alessandro Rubini (maintainer)

A

This HOWTO describes how to install and configure the Linux networking software and associated tools.

1. Introduction
2. Document History
    2.1 Feedback
3. How to use this HOWTO
    3.1 Conventions used in this document
4. General Information about Linux Networking
    4.1 A brief history of Linux Networking Kernel Development
    4.2 Linux Networking Resources
    4.3 Where to get some non-Linux-specific network information
5. Generic Network Configuration Information
    5.1 What do I need to start?
        5.1.1 Current Kernel source (Optional)
        5.1.2 Current Network tools
        5.1.3 Network Application Programs
        5.1.4 IP Addresses, an Explanation
    5.2 Where should I put the configuration commands?
    5.3 Creating your network interfaces
    5.4 Configuring a network interface
    5.5 Configuring your Name Resolver
        5.5.1 What's in a name?
        5.5.2 What information you will need
        5.5.3 /etc/resolv.conf
        5.5.4 /etc/host.conf
        5.5.5 /etc/hosts
        5.5.6 Running a name server
    5.6 Configuring your loopback interface
    5.7 Routing
        5.7.1 So what does the routed program do?
    5.8 Configuring your network servers and services.
        5.8.1 /etc/services
            5.8.1.1 An example /etc/services File
        5.8.2 /etc/inetd.conf
            5.8.2.1 An example /etc/inetd.conf
    5.9 Other miscellaneous network related configuration files
        5.9.1 /etc/protocols
        5.9.2 /etc/networks
    5.10 Network Security and access control
        5.10.1 /etc/ftpusers
        5.10.2 /etc/securetty
        5.10.3 The tcpd hosts access control mechanism
            5.10.3.1 /etc/hosts.allow

5.10.3.2 /etc/hosts.deny
5.10.4 /etc/hosts.equiv
5.10.5 Configure your
5.10.6 Network Firewalling
5.10.7 Other suggestions
6. IP- and Ethernet-Related Information
6.1 Ethernet
6.2 EQL - multiple line traffic equalizer
6.3 IP Accounting (for Linux-2.0)
6.4 IP Accounting (for Linux-2.2)
6.5 IP Aliasing
6.6 IP Firewall (for Linux-2.0)
6.7 IP Firewall (for Linux-2.2)
6.8 IPIP Encapsulation
6.8.1 A tunneled network configuration
6.8.2 A tunneled host configuration
6.9 IP Masquerade
6.10 IP Transparent Proxy
6.11 IPv6
6.12 Mobile IP
6.13 Multicast
6.14 NAT - Network Address Translation
6.15 Traffic Shaper - Changing allowed bandwidth
6.16 Routing in Linux-2.2
7. Using common PC hardware
7.1 ISDN
7.2 PLIP for Linux-2.0
7.3 PLIP for Linux-2.2
7.4 PPP
7.4.1 Maintaining a permanent connection to the net with pppd
7.5 SLIP client
7.5.1 dip
7.5.2 slattach
7.5.3 When do I use which?
7.5.4 Static SLIP server with a dialup line and DIP
7.5.5 Dynamic SLIP server with a dialup line and DIP
7.5.6 Using DIP
7.5.7 Permanent SLIP connection using a leased line and slattach
7.6 SLIP server
7.6.1 SLIP Server using sliplogin
7.6.1.1 Where to get sliplogin
7.6.1.2 Configuring /etc/passwd for SLIP hosts

A

7.6.1.3 Configuring /etc/slip.hosts
7.6.1.4 Configuring the /etc/slip.login File
7.6.1.5 Configuring the /etc/slip.logout File
7.6.1.6 Configuring the /etc/slip.tty File
7.6.2 SLIP Server using dip
7.6.2.1 Configuring /etc/diphosts
7.6.3 SLIP server using the dSIP package
8. Other Network Technologies
8.1 ARCNet
8.2 Appletalk
8.2.1 Configuring the Appletalk software
8.2.2 Exporting a Linux filesystems via Appletalk
8.2.3 Sharing your Linux printer across Appletalk
8.2.4 Starting the Appletalk software
8.2.5 Testing the Appletalk software
8.2.6 Caveats of the Appletalk software
8.2.7 More information
8.3 ATM
8.4 AX25
8.5 DECNet
8.6 FDDI
8.7 Frame Relay
8.8 IPX
8.9 NetRom
8.10 Rose protocol
8.11 SAMBA—'NetBEUI', 'NetBios', 'CIFS' support
8.12 STRIP support (Starmode Radio IP)
8.13 Token Ring
8.14 X.25
8.15 WaveLan Card
9. Cables and Cabling
9.1 Serial NULL Modem cable
9.2 Parallel port cable (PLIP cable)
9.3 10base2 (thin coax) Ethernet Cabling
9.4 Twisted Pair Ethernet Cable
10. Glossary of Terms used in this document
11. Linux for an ISP?
12. Acknowledgements
13. Copyright

The Linux Networking Overview HOWTO

Daniel López Ridruejo, ridruejo@esi.us.es

v 0.2, July 1998

This HOWTO gives an overview of the networking capabilities of the Linux Operating System and provides pointers for further information and implementation details.

1. Introduction
2. Linux
    2.1 What is Linux?
    2.2 What makes Linux different?
3. Networking protocols
    3.1 TCP/IP
    3.2 TCP/IP version 6
    3.3 IPX/SPX
    3.4 AppleTalk Protocol Suite
    3.5 WAN Networking: X.25, Frame-relay, etc.
    3.6 ISDN
    3.7 PPP, SLIP, PLIP
    3.8 Amateur Radio
    3.9 ATM
4. Networking hardware supported
5. File Sharing and Printing
    5.1 Apple environment
    5.2 Windows Environment
    5.3 Novell Environment
    5.4 UNIX Environment
6. Internet/Intranet
    6.1 Mail
        6.1.1 Mail servers
        6.1.2 Remote Access to mail
        6.1.3 Mail User Agents
        6.1.4 Mailing list software
        6.1.5 Fetch-mail
    6.2 Web Servers
    6.3 Web Browsers
    6.4 FTP Servers and clients
    6.5 News service
    6.6 Domain Name System
    6.7 DHCP, bootp
    6.8 NIS
    6.9 Authentication

7. Remote execution of applications
  7.1 Telnet
  7.2 Remote commands
  7.3 X-Window
8. Network Interconnection
  8.1 Router
  8.2 Bridge
  8.3 IP-Masquerading
  8.4 IP-Accounting
  8.5 IP aliasing
  8.6 Traffic Shaping
  8.7 Firewall
  8.8 Port forwarding
  8.9 Load Balancing
  8.10 EQL
  8.11 Proxy Server
  8.12 Diald on demand
  8.13 Tunnelling, mobile IP and virtual private networks
9. Network Management
  9.1 Network management applications
  9.2 SNMP
10. Enterprise Linux Networking
  10.1 High Availability
  10.2 RAID
  10.3 Redundant networking
11. Sources of Information
12. Acknowledgements and disclaimer

NFS HOWTO

Nicolai Langfeldt, janl@math.uio.no

v 0.7, November 1997

This HOWTO shows the method for doing the set up for NFS clients and servers.

1. Preamble
  1.1 Legal stuff
  1.2 Other stuff
  1.3 Dedication
2. README.first
3. Setting up a NFS server
  3.1 Prerequisites

3.2 First step
3.3 The portmapper
3.4 Mountd and nfsd
4. Setting up a NFS client
4.1 Mount options
4.2 Optimizing NFS
5. NFS over slow lines
6. Security and NFS
6.1 Client Security
6.2 Server security: nfsd
6.3 Server security: the portmapper
6.4 NFS and firewalls
6.5 Summary
7. Mount Checklist
8. FAQs
9. Exporting filesystems
9.1 IRIX, HP-UX, Digital-UNIX, Ultrix, SunOS 4 (Solaris 1), AIX
9.2 Solaris 2
10. PC-NFS

The Linux NIS(YP)/NYS/NIS+ HOWTO

Thorsten Kukuk

v 1.0, March 1999

This HOWTO describes how to configure Linux as NIS (YP) or NIS+ client and how to install as NIS server.

1. Introduction
1.1 New Versions of this Document
1.2 Disclaimer
1.3 Feedback and Corrections
1.4 Acknowledgements
2. Glossary and General Information
2.1 Glossary of Terms
2.2 Some General Information
3. NIS, NYS, or NIS+?
3.1 libc 4/5 with traditional NIS or NYS?
3.2 glibc 2 and NIS/NIS+
3.3 NIS or NIS+?
4. How it works
4.1 How NIS works
4.2 How NIS+ works

A

5. The RPC Portmapper
6. What do you need to set up NIS?
    6.1 Determine whether you are a Server, Slave or Client
    6.2 The Software
    6.3 The ypbind daemon
    6.4 Setting up a NIS Client using Traditional NIS
    6.5 Setting up a NIS Client using NYS
    6.6 Setting up a NIS Client using glibc 2.x
    6.7 The nsswitch.conf File
    6.8 Shadow Passwords with NIS
        6.8.1 Linux
        6.8.2 Solaris
        6.8.3 PAM
7. What do you need to set up NIS+?
    7.1 The Software
    7.2 Setting up a NIS+ client
    7.3 NIS+, keylogin, login and PAM
    7.4 The nsswitch.conf File
8. Setting up a NIS Server
    8.1 The Server Program ypserv
    8.2 The Server Program yps
    8.3 The Program rpc.ypxfrd
    8.4 The Program rpc.yppasswdd
9. Verifying the NIS/NYS Installation
10. Common Problems and Troubleshooting NIS
11. Frequently Asked Questions

Linux PCMCIA HOWTO

David Hinds, dhinds@hyper.stanford.edu.

v 2.32, May 1999

This HOWTO describes how to install and use PCMCIA Card Services for Linux.

1. General information and hardware requirements
    1.1 Introduction
    1.2 Copyright notice and disclaimer
    1.3 What is the latest version, and where can I get it?
    1.4 What systems are supported?
    1.5 What cards are supported?
    1.6 When will my favorite (unsupported) card become supported?
    1.7 Mailing lists and other information sources

- 1.8 Why don't you distribute binaries?
- 1.9 Why is the package so darned big?

2. Compilation and installation
    - 2.1 Prerequisites and kernel setup
    - 2.2 Installation
    - 2.3 Startup options
    - 2.4 System resource settings
    - 2.5 Notes about specific Linux distributions
        - 2.5.1 Debian
        - 2.5.2 Red Hat, and Caldera Open Desktop
        - 2.5.3 Slackware
        - 2.5.4 SuSE
3. Resolving installation and configuration problems
    - 3.1 Base PCMCIA kernel modules do not load
    - 3.2 Some client driver modules do not load
    - 3.3 Interrupt scan failures
    - 3.4 IO port scan failures
    - 3.5 Memory probe failures
    - 3.6 Failure to detect card insertions and removals
    - 3.7 System resource starvation
    - 3.8 Resource conflict between two cards
    - 3.9 Device configuration does not complete
4. Usage and features
    - 4.1 Tools for configuring and monitoring PCMCIA devices
        - 4.1.1 The cardmgr configuration daemon
        - 4.1.2 The cardctl and cardinfo utilities
        - 4.1.3 Inserting and ejecting cards
        - 4.1.4 Card Services and Advanced Power Management
        - 4.1.5 Shutting down the PCMCIA system
    - 4.2 Overview of the PCMCIA configuration scripts
    - 4.3 PCMCIA network adapters
        - 4.3.1 Network device parameters
        - 4.3.2 Comments about specific cards
        - 4.3.3 Diagnosing problems with network adapters
    - 4.4 PCMCIA serial and modem devices
        - 4.4.1 Serial device parameters
        - 4.4.2 Diagnosing problems with serial devices
    - 4.5 PCMCIA SCSI adapters
        - 4.5.1 SCSI device parameters
        - 4.5.2 Comments about specific cards
        - 4.5.3 Diagnosing problems with SCSI adapters
    - 4.6 PCMCIA memory cards
        - 4.6.1 Memory device parameters

4.6.2 Using flash memory cards
4.7 PCMCIA ATA/IDE card drives
4.7.1 ATA/IDE fixed-disk device parameters
4.7.2 Diagnosing problems with ATA/IDE adapters
4.8 Multifunction cards
5. Advanced topics
5.1 Resource allocation for PCMCIA devices
5.2 How can I have separate device setups for home and work?
5.3 Booting from a PCMCIA device
5.3.1 The pcinitrd helper script
5.3.2 Creating an initrd boot floppy
5.3.3 Installing an initrd image on a non-Linux drive
6. Dealing with unsupported cards
6.1 Configuring unrecognized cards
6.2 Adding support for an NE2000-compatible Ethernet card
6.3 PCMCIA floppy interface cards
6.4 What's up with support for Xircom cards?
7. Debugging tips and programming information
7.1 Submitting useful bug reports
7.2 Interpreting kernel trap reports
7.3 Low level PCMCIA debugging aids
7.4 /proc/bus/pccard
7.5 Writing Card Services drivers for new cards
7.6 Guidelines for PCMCIA client driver authors
7.7 Guidelines for Linux distribution maintainers

The Linux Plug-and-Play-HOWTO

David S. Lawyer, <mailto:bf347@lafn.org>

v 0.05, August 1999

This HOWTO shows how to get your Linux system to support Plug-and-Play.

1. Introduction
1.1 Copyright, Trademarks, Disclaimer, and Credits
1.1.1 Copyright
1.1.2 Trademarks
1.1.3 Disclaimer
1.2 Future Plans; You Can Help
1.3 New Versions of this HOWTO
2. What PnP Should Do: Allocate "Resources"
2.1 What is Plug-and-Play (PnP)?

- 2.2 How a Computer Finds Devices (and conversely)
- 2.3 I/O Addresses, etc.
- 2.4 IRQs—Overview
- 2.5 DMA Channels
- 2.6 Memory Ranges
- 2.7 "Resources" to both Device and Driver
- 2.8 The Problem
- 2.9 PnP Finds Devices Plugged Into Serial Ports

3. The Plug-and-Play (PnP) Solution
   - 3.1 Introduction to PnP
   - 3.2 How It Works (simplified)
   - 3.3 Starting Up the PC
   - 3.4 Buses
   - 3.5 Linux Needs to Cope Better with PnP
4. Configuring a PnP BIOS
   - 4.1 Do you have a PnP operating system?
     - 4.1.1 Interoperability with Windows9x
   - 4.2 How are resources to be controlled?
   - 4.3 Reset the configuration?
5. How to Deal with PnP Cards
   - 5.1 Introduction to Dealing with PnP Cards
   - 5.2 Disable PnP?
   - 5.3 BIOS Configures PnP
     - 5.3.1 Intro to Using the BIOS to Configure PnP
     - 5.3.2 The BIOS's ESCD Database
     - 5.3.3 Using Windows to set the ESCD
     - 5.3.4 Adding a New Device (under Linux or Windows)
   - 5.4 Isapnp (part of isapnptools)
   - 5.5 PCI Utilities
   - 5.6 Patch the Kernel to Make Linux PnP
   - 5.7 Windows Configures
   - 5.8 Device Driver Configures
   - 5.9 PnP Software/Documents
6. Tell the Driver the Configuration
   - 6.1 Introduction
   - 6.2 Serial Port Driver: setserial
   - 6.3 Sound Card Drivers
     - 6.3.1 OSS-Lite
     - 6.3.2 OSS (Open Sound System) and ALSA
7. What Is My Current Configuration?
   - 7.1 How Are My Device Drivers Configured?
   - 7.2 How Are My Hardware Devices Configured?
8. Appendix

8.1 Addresses
8.1.1 ISA Bus Configuration Address (Read-Port etc.)
8.1.2 Address ranges
8.1.3 Address space
8.1.4 Range Check (ISA Testing for IO Address Conflicts)
8.1.5 Communicating Directly via Memory
8.2 Interrupts—Details
8.3 PCI Interrupts
8.4 Isolation

Linux PPP HOWTO

Robert Hart, hartr@interweft.com.au

v 3.0, March 1997

This HOWTO shows how to connect a Linux PC to a PPP server, how to use PPP to link two LANs together, and provides one method of setting up your Linux computer as a PPP server.

1. Introduction
1.1 Clients and Servers
1.2 Differences between Linux distributions
1.3 Distribution specific PPP configuration tools
2. IP Numbers
3. Aims of this Document
3.1 Setting up a PPP Client
3.2 Linking two LANs or a LAN to the Internet using PPP
3.3 Setting up a PPP server
3.4 Using PPP over a direct null modem connection
3.5 This document at present does NOT cover...
4. Software versions covered
5. Other Useful/Important Documents
5.1 Useful Linux Mailing Lists
6. Overview of what has to be done to get PPP working as a client
6.1 Obtaining/Installing the software
6.2 Compiling PPP support into the kernel
6.3 Obtaining information from your ISP
6.4 Configuring your modem and serial port
6.5 Setting up Name to Address Resolution (DNS)
6.6 PPP and root Privileges
6.7 Checking your distribution PPP Files and setting up the PPP Options
6.8 If your PPP server uses PAP (Password Authentication Protocol)

6.9 Connecting to the PPP server by hand
6.10 Automating your PPP Connection
6.11 Shutting down the link
6.12 If you have problems
6.13 After the link comes up
6.14 Problems with standard IP services on a Dynamic IP number PPP link
7. Configuring your Linux Kernel
7.1 Installing the Linux Kernel source
7.2 Knowing your hardware
7.3 Kernel compilation - the Linux 1.2.13 kernel
7.4 Kernel compilation - the Linux 1.3.x and 2.0.x kernels
7.5 Note on PPP-2.2 and /proc/net/dev
7.6 General kernel config considerations for PPP
8. Getting the Information you need about the PPP server
9. Configuring your modem and serial port
9.1 A note about serial ports and speed capabilities
9.2 Serial Port Names
9.3 Configuring your modem
9.4 Note on Serial Flow Control
9.5 Testing your modem for dial out
10. Setting up Name to Address Resolution (DNS)
10.1 The /etc/resolv.conf file
10.2 The /etc/host.conf file
11. Using PPP and root privileges
12. Setting up the PPP connection files
12.1 The supplied options.tpl file
12.2 What options should I use? (No PAP/CHAP)
13. If your PPP server uses PAP (Password Authentication Protocol)
13.1 Using MSCHAP
13.2 The PAP/CHAP secrets file
13.3 The PAP secrets file
13.4 The CHAP secrets file
13.5 Handling multiple PAP-authenticated connections
14. Setting up the PPP connection manually
15. Automating your connections - Creating the connection scripts
15.1 Connection scripts for User name/Password Authentication
15.2 The ppp-on script
15.3 Editing the supplied PPP startup scripts
15.4 What a Chat script means...
15.5 A chat script for PAP/CHAP authenticated connections
15.6 The pppd debug and file option_file options
16. Testing your connection script

A

17. Shutting down the PPP link
18. Debugging
    18.1 I have compiled PPP support into the kernel, but...
    18.2 My modem connects but ppp never starts up
    18.3 The syslog says "serial line is not 8 bit clean..."
    18.4 Default route not set
    18.5 Other Problems
19. Getting Help when totally stuck
20. Common Problems once the link is working
    20.1 I can't see beyond the PPP server I connect to
    20.2 I can send email, but not receive it
    20.3 Why can't people finger, WWW, gopher, talk etc to my machine?
21. Using Internet services with Dynamic IP numbers
    21.1 Setting up email
    21.2 Setting Up a local Name server
22. Linking two networks using PPP
    22.1 Setting up the IP numbers
    22.2 Setting up the routing
    22.3 Network security
23. After the link comes up - the /etc/ppp/ip-up script
    23.1 Special routing
    23.2 Handling email queues
    23.3 A sample /etc/ppp/ip-up script
    23.4 Handling email
24. Using /etc/ppp/ip-down
25. Routing issues on a LAN
    25.1 Note on Security
26. Setting up a PPP server
    26.1 Kernel compilation
    26.2 Overview of the server system
    26.3 Getting the software together
    26.4 Setting up standard (shell access) dialup
    26.5 Setting up the PPP options files
    26.6 Setting pppd up to allow users to (successfully) run it
    26.7 Setting up the global alias for pppd
27. Using PPP across a null modem (direct serial) connection

The Linux Printing HOWTO

Grant Taylor, <gtaylor+pht@picante.com>

v 3.29, March 1999

This HOWTO is a collection of information on how to generate, preview, print, and fax anything under Linux.

1. Introduction
    - 1.1 History
    - 1.2 Copyright
2. How to print
3. Kernel printer devices
    - 3.1 The lp device (kernels <=2.1.32)
    - 3.2 The parport device (kernels >= 2.1.33)
    - 3.3 Serial devices
4. Supported Printers
    - 4.1 Postscript
    - 4.2 Non-Postscript
    - 4.3 What printers work?
        - 4.3.1 Printer compatibility list
5. Which spooling software?
6. How it works, basic
7. How to set things up, basic
    - 7.1 Traditional lpd configuration
    - 7.2 File Permissions
8. Getting Printing Software
9. Vendor Solutions
    - 9.1 Red Hat
    - 9.2 Debian
    - 9.3 Other Distributions
10. Ghostscript
    - 10.1 Invoking Ghostscript
    - 10.2 Ghostscript output tuning
        - 10.2.1 Output location and size
        - 10.2.2 Gamma, dotsizes, etc.
11. How to print to a printer over the network
    - 11.1 To a Unix/lpd host
        - 11.1.1 With lpd
        - 11.1.2 With rlpr
    - 11.2 To a Win95, WinNT, LanManager, or Samba printer
    - 11.3 To a NetWare Printer
    - 11.4 To an EtherTalk (Apple) printer
    - 11.5 To an HP or other ethernet printer
        - 11.5.1 To older HPs
    - 11.6 Running an if for remote printers
    - 11.7 From Windows
    - 11.8 From an Apple
    - 11.9 From Netware

12. Windows-only printers
    12.1 The Ghostscript Windows redirector
    12.2 The pbm2ppa program
    12.3 The pbm2l7k program
13. How to print to a fax machine
    13.1 Using a faxmodem
    13.2 Using the Remote Printing Service
14. How to generate something worth printing
    14.1 Markup languages
    14.2 WYSIWYG Word Processors
15. On-screen previewing of printable things
    15.1 PostScript
    15.2 TeX dvi
    15.3 Adobe PDF
16. Serial printers under lpd
    16.1 Setting up in printcap
    16.2 Older serial printers that drop characters
17. Credits

RPM HOWTO (RPM at Idle)

Donnie Barnes, djb@redhat.com

v 2.0, 8 April 1997

This HOWTO discusses the functionality of the Red Hat Package Manager (RPM). While RPM was originally developed by Red Hat, it is completely intended to be an open packaging system available for anyone to use.

1. Introduction
2. Overview
3. General Information
    3.1 Acquiring RPM
    3.2 RPM Requirements
4. Using RPM
5. Now what can I really do with RPM?
6. Building RPMs
    6.1 The rpmrc File
    6.2 The spec File
    6.3 The Header
    6.4 Prep
    6.5 Build
    6.6 Install

6.7 Option pre and post Install/Uninstall Scripts
6.8 Files
6.9 Building It
6.9.1 The Source Directory Tree
6.9.2 Test Building
6.9.3 Generating the File List
6.9.4 Building the Package with RPM
6.10 Testing It
6.11 What to do with your new RPMs
6.12 What Now?
7. Multi-architectural RPM Building
7.1 Sample spec File
7.2 Optflags
7.3 Macros
7.4 Excluding Architecture
7.5 Finishing Up
8. Copyright Notice

The Linux SCSI Programming HOWTO

Heiko Eißfeldt, heiko@colossus.escape.de

v 1.5, May 1996

This HOWTO deals with programming the Linux generic SCSI interface.

1. What's New?
2. Introduction
3. What Is the Generic SCSI Interface?
4. What Are the Requirements To Use It?
4.1 Kernel Configuration
4.2 Device Files
4.3 Device Mapping
5. Programmers Guide
6. Overview of Device Programming
7. Opening the Device
8. The Header Structure
9. Inquiry Command Example
10. The Sense Buffer
11. Example Using Sense Buffer
12. Ioctl Functions
13. Driver Defaults
13.1 Transfer Lengths
13.2 Timeout and Retry Values

A

14. Obtaining the SCSI Specifications
15. Related Information Sources
    15.1 HOWTOs and FAQs
    15.2 Mailing list
    15.3 Example code
16. Other useful stuff
    16.1 Device driver writer helpers
    16.2 Utilities
17. Other SCSI Access Interfaces
18. Final Comments
19. Acknowledgments
20. Appendix
21. Error handling
    21.1 Error status decoding
    21.2 Status codes
    21.3 SCSI Sense Keys
    21.4 Host codes
    21.5 Driver codes
22. Additional sense codes and additional sense code qualifiers
    22.1 ASC and ASCQ in lexical order
    22.2 ASC and ASCQ in numerical order
23. A SCSI command code quick reference
24. Example programs

Linux Security HOWTO

Kevin Fenzi, kevin@scrye.com, and Dave Wreski, dave@nic.com

v 1.0.2, April 1999

This HOWTO is a general overview of security issues that face the Linux filesystem administrator.

1. Introduction
    1.1 New Versions of this Document
    1.2 Feedback
    1.3 Disclaimer
    1.4 Copyright Information
2. Overview
    2.1 Why Do We Need Security?
    2.2 How Secure Is Secure?
    2.3 What Are You Trying to Protect?
    2.4 Developing A Security Policy
    2.5 Means of Securing Your Site

2.5.1 Host Security
2.5.2 Network Security
2.5.3 Security Through Obscurity
2.6 Organization of This Document
3. Physical Security
3.1 Computer locks
3.2 BIOS Security
3.3 Boot Loader Security
3.4 xlock and vlock
3.5 Detecting Physical Security Compromises
4. Local Security
4.1 Creating New Accounts
4.2 Root Security
5. Files and Filesystem Security
5.1 Umask Settings
5.2 File Permissions
5.3 Integrity Checking with Tripwire
5.4 Trojan Horses
6. Password Security and Encryption
6.1 PGP and Public-Key Cryptography
6.2 SSL, S-HTTP, HTTPS and S/MIME
6.3 Linux IPSEC Implementations
6.4 ssh (Secure Shell) and stelnet
6.5 PAM - Pluggable Authentication Modules
6.6 Cryptographic IP Encapsulation (CIPE)
6.7 Kerberos
6.8 Shadow Passwords.
6.9 "Crack" and "John the Ripper"
6.10 CFS - Cryptographic File System and TCFS - Transparent Cryptographic File System
6.11 X11, SVGA and display security
6.11.1 X11
6.11.2 SVGA
6.11.3 GGI (Generic Graphics Interface project)
7. Kernel Security
7.1 2.0 Kernel Compile Options
7.2 2.2 Kernel Compile Options
7.3 Kernel Devices
8. Network Security
8.1 Packet Sniffers
8.2 System services and tcp_wrappers
8.3 Verify Your DNS Information
8.4 identd

A

8.5 SATAN, ISS, and Other Network Scanners
8.5.1 Detecting Port Scans
8.6 Sendmail, qmail, and MTA's
8.7 Denial of Service Attacks
8.8 NFS (Network File System) Security
8.9 NIS (Network Information Service) (formerly YP)
8.10 Firewalls
8.11 IP Chains - Linux Kernel 2.2.x Firewalling
8.12 VPN's - Virtual Private Networks
9. Security Preparation (before you go on-line)
9.1 Make a Full Backup of Your Machine
9.2 Choosing a Good Backup Schedule
9.3 Backup Your RPM or Debian File Database
9.4 Keep Track of Your System Accounting Data
9.5 Apply All New System Updates
10. What To Do During and After a Break in
10.1 Security Compromise Underway
10.2 Security Compromise has already happened
10.2.1 Closing the Hole
10.2.2 Assessing the Damage
10.2.3 Backups, Backups, Backups!
10.2.4 Tracking Down the Intruder
11. Security Sources
11.1 FTP Sites
11.2 Web Sites
11.3 Mailing Lists
11.4 Books - Printed Reading Material
12. Glossary
13. Frequently Asked Questions
14. Conclusion
15. Acknowledgements

The Linux Serial HOWTO

David S. Lawyer, bf347@lafn.org; original by Greg Hankins

v 2.01, August 1999

This HOWTO describes serial port features other than those covered by the Modem-HOWTO, PPP-HOWTO, Serial-Programming-HOWTO, or Text-Terminal-HOWTO. It lists information on multiport serial cards.

1. Introduction
1.1 Copyright, Disclaimer, and Credits

- 1.1.1 Copyright
- 1.1.2 Disclaimer
- 1.1.3 Credits
- 1.2 Release Notes
- 1.3 New Versions of this Serial-HOWTO
- 1.4 Related HOWTO's re the Serial Port
- 1.5 Feedback
- 1.6 What is a Serial Port?

2. How the Hardware Transfers Bytes
- 2.1 Transmitting
- 2.2 Receiving
- 2.3 The Large Serial Buffers

3. Serial Port Basics
- 3.1 What is a Serial Port?
  - 3.1.1 Intro to Serial
  - 3.1.2 Pins and Wires
  - 3.1.3 RS-232 or EIA-232, etc.
- 3.2 IO Address and IRQ
- 3.3 Names: ttyS0, ttyS1, etc.
- 3.4 Interrupts
- 3.5 Data Flow (Speeds)
- 3.6 Flow Control
  - 3.6.1 Example of Flow Control
  - 3.6.2 Symptoms of No Flow Control
  - 3.6.3 Hardware vs. Software Flow Control
- 3.7 Data Flow Path; Buffers
- 3.8 Complex Flow Control Example
- 3.9 Serial Software: Device Driver Module

4. Is the Serial Port Obsolete?
- 4.1 Introduction
- 4.2 EIA-232 Cable Is Low Speed and Short Distance
- 4.3 Inefficient Interface to the Computer

5. Multiport Serial Boards/Cards/Adapters
- 5.1 Intro to Multiport Serial
- 5.2 Making "devices" in the /dev directory
- 5.3 Standard PC Serial Boards
- 5.4 Dumb Multiport Serial Boards (with 8250/16450/16550A UART's)
- 5.5 Intelligent Multiport Serial Boards

6. Configuring the Serial Port
- 6.1 Configuring Overview
- 6.2 Common mistakes made re low-level configuring
- 6.3 I/O Address and IRQ: Boot-time messages

A

6.4 What is the current IO address and IRQ of my Serial Port?
6.4.1 What does the device driver think?
6.4.2 What is set in my serial port hardware?
6.4.3 What is set in my PnP serial port hardware?
6.5 Choosing Serial IRQs
6.5.1 IRQ 0 is not an IRQ
6.5.2 Interrupt sharing and Kernels 2.2+
6.5.3 What IRQs to choose?
6.6 Choosing Addresses—Video card conflict with ttyS3
6.7 Set IO Address and IRQ in the hardware (mostly for PnP)
6.7.1 Using a PnP BIOS to I0-IRQ Configure
6.8 Giving the IRQ and IO Address to Setserial
6.9 High-level Configuring: stty, etc.
6.9.1 Configuring Flow Control: Hardware Flow Control is Best
7. Serial Port Devices /dev/ttyS2, etc.
7.1 Serial Port Device Names and Numbers
7.2 Link ttySN to /dev/modem?
7.3 Notes For Multiport Boards
7.4 Creating Devices In the /dev directory
8. Interesting Programs You Should Know About
8.1 Serial Monitoring/Diagnostics Programs
8.2 Changing Interrupt Priority
8.3 What is Setserial?
8.3.1 Introduction
8.3.2 Probing
8.3.3 Can Linux Configure the Serial Devices Automatically?
8.3.4 Boot-time Configuration
8.3.4.1 New configuration method using /etc/serial.conf
8.3.4.2 Old configuration method: edit a script
8.3.5 IRQs
8.3.6 Where to Run Setserial?
8.3.6.1 Prior to version 2.15
8.3.6.2 Version 2.15 and later
8.4 Stty
8.4.1 Introduction
8.4.2 Using stty for another port
8.4.3 Two interfaces at a terminal
8.4.4 Where to put the stty command?
8.5 What is isapnp?
9. Speed (Flow Rate)
9.1 Can't Set a High Enough Speed

9.1.1 How speed is set in hardware: the divisor and baud_base
9.1.2 Work-arounds for setting speed
9.1.3 Crystal frequency is not baud_base
9.2 Higher Serial Throughput
10. Communications Programs and Utilities
10.1 List of Software
10.2 kermit and zmodem
11. Serial Tips and Miscellany
11.1 Line Drivers
11.2 Known Defective Hardware
11.2.1 Avoiding IO Address Conflicts with Certain Video Boards
11.2.2 Problem with AMD Elan SC400 CPU (PC-on-a-chip)
11.3 What Are Lock Files?
12. Troubleshooting
12.1 Serial Electrical Test Equipment
12.1.1 Breakout Gadgets, etc.
12.1.2 Measuring Voltages
12.1.3 Taste Voltage
12.2 Serial Monitoring/Diagnostics
12.3 The following subsections are in both the Serial and Modem HOWTOs:
12.4 My Serial Port is Physically There but Can't be Found
12.5 Slow: Text appears on the screen slowly after long delays
12.6 The Startup Screen Show Wrong IRQs for the Serial Ports.
12.7 "Cannot open /dev/ttyS?: Permission denied"
12.8 "Operation not supported by device" (error message) for ttySx
12.9 "Cannot create lockfile. Sorry" (error message)
12.10 Software which may help
13. Interrupt Problem Details
13.1 Symptoms of Mis-set or Conflicting Interrupts
13.2 Mis-set Interrupts
13.3 Interrupt Conflicts
13.4 Resolving Interrupt Problems
14. What Are UARTs? How Do They Affect Performance?
14.1 Introduction to UARTS
14.2 Two Types of UARTs
14.3 FIFOs
14.4 UART Model Numbers
15. Pinout and Signals
15.1 Pinout

A

15.2 Signals May Have No Fixed Meaning
15.3 Cabling Between Serial Ports
15.4 RTS/CTS and DTR/DSR Flow Control
15.4.1 The DTR and DSR Pins
15.5 Preventing a Port From Opening
16. Voltage Waveshapes
16.1 Voltage for a Bit
16.2 Voltage Sequence for a Byte
16.3 Parity Explained
16.4 Forming a Byte (Framing)
16.5 How "Asynchronous" is Synchronized
17. Other Serial Devices (not async EIA-232)
17.1 Successors to EIA-232
17.2 EIA-422-A (balanced) and EIA-423-A (unbalanced)
17.3 EIA-485
17.4 EIA-530
17.5 EIA-612/613
17.6 The Universal Serial Bus (USB)
17.7 Synchronization and Synchronous
17.7.1 Defining Asynchronous versus Synchronous
17.7.2 Synchronous Communication
18. Other Sources of Information
18.1 Books
18.2 Serial Software
18.3 Linux Documents
18.4 Usenet newsgroups
18.5 Serial Mailing List
18.6 Internet

Linux Shadow Password HOWTO

Michael H. Jackson, mhjack@tscnet.com

v 1.3, April 1996

This HOWTO describes how to obtain, install, and configure the Linux password Shadow Suite. It also discusses obtaining, and reinstalling other software and network daemons that require access to user passwords.

1. Introduction
1.1 Changes from the previous release
1.2 New versions of this document
1.3 Feedback

2. Why shadow your passwd file?
    2.1 Why you might NOT want to shadow your passwd file
    2.2 Format of the /etc/passwd file
    2.3 Format of the shadow file
    2.4 Review of crypt(3)
3. Getting the Shadow Suite
    3.1 History of the Shadow Suite for Linux
    3.2 Where to get the Shadow Suite
    3.3 What is included with the Shadow Suite?
4. Compiling the programs
    4.1 Unpacking the archive
    4.2 Configuring with the config.h file
    4.3 Making backup copies of your original programs
    4.4 Running make
5. Installing
    5.1 Have a boot disk handy in case you break anything
    5.2 Removing duplicate man pages
    5.3 Running make install
    5.4 Running pwconv
    5.5 Renaming npasswd and nshadow
6. Other programs you may need to upgrade or patch
    6.1 Slackware adduser program
    6.2 The wu_ftpd Server
    6.3 Standard ftpd
    6.4 pop3d (Post Office Protocol 3)
    6.5 xlock
    6.6 xdm
    6.7 sudo
    6.8 imapd (E-Mail pine package])
    6.9 pppd (Point-to-Point Protocol Server)
7. Putting the Shadow Suite to use.
    7.1 Adding, Modifying, and deleting users
    7.2 The passwd command and passwd aging
    7.3 The login.defs file
    7.4 Group passwords
    7.5 Consistency checking programs
    7.6 Dial-up passwords
8. Adding shadow support to a C program
    8.1 Header files
    8.2 libshadow.a library
    8.3 Shadow Structure
    8.4 Shadow Functions
    8.5 Example

9. Frequently Asked Questions
10. Copyright Message
11. Miscellaneous and Acknowledgments

SMB HOWTO

David Wood, dwood@plugged.net.au

v 1.1.1, June 1999

This HOWTO describes how to use the Server Message Block (SMB) protocol, also called the Session Message Block, NetBIOS or LanManager protocol, with Linux. It is also known as Samba.

1. Introduction
2. Further Information
3. Installation
4. Running the Daemons
5. General Configuration (/etc/smb.conf)
6. Sharing A Linux Drive with Windows Machines
7. Sharing A Windows Drive with Linux Machines
8. Sharing A Linux Printer with Windows Machines
9. Sharing A Windows Printer with Linux Machines
10. Backing Up Windows Machines to a Linux Host
11. Copyright
12. Acknowledgements

Building and Installing Software Packages for Linux

Mendel Cooper, <mailto:thegrendel@theriver.com>

v 1.91, July 1999

This HOWTO is a comprehensive guide to building and installing "generic" UNIX software distributions under Linux. Additionally, there is some coverage of "rpm" and "deb" pre-packaged binaries.

1. Introduction
2. Unpacking the Files
3. Using Make
4. Prepackaged Binaries
    4.1 Whats wrong with rpms?
    4.2 Problems with rpms: an example
5. Termcap and Terminfo Issues
6. Backward Compatibility With a.out Binaries
    6.1 An Example

7. Troubleshooting
    7.1 Link Errors
    7.2 Other Problems
    7.3 Tweaking and fine tuning
    7.4 Where to go for more help
8. Final Steps
9. First Example: Xscrabble
10. Second Example: Xloadimage
11. Third Example: Fortune
12. Fourth Example: Hearts
13. Fifth Example: XmDipmon
14. Where to Find Source Archives
15. Final Words
16. References and Further Reading
17. Credits

The Linux Sound HOWTO

Jeff Tranter, tranter@pobox.com

v 1.20, March 1999

This HOWTO describes sound support for Linux. It lists the supported sound hardware, describes how to configure the kernel drivers, and answers frequently asked questions.

1. Introduction
    1.1 Acknowledgments
    1.2 New versions of this document
    1.3 Feedback
    1.4 Distribution Policy
2. Sound Card Technology
3. Supported Hardware
    3.1 Sound Cards
    3.2 Alternate Sound Drivers
    3.3 PC Speaker
    3.4 Parallel Port
4. Installation
    4.1 Installing the Sound Card
    4.2 Configuring Plug and Play
    4.3 Configuring the Kernel
    4.4 Creating the Device Files
    4.5 Booting Linux and Testing the Installation
    4.6 Troubleshooting

A

        4.6.1 Step 1: Make sure you are really running the kernel you compiled
        4.6.2 Step 2: Make sure the kernel sound drivers are compiled in
        4.6.3 Step 3: Did the kernel detect your sound card during booting?
        4.6.4 Step 4: Can you read data from the dsp device?
        4.6.5 When All Else Fails

5. Applications Supporting Sound

6. Answers To Frequently Asked Questions
    6.1 What are the various sound device files?
    6.2 How can I play a sound sample?
    6.3 How can I record a sample?
    6.4 Can I have more than one sound card?
    6.5 Error: No such file or directory for sound devices
    6.6 Error: No such device for sound devices
    6.7 Error: No space left on device for sound devices
    6.8 Error: Device busy for sound devices
    6.9 I still get device busy errors!
    6.10 Partial playback of digitized sound file
    6.11 There are pauses when playing MOD files
    6.12 Compile errors when compiling sound applications
    6.13 SEGV when running sound binaries that worked previously
    6.14 What known bugs or limitations are there in the sound driver?
    6.15 Where are the sound driver ioctls() etc. documented?
    6.16 What CPU resources are needed to play or record without pauses?
    6.17 Problems with a PAS16 and an Adaptec 1542 SCSI host adapter
    6.18 Is it possible to read and write samples simultaneously?
    6.19 My SB16 is set to IRQ 2, but configure does not allow this value
    6.20 If I run Linux, then boot DOS, I get errors and/or sound applications do not work properly
    6.21 Problems running DOOM under Linux
    6.22 How can I reduce noise picked up by my sound card?
    6.23 I can play sounds, but not record
    6.24 My “compatible” sound card only works if I first initialize under MS-DOS
    6.25 My 16-bit SoundBlaster “compatible” sound card only works in 8-bit mode under Linux
    6.26 Where can I find sound applications for Linux?

6.27 Can the sound driver be compiled as a loadable module?
6.28 Can I use a sound card to replace the system console beep?
6.29 What is VoxWare?
6.30 Sox/Play/Vplay reports "invalid block size 1024"
6.31 The mixer settings are reset whenever I load the sound driver module
6.32 Only user root can record sound
6.33 Is the sound hardware on the IBM ThinkPad supported?
6.34 Applications fail because my sound card has no mixer
6.35 Problems with a SB16 CT4170
6.36 How to connect a MIDI keyboard to a soundcard
6.37 Problems with IRQ 15 and Ensoniq PCI 128
6.38 Where can I get freely available MIDI patches to run SoftOSS?
7. References

The Linux UUCP HOWTO

Guylhem Aznar, <guylhem@oeil.qc.ca>

v 2.0, 6 February 1998

This HOWTO describes the setup and maintenance of UUCP under Linux.

1. Introduction, copyright and standard disclaimer
1.1 Email and spamming
1.2 Goals
1.3 New versions
1.4 Feedback
1.5 Copyright
1.6 Limited warranty
2. Other sources of information
2.1 USENET
2.2 Mailing Lists
2.3 Other documents from LDP
2.4 Books
3. Requirements
3.1 Hardware
3.2 Software
4. Setting up the config files
4.1 Installing config files
4.2 "Poll" file
4.3 "call" file

A

4.4 "config" file
4.5 "crontab" file
4.6 "dial" file
4.7 "passwd" file
4.8 "port" file
4.9 "sys" file
4.10 Now let's test all this
4.11 Additional information
5. It doesn't work - now what?
6. Frequently Asked Questions about Linux UUCP
6.1 Why is all the info here for UUCPs configured in "Taylor" rather than "HDB" mode?
6.2 Why do I get "timeout" on connections when I upgraded to uucp-1.04?
6.3 Why doesn't HDB anonymous UUCP seem to work?
6.4 What does "no matching ports found" mean?
6.5 What are known good config files for HDB mode?
6.6 Getting uucico to call alternate numbers
7. Acknowledgements

Virtual Services HOWTO

Brian Ackerman, brian@nycrc.net

v 2.1, August 1998

This HOWTO describes how to create a virtual service.

1. Introduction
1.1 Knowledge Required
1.2 Purpose
1.3 Feedback
1.4 Revision History
1.5 Copyright/Distribution
2. IP Aliasing
3. Virtuald
3.1 Introduction
3.2 Inetd
3.3 Config File
3.4 Source
4. Shell Scripts
4.1 Virtfs
4.2 Virtexec
4.3 Notes

5. DNS
6. Syslogd
  6.1 Problem
  6.2 Solution
    6.2.1 Setup Links
    6.2.2 Syslogd.init
  6.3 Multiple Syslogd's
    6.3.1 One Per Disk
    6.3.2 One Per Domain
7. Virtual FTP
  7.1 Inetd
  7.2 Anonymous FTP
  7.3 Virtual FTP Users
8. Virtual Web
  8.1 Running With Virtuald
    8.1.1 Not recommended
    8.1.2 Inetd
    8.1.3 Httpd.conf
    8.1.4 Configuration
    8.1.5 Httpd.init
  8.2 Running With Apache VirtualHost
    8.2.1 Access.conf
    8.2.2 Httpd.conf
    8.2.3 Srm.conf
    8.2.4 Httpd.init
  8.3 File Descriptor Overflow
    8.3.1 Warning
    8.3.2 Multiple Apache Servers
  8.4 Sharing Servers with One IP
    8.4.1 Saving IPs
    8.4.2 Drawback
  8.5 More Information
9. Virtual Mail/Pop
  9.1 Problem
  9.2 Solution
  9.3 Sendmail Solution
    9.3.1 Introduction
    9.3.2 Create Sendmail Configuration File
    9.3.3 Edit Sendmail Configuration File
    9.3.4 Sendmail Local Delivery
    9.3.5 Sendmail between Virtual Domains: The Hack (PRE8.8.6)

9.3.6 Sendmail between Virtual Domains: New Sendmail Feature (POST8.8.6)
9.3.7 Sendmail.init
9.3.8 Inetd Setup
9.4 Qmail Solution
9.4.1 Introduction
9.4.2 Setup Virtual Domains
9.4.3 Setup Domain Master User
9.4.4 Tcpserver
9.4.5 Qmail.init
9.4.6 Source
9.4.7 Source
9.5 Acknowledgement
10. Virtual Samba
10.1 Setup
10.2 Inetd
10.3 Smb.init
11. Virtual Other
12. Conclusion
13. FAQ

Linux VPN Masquerade HOWTO

John D. Hardin, <jhardin@wolfenet.com>

v 2.2, September 1999

This HOWTO describes how to configure a Linux firewall to masquerade IP addresses and PPTP-based Virtual Private Network traffic. In addition, information on configuring the VPN client and server is given.

1. Introduction
1.1 Introduction
1.2 Feedback, Credits and Resources
1.3 Copyright and Disclaimer
2. Background Knowledge
2.1 What is a VPN?
2.2 What is IPsec?
2.3 What is PPTP?
2.4 Why masquerade a VPN client?
2.5 Can several clients on my local network use IPsec simultaneously?
2.6 Can several clients on my local network use PPTP simultaneously?

- 2.7 Can I access the remote network from my entire local network?
- 2.8 Why masquerade the VPN server?
- 2.9 Why patch the Linux kernel?
- 2.10 Current Status

3. Configuring the Linux firewall
   - 3.1 Example network
   - 3.2 Determining what needs to be done on the firewall
   - 3.3 Patching and configuring the 2.0.x kernel for VPN Masquerade support
   - 3.4 Patching and configuring the 2.2.x kernel for VPN Masquerade support
   - 3.5 ipfwadm setup for a Private-IP VPN Client or Server
   - 3.6 ipchains setup for a Private-IP VPN Client or Server
   - 3.7 A note about dynamic IP addressing
   - 3.8 Additional setup for a Private-IP VPN Server
   - 3.9 ipfwadm setup for a Registered-IP VPN Server
   - 3.10 ipfwadm setup for a Registered-IP VPN Client
4. Configuring the VPN client
   - 4.1 Configuring a MS W'95 or W'98 client
   - 4.2 Configuring a MS NT client
5. Troubleshooting
   - 5.1 Testing
   - 5.2 Possible problems
   - 5.3 Troubleshooting
   - 5.4 MS PPTP Clients and domain-name issues
   - 5.5 MS PPTP Clients and Novell IPX
   - 5.6 MS network password issues
   - 5.7 If your IPsec session always dies after a certain amount of time
6. IPsec masquerade technical notes and special security considerations
   - 6.1 Limitations and weaknesses of IPsec masquerade
   - 6.2 Proper routing of inbound encrypted traffic

Linux WWW HOWTO

Mr. Poet, poet@linuxports.com

v 0.85, August 1999

This HOWTO contains information about setting up WWW services under Linux (both server and client).

1. Introduction
   - 1.1 Copyright

A

- 1.2 Feedback
- 1.3 New versions of this Document
2. Setting up WWW client software (Antiquated)
    - 2.1 Overview
3. Lynx
    - 3.1 Where to get
4. Emacs-W3
    - 4.1 Where to get
5. Netscape Navigator/Communicator
    - 5.1 Different versions and options
    - 5.2 Where to get
    - 5.3 Installing
6. Setting up WWW server systems
    - 6.1 Overview
7. Apache
    - 7.1 Where to get
    - 7.2 Compiling and Installing
    - 7.3 Configuring
    - 7.4 Hosting virtual Web sites
        - 7.4.1 IP based virtual hosting
        - 7.4.2 Shared IP virtual hosting
    - 7.5 CGI scripts
    - 7.6 Users Web Directories
    - 7.7 Daemon mode vs. inetd mode
    - 7.8 Allowing put and delete commands
    - 7.9 User Authentication/Access Control
    - 7.10 su-exec
    - 7.11 Imagemaps
    - 7.12 SSI/XSSI
    - 7.13 Module system
8. Web Server Add-ons
9. Intranet Section
    - 9.1 What is required?
    - 9.2 New versions of this document
    - 9.3 Feedback
10. Install the HTTP server
    - 10.1 Preparation before downloading
        - 10.1.1 The Operating System
        - 10.1.2 Process type (ServerType)
        - 10.1.3 Binding Port (Port)
        - 10.1.4 Server user identity (User)
        - 10.1.5 Server group identity (Group)
        - 10.1.6 Server administrator email address (ServerAdmin)

10.1.7 Location of server directory (ServerRoot)
10.1.8 Location of HTML files (DocumentRoot)
10.2 Compiling HTTPd
11. Testing HTTPd
12. Connecting to the Linux Server
12.1 Setup the Linux server
12.2 Setup the Netware server
12.3 Setup the Netware Client
12.3.1 Windows 3.x
12.3.2 Windows 95
12.4 Setup Microsoft Client
12.4.1 Windows for Workgroups
12.4.2 Windows 95
12.4.3 Windows NT
12.5 Setup TCP/IP on Macintosh
12.5.1 MacTCP
13. Setting up the Intranet
13.1 NCPFS
13.1.1 Installation
13.1.2 Mounting NCPFS
13.2 SMBFS
13.2.1 Installation
13.2.2 Mounting SMBFS
13.3 NFS
14. Accessing the Web
14.1 Accessing the mounted filesystems
14.2 Connecting to the Internet
14.3 Other uses
15. More things to do
16. Credits and Legalities
16.1 Thanks
16.2 Copyright information
17. For further reading
17.1 O'Reilly and Associates Books
17.2 Internet Request For Comments (RFC)

The X Window User HOWTO

Ray Brigleb, ray@aracnet.com

v 2.0, September 1999

A

This HOWTO contains information on configuring the X Window environment for the Linux user, as well as for the beginning system administrator attempting to sort through the many configuration options and details of X Window.

1. Introduction
   1.1 Other Sources of Information
   1.2 Versions of This Document
   1.3 Feedback and Corrections
   1.4 Acknowledgments
   1.5 Copyright
2. Getting Started
   2.1 The X Window System: History and Architecture
   2.2 Anatomy of Your Desktop
   2.3 Invoking X Window
   2.4 The X Display Manager
3. Choosing a Window Manager
   3.1 FVWM and Its Ancestors
   3.2 The Wide World of Window Systems
   3.3 The X Graphical Interfaces
   3.4 The X Desktop Environments
   3.5 The Flashy Window Managers
4. Working In X
   4.1 Command Line Options
   4.2 Display Names
   4.3 XTerm versus Rxvt, or, Know Thy Terminal Emulator
5. X Startup
   5.1 A Sample Starting Configuration
   5.2 A More Intelligent Startup
   5.3 Getting the Windows Where You Want Them
6. Configuring the Window Manager
   6.1 Basic FVWM2 Configuration
   6.2 Advanced FVWM2 Configuration
   6.3 FVWM2 Configuration Shortcuts
   6.4 FVWM2 Themes
7. Fonts and Colors
   7.1 Fonts Demystified
   7.2 Font Aliases and Configuration
   7.3 Using Type 1 Fonts in X
   7.4 Using TrueType Fonts in X
   7.5 Colors
8. The X Resources
   8.1 X Resources: The Basics
   8.2 Inside The X Resource Database With

- 8.3 The Anatomy of X Resources
- 8.4 Making Your Changes Last With
- 8.5 Your Own User Resource Directory

9. Clients and Application Tips
   - 9.1 Screen Savers for X
   - 9.2 Emacs and XEmacs
   - 9.3 Some Useful Programs and Tricks
10. Advanced X Usage
    - 10.1 Libraries and Compiling X Applications
    - 10.2 Basic X Security
    - 10.3 More About X Authority
11. Bibliography and Other Resources

Appendix B

Listing of Man Pages for Networking Administration and Maintenance

This appendix is primarily for the person who is a day-to-day system administrator. However, a user who has a workstation and has to act on occasion as system administrator may also find this appendix useful. The appendix lists some 400 commands, users, functions, and files with highly abbreviated descriptions that relate to networking. These man pages may be available.

Red Hat Linux divides the man pages into ten sections. The sections are:

1	User commands
2	System calls
3	Functions and library routines
4	Special files, device drivers, and hardware
5	Configuration files and file formats
6	Games and demos
7	Miscellaneous
8	System administration and maintenance commands
9	Kernel internals
n	Tcl/Tk commands

A

abort (3)	Terminate the process abnormally
accept (2)	Accept a connection on a socket
access (2)	Check user's file permissions
acct (2)	Switch process accounting on or off
addmntent (3)	Add filesystem description file entry
alarm (2)	Set a process alarm clock in seconds
alloca (3)	Allocate size bytes of space
answer (1)	Phone message transcription system on Elm

appres (1)	List X application resource database
ar (1)	Maintain portable archive on library
arch (1)	Display the current host's architecture
assert (3)	Verify program assertion
at (1)	Batch jobs for later execution
atq (1)	List queued jobs to run at a specifc time
atrm (1)	Delete spooled jobs
atrun (8)	Run queued jobs

B

badblocks (8)	Search a device for bad blocks
batch (1)	Execute commands when the system permits
bdflush (8)	Kernel daemon to flush dirty buffers back to disk
bind (2)	Bind a name to a socket
brk (2)	Change data segment size

C

cacheflush (2)	Flush contents of instruction or data cache
calloc (3)	Allocate space for an array
catclose (3)	Close a message catalog
catgets (3)	Get message from a message catalog
catopen (3)	Open a message catalog
cfgetispeed (2)	Get input baud rate
cfgetospeed (2)	Get output baud rate
cfsetispeed (2)	Set input baud rate
cfsetospeed (2)	Set output baud rate
chat (8)	Automated conversational script with a modem
chattr (1)	Change file attributes on a Linux second extended filesystem
chdir (2)	Change working directory
chgrp (1)	Change the group ownership of files
chmod (1)	Change the file access permissions
chmod (2)	Change file permissions
chown (1)	Change the user and group ownership of files
chown (2)	Change ownership of a file
chroot (2)	Change root directory
chroot (8)	Change root directory and execute a program there
chsh (1)	Change your login shell
clearerr (3)	Clear end-of-file and error indicators
clock (1)	Display the time in an icon or window
clock (3)	Determine processor time
clock (8)	Manipulate the CMOS clock
closelog (3)	Close the descriptor to the system logger

confstr (3)	Get configuration dependent string variables
connect (2)	Initiate a connection on a socket
console (4)	Console terminal and virtual consoles
crypt (3)	Password and data encryption
csplit (1)	Split a file into sections determined by context lines
ctermid (3)	Get controlling terminal name
ctrlaltdel (8)	Set the function of the Ctrl-Alt-Del combination

D

date (1)	Print and set date and time
depmod (1)	Handle loadable modules automatically
df (1)	Report filesystem disk space usage
dialog (1)	Display dialog boxes from shell scripts
dig (1)	Send domain name query packets to name servers
dirname (1)	Strip non-directory suffix from filename
dmesg (8)	Print or control the kernel ring buffer
dnsdomainname (1)	Display the system's DNS domain name
dnsquery (1)	Query domain name servers using resolver
dos (1)	Invoke the Linux DOS emulator
dumpkeys (1)	Dump keyboard translation tables
dup (2)	Duplicate a file descriptor

E

echo (1)	Display a line of text
elm (1)	Interactive mail system
elmalias (1)	Expand and display Elm address aliases
emacs (1)	GNU project Emacs
endgrent (3)	Close group file entry
endhostent (3)	Close network host entry
endmntent (3)	Close filesystem description file entry
endnetent (3)	Close network entry
endprotoent (3)	Close protocol entry
endpwent (3)	Close /etc/passwd file
endservent (3)	Close service entry
endusershell (3)	Close legal user shells

F

fchmod (2)	Change permissions of a file
fchown (2)	Change ownership of a file
fclose (3)	Close a stream
fdisk (8)	Partition table manipulator for Linux

feof (3)	Test stream status on detecting an EOF error
ferror (3)	Test the error indicator
fflush (3)	Flush a stream
fgetgrent (3)	Get group file entry
fgetpwent (3)	Get password file entry
fileno (3)	Examine the argument stream
formail (1)	Mail (re)formatter
form_cursor (3)	Position a form window cursor
form_driver (3)	Command-processing loop of the form system
form_field (3)	Make and break connections between fields and forms
form_field_	Color and attribute control for form fields attributes (3)
form_field_buffer (3)	Field buffer control
form_field_info (3)	Retrieve field characteristics
free (1)	Free the memory space

G

getdomainname (2)	Get domain name
getegid (2)	Get group identity
getenv (3)	Get an environment variable
geteuid (2)	Get user identity
getgid (2)	Get group identity
getgrent (3)	Get group file entry
getgrgid (3)	Get group file entry ID
getgrnam (3)	Get group file entry name
getgroups (2)	Get list of supplementary group IDs
gethostbyaddr (3)	Get network host's address
gethostbyname (3)	Get network host's name
gethostid (2)	Get the unique identifier of the current host
gethostname (2)	Get host name
getitimer (2)	Get value of an interval timer
getmntent (3)	Read next line of the filesystem descriptor file entry
getopt (1)	Parse command options
getopt (3)	Read command line options
getpagesize (2)	Get system page size
getpass (3)	Get a password
getpeername (1)	Get name of connected peer
getpgrp (2)	Get process group
getpid (2)	Get process identification
getppid (2)	Get parent process identification
getpriority (2)	Get program scheduling priority
getprotobyname (3)	Get protocol's name
getprotobynumber (3)	Get protocol's number
getprotoent (3)	Get protocol entry

getpwent (3)	Get password file entry from /etc/passwd
getpwnam (3)	Get password file entry with specified login name
getpwuid (3)	Get user's password ID
getrlimit (2)	Get resource limits
getrusage (2)	Get resource usage
getservbyname (3)	Get service name
getservbyport (3)	Get service port
getservent (3)	Get service entry
getsockname (2)	Get socket name
getsockopt (2)	Get options on sockets
gettimeofday (2)	Get time of day
getty (1)	Set terminal mode, speed, and line discipline
gettydefs (5)	Speed and tty settings used by getty
getusershell (3)	Get next line from /etc/shells file
gpm (1)	Cut and paste utility and mouse server for virtual consoles
groups (1)	Print the groups a user is in

H

halt (8)	Stop the system
hcreate (3)	Create hash table
hd (4)	MFM/IDE hard disk device
hdestroy (3)	Destroy hash table
hdparm (8)	Get or set hard disk parameters
herror (3)	Get network host entry
hexdump (1)	ASCII, decimal, hexadecimal, octal dump
hostname (1)	Show or set the system's host name
hosts_access (3)	Access control tables
hosts_access (5)	Format of host access control files
hosts_options (5)	Host access control language extensions
hsearch (3)	Search hash table
htonl (3)	Convert long integers between host and network byte order
htons (3)	Convert short integers between host and network byte order

I

id (1)	Print real and effective UIDs and GIDs
ident (1)	Identify RCS keyword strings in files
ifconfig (8)	Configure a network interface
indxbib (1)	Make inverted index for bibliographic databases
inetd (8)	Internet "super-server"
inet_atm (3)	Store converted Internet address

inet_addr (3)	Convert numbers-and-dots Internet address into binary data
inet_lnaof (3)	Return local host address part of Internet address
inet_makeaddr (3)	Make an Internet address into network byte order
inet_network (3)	Extract the network number in host byte order
inet_ntoa (3)	Convert network byte order into a string
info (1)	Return info about state of Tcl interpreter
init (8)	Process control initialization
initgroups (3)	Initialize the supplementary group access list
initscript (5)	Script that executes inittab commands
init_module (2)	Initialize loadable module support
insmod (1)	Install loadable modules (aout and Elf format)
install (1)	Copy files and set their attributes
intro (1)	Introduction to user commands
intro (2)	Introduction to system calls
intro (3)	Introduction to library functions
intro (4)	Introduction to special files
intro (5)	Introduction to file formats
intro (7)	Introduction to miscellany section
intro (8)	Introduction to administration and privileged commands
ioctl (2)	Control device
ioperm (2)	Set port input or output permissions
iopl (2)	Change input and output privilege level
ipc (5)	System V interprocess communication calls
ipcs (8)	Provide information on ipc facilities
ipfw (4)	IP firewall and accounting administration
ipfw (8)	Controlling utility for ipfw/ipacct facilities
iso_8859_1 (7)	Map of character set

J

jpegtran (1)	Lossless transcoding of JPEG files

K

kerneld (8)	Perform kernel action in user space
kill (1)	Terminate a process
kill (2)	Send signal to a process
killall (1)	Kill processes by name
killall5 (8)	Send a signal to all processes
killpg (2)	Kill a process group
killpg (3)	Send signal to all members of a process group
klogd (8)	Kernel log daemon
kmem (4)	Access kernel memory
ksyms (1)	Display the exported kernel symbols

L

lchown (2)	Change ownership of a file
ldconfig (8)	Determine runtime link bindings
ldd (1)	Print shared library dependencies
lilo (8)	Install boot loader
listalias (1)	List user and system aliases
listen (2)	Listen for connections on a socket
listres (1)	List resources in widgets
lkbib (1)	Search bibliographic databases
loadkeys (1)	Load keyboard translation tables
locate (1)	List files in databases that match a pattern
logger (1)	Make entries in the system log
lookbib (1)	Search bibliographic databases
losetup (8)	Set up and control loop devices
lsmod (1)	List loaded modules

M

mailcap (4)	Metamail capabilities file
mailto (1)	Simple multimedia mail sending program
make (1)	GNU make utility to maintain groups of programs
makemap (8)	Create database maps for sendmail
malloc (3)	Point to smallest block of bytes for allocation
mem (4)	Access system memory
menu_hook (3)	Set hooks for automatic invocation by applications
menu_items (3)	Make and break connections between items and menus
menu_mark (3)	Get and set the menu mark string
menu_new (3)	Create and destroy menus
menu_opts (3)	Set and get menu options
menu_pattern (3)	Get and set a menu's pattern buffer
menu_post (3)	Write or erase menus from associated subwindows
menu_userptr (3)	Associate application data with a menu item
menu_win (3)	Make and break menu window and subwindow associations
messages (1)	Quick count of messages in mailbox or folder
metamail (1)	Infrastructure for mailcap-based multimedia mail handling
minicom (1)	Serial communication program
mkfs (8)	Build a Linux filesystem
mkswap (8)	Set up a Linux swap device
mktemp (3)	Make a unique temporary filename
mmap (2)	Map files or devices into memory
motd (5)	Message of the day

msgctl (2)	Message control operations
msgget (2)	Get a message queue identifier
msgop (2)	Message operations
munmap (2)	Unmap files or devices from memory

N

namei (1)	Follow a pathname until a terminal point is found
netstat (8)	Display active network connections
newalias (1)	Install new elm aliases for user or system
nice (1)	Run a program with modified scheduling priority
nice (2)	Change process priority
nodename (1)	Show or set the system's DECnet node name
nohup (1)	Run a command immune to hangups, with output to a non-tty
nologin (5)	Prevent usual users from logging into the system
ntonl (3)	Convert long integer between network and host byte order
ntons (3)	Convert short integer between network and host byte order

O

openlog (3)	Open a connection to the system logger

P

passwd (5)	Update a user's authentication
pooltype (1)	Display a Web pool file
popen (3)	Open a process
port (4)	Access system ports
poweroff (8)	Stop the system
pppd (8)	Point-to-Point Protocol daemon
printcap (5)	Printer capability database
printenv (1)	Print all or part of environment
procmail (1)	Autonomous mail processor
procmailex (5)	Procmail rcfile examples
procmailrc (5)	Procmail rcfile
procmailsc (5)	Procmail weighted scoring technique
pstree (1)	Display a tree of processes
ptrace (2)	Process trace

Q

qsort (3)	Sort an array
quota (1)	Display disk usage and limits
quotacheck (8)	Scan a filesystem for disk usages
quotaon (8)	Turn filesystem quotas on
quotaoff (8)	Turn filesystem quotas off

R

ranlib (1)	Generate index to archive
rarp (8)	Manipulate the system RARP table
rcsintro (1)	Introduction to RCS commands
readprofile (1)	Tool to read kernel profiling information
readv (3)	Read data into multiple buffers
realloc (3)	Return a pointer to newly allocated memory
realpath (3)	Returns the canonical absolute pathname
reboot (8)	Stop the system
recv (2)	Receive a message from a connected socket
recvfrom (2)	Receive a message from a socket
recvmsg (2)	Receive a message from a socket
renice (8)	Alter priority of running processes
repquota (8)	Summarize quotas for a filesystem
request_init (3)	Intialize a structure with information about a client request
rewind (3)	Set file position indicator to beginning of file
rewinddir (3)	Reset directory stream
rexecd (8)	Remote execution server
route (8)	Show or manipulate the IP routing table
routed (8)	Network routing daemon
rquota (3)	Implement quotas on remote machines
rquotad (8)	Remote quota server
rsh (1)	Remote shell
runlevel (8)	Find the current and previous system runlevel
runscript (1)	Script interpreter for minicom
ruptime (1)	Show host status of local machines
rusers (1)	Who is logged in to machines on local network
rwho (1)	Who is logged in on local machines
rwhod (8)	System status server

S

securetty (5)	File that lists ttys from which root can log in
send (2)	Send a message from a connected socket
sendmail (8)	Mail transport agent

sendmsg (2)	Send a message from a socket
sendto (2)	Send a message to a socket
setdomainname (2)	Set domain name
setegid (2)	Set effective group ID
setenv (3)	Set an environment variable
seteuid (2)	Set effective user ID
setfsgid (2)	Set group identity used for filesystem checks
setfsuid (2)	Set user identity used for filesystem checks
setgid (2)	Set group identity
setgrent (3)	Set group file entry
setgroups (2)	Set list of supplementary group IDs
sethostent (3)	Set network host entry
sethostid (2)	Set the unique identifier of the current host
sethostname (2)	Set host name
setlocale (3)	Set the current locale
setmetamode (1)	Set the keyboard meta key handling
setmntent (3)	Open filesystem description file entry
setnetent (3)	Set network entry
setpgid (2)	Set process group ID
setpgrp (2)	Set process group
setpriority (2)	Set program scheduling priority
setprotoent (3)	Set protocol entry
setpwent (3)	Set password file entry to beginning
setregid (2)	Set real group ID
setreuid (2)	Set real user ID
setrlimit (2)	Set resource limits
setrusage (2)	Set resource usage
setserial (8)	Set Linux serial port information
setservent (3)	Set /etc/services file to beginning
setsockopt (2)	Set options on sockets
setstate (3)	Change the state array used by the random number generator
setterm (1)	Set terminal attributes
settimeofday (2)	Set time of day
setuid (2)	Set user identity
setusershell (3)	Set /etc/shells file to beginning
setvbuf (3)	Stream buffering operations
shar (1)	Create shell archives
shmctl (2)	Shared memory control
shmget (2)	Allocate a shared memory segment
shmop (2)	Shared memory operations
shutdown (8)	Bring the system down
skill (1)	Signal specified processes
slattach (8)	Attach a network interface to a serial line
smproxy (1)	Session Manager Proxy
snice (1)	Reprioritize specified processes
sockdown (1)	Shutdown (2) a socket
socket (2)	Create an endpoint for communication

socketpair (2)	Create a pair of connected sockets
statfs (2)	Get filesystem statistics
stdio (3)	Standard input and output library functions
strace (1)	Trace system calls and signals
stty (1)	Change and print terminal line settings
su (1)	Run a shell with substitute user and group IDs
sysinfo (2)	Return information on overall system statistics
sysklogd (8)	Linux system logging utilities
syslog (3)	Generate messages to the system logger
system (3)	Execute a shell command

T

tcdrain (2)	Wait until all output has been transmitted
tcflow (2)	Suspend data flow
tcflush (2)	Discard data written
tcgetattr (2)	Get terminal attributes
tcgetpgrp (2)	Get process group ID
tcpd (8)	Access control facility for Internet services
tcpdchk (8)	Tcp wrapper configuration checker
tcpdmatch (8)	Tcp wrapper oracle
tcpdump (1)	Dump traffic on a network
tcsendbreak (2)	Send a continuous stream of zero-valued bits for a specific duration
tcsetattr (2)	Set terminal attributes
tcsetpgrp (2)	Set process group ID
telldir (3)	Return current location in directory stream
telnet (1)	User interface to the Telnet protocol
telnetd (8)	DARPA Telnet protocol server
termios (2)	Set terminal attributes
timed (8)	Time server daemon
timedc (8)	Timed control program
times (2)	Get process times
tin (1)	Usenet newsreader

U

uname (1)	Print system information
uname (2)	Get name and information about current kernel
uptime (1)	Tell how long the system has been running
users (1)	Print the user names of users currently logged in to the current host
ustat (2)	Get filesystem statistics
utmp (5)	Login records of current users

V

vhangup (2)	Virtually hangup the current tty
vmstat (8)	Report virtual memory statistics

W

w (1)	Show who is logged on and what they are doing
wall (1)	Write a message to users
whatis (1)	Search the whatis database for complete words
whereis (1)	Locate the binary, source, and manual page files for a command
which (1)	Show full path of commands
who (1)	Show who is logged on
whoami (1)	Print effective userid
writev (w)	Write data into multiple buffers

X

xdos (1)	Start DOSEMU in its own X window
x11perf (1)	X11 server performance test program
x11perfcomp (1)	X11 server performance comparison program
xauth (1)	X authority file utility
xtermdoc 91)	Bring up DOSEMU in an xterm

Y

ypdomainname (1)	Show or set the system's NIS/YP domain name

Z

zic (8)	Time zone compiler

Appendix C

Networking Request for Comments (RFCs)

A Request for Comments (RFC) is a document that defines aspects of protocols, management, and policies about the Internet. They were started for ARPANET, the original Internet, in 1969. An RFC is the first step in creating a new Internet standard. The steps are:

1. RFC Draft
2. Internet Draft (as many refinements as required)
3. Proposed Standard (as many refinements as required; at least two implementations)
4. Draft Standard (as many refinements as required; wide implementation)
5. Official Standard

There are many ways to get RFCs electronically. One way is http://www.rfc-editor.org/categories/rfc-standard.html

Note: RFCs are being revised all the time. A revision gets a new RFC number, not a version number.

There are four lists below: standards, proposed standards, draft standards, and other RFCs.

Standards

791	Internet Protocol (1981)
793	Transmission Control Protocol (1981)
821	Simple Mail Transfer Protocol (1982)
950	Internet Standard Subnetting Procedure (1985)
959	File Transfer Protocol (1985)
974	Mail routing and the domain system (1986)

1155	Structure and identification of management information for TCP/IP-based Internets (1990)
1157	Simple Network Management Protocol (SNMP) (1990)
1661	The Point-to-Point Protocol (PPP) (1994)
1869	SMTP Service Extensions (1995)
1870	SMTP Service Extension for Message Size Declaration (1995)
1957	Some Observations on Implementations of the Post Office Protocol (POP3) (1996)

Proposed Standards

1757	Remote Network Monitoring Management Information Base (1995)
1762	The PPP DECnet Phase IV Control Protocol (DNCP) (1995)
1771	A Border Gateway Protocol 4 (BGP-4) (1995)
1772	Application of the Border Gateway Protocol in the Internet (1995)
1777	Lightweight Directory Access Protocol (1995)
1957	Some Observations on Implementations of the Post Office Protocol (POP3) (1996)
2045	Multipurpose Internet Mail Extensions (MIME) Part One: Format of Internet Message Bodies (1996)
2046	Multipurpose Internet Mail Extensions (MIME) Part Two: Media Types (1996)
2047	MIME (Multipurpose Internet Mail Extensions) Part Three: Message Header Extensions for Non-ASCII Text (1996)
2048	Multipurpose Internet Mail Extension (MIME) Part Four: Registration Procedures (1996)
2049	Multipurpose Internet Mail Extensions (MIME) Part Five: Conformance Criteria and Examples (1996)

Draft Standards

977	Network News Transfer Protocol (1986)
1234	Tunneling IPX traffic through IP networks (1991)
1332	The PPP Internet Protocol Control Protocol (IPCP) (1992)
1349	Type of Service in the Internet Protocol Suite (1992)
1421	Privacy Enhancement for Internet Electronic Mail: Part I: Message Encryption and Authentication Procedures (1993)

1422	Privacy Enhancement for Internet Electronic Mail: Part II: Certificate-Based Key Management (1993)
1423	Privacy Enhancement for Internet Electronic Mail: Part III: Algorithms, Modes, and Identifiers (1993)
1424	Privacy Enhancement for Internet Electronic Mail: Part IV: Key Certification and Related Services (1993)
1425	SMTP Service Extensions (1993)
1513	Token Ring Extensions to the Remote Network Monitoring MIB (1993)
1524	A User Agent Configuration Mechanism For Multimedia Mail Format Information (1993)
1552	The PPP Internetworking Packet Exchange Control Protocol (IPXCP) (1993)
1565	Network Services Monitoring MIB (1994)
1566	Mail Monitoring MIB (1994)
1598	PPP in X.25 (1994)
1611	DNS Server MIB Extensions (1994)
1612	DNS Resolver MIB Extensions (1994)
1638	PPP Bridging Control Protocol (BCP) (1994)
1731	IMAP4 Authentication Mechanisms (1994)
1738	Uniform Resource Locators (URL) (1994)
1752	The Recommendation for the IP Next Generation Protocol (1995)
1812	Requirements for IP Version 4 Routers (1995)
1825	Security Architecture for the Internet Protocol (1995)
1826	IP Authentication Header (1995)
1827	IP Encapsulating Security Payload (ESP) (1995)
1848	MIME Object Security Services (1995)
1883	Internet Protocol, Version 6 (IPv6) Specification (1995)
1886	DNS Extensions to support IP version 6 (1995)
1929	Username/Password Authentication for SOCKS V5 (1996)
1938	A One-Time Password System (1996)
1968	The PPP Encryption Control Protocol (ECP) (1996)
1994	PPP Challenge Handshake Authentication Protocol (CHAP) (1996)
2002	IP Mobility Support (1996)
2011	SNMPv2 Management Information Base for the Internet Protocol using SMIv2 (1996)
2012	SNMPv2 Management Information Base for the Transmission Control Protocol using SMIv2 (1996)

2013 SNMPv2 Management Information Base for the User Datagram Protocol using SMIv2 (1996)
2065 Domain Name System Security Extensions (1997)
2078 Generic Security Service Application Program Interface, Version 2 (1997)
2136 Dynamic Updates in the Domain Name System (DNS UPDATE) (1997)
2137 Secure Domain Name System Dynamic Update (1997)
2142 Mailbox Names for Common Services, Roles and Functions (1997)

Other RFCs

799 Internet Name Domains (1981)
896 Congestion Control in IP/TCP Internetworks (1984)
903 Reverse Address Resolution Protocol (1984)
1011 Official Internet Protocols (1987)
1027 Using ARP to Implement Transparent Subnet Gateways (1987)
1032 Domain Administrators Guide (1987)
1033 Domain Administrators Operations Guide (1987)
1036 Standard for Interchange of USENET Messages (1987)
1074 NSFNET Backbone SPF-Based Interior Gateway Protocol (1988)
1090 SMTP on X.25 (1989)
1094 NFS: Network File System Protocol Specification (1989)
1104 Models of Policy Based Routing (1989)
1124 Policy Issues in Interconnecting Networks (1989)
1173 Responsibilities of Host and Network Managers: A Summary of the "Oral Tradition" of the Internet (1990)
1180 TCP/IP Tutorial (1991)
1206 FYI on Questions and Answers: Answers to Commonly Asked "New Internet User" Questions (1991)
1207 FYI on Questions and Answers: Answers to Commonly Asked "Experienced Internet User" Questions (1991)
1208 Glossary of Networking Terms (1991)
1241 A Scheme for an Internet Encapsulation Protocol: Version 1 (1991)
1244 Site Security Handbook (1991)
1267 A Border Gateway Protocol 3 (BGP-3) (1991)
1704 On Internet Authentication (1994)

1726	Technical Criteria for Choosing IP: The Next Generation (Ipng) (1994)
1746	Ways to Define User Expectations (1994)
1774	BGP-4 Protocol Analysis (1995)
1791	TCP and UDP over IPX Networks with Fixed Path MTU (1995)
1792	TCP/IPX Connection Mib Specification (1995)
1813	NFS Version 3 Protocol Specification (1995)
1853	IP in IP Tunneling (1995)
1855	Netiquette Guidelines (1995)
1944	Benchmarking Methodology for Network Interconnect Devices (1996)
1955	New Scheme for Internet Routing and Addressing (ENCAPS) for IPN (1996)
1958	Architectural Principles of the Internet (1996)
1963	PPP Serial Data Transport Protocol (SDTP) (1996)
1983	Internet Users' Glossary (1996)
1984	IAB and IESG Statement on Cryptograhic Technology and the Internet (1996)
2007	Catalogue of Network Training Materials (1996)
2026	The Internet Standards Process – Revision 3 (1996)
2030	Simple Network Time Protocol (SNTP) Version 4 for Ipv4, Ipv6 and OSI (1996)
2033	Local Mail Transfer Protocol (1996)
2057	Sources Directed Access Control on the Internet (1996)
2063	Traffic Flow Measurement: Architecture (1997)
2064	Traffic Flow Measurement: Meter MIB (1997)
2072	Router Renumbering Guide (1997)
2084	Considerations for Web Translation Security (1997)
2107	Ascend Tunnel Management Protocol – ATMP (1997)
2119	Key Words for Use in RFCs to Indicate Requirement Levels (1997)

Appendix D

List of Linux 6.0 Server Packages

D

This appendix lists the 270-plus packages available in the original installation. Notice that Linux is case sensitive so package names have to be entered as stated below in any command.

To get package information in alphabetical order from your server, enter rpm –qa. The following list is from *The Official Red Hat Linux Installation Guide*. If there is a second version number with a package, it is the version that comes with Linux 6.0.

If you enter rpm –q package-name, you also get the release number. For example, if you enter rpm –q xbanner; you get xbanner-1.31-7.

Graphics

xbanner (Version 1.31)

Archiving

cpio (Version 2.4.2)
ncompress (Version 4.2.4)
rmt (Version 0.4b4)
sharutils (Version 4.2)
tar (Version 1.12)

Communication

dip (Version 3.3.7o)
getty_ps (Version 2.0.7j)
lrzsz (Version 0.12.20)
minicom (Version 1.82)
uucp (Version 1.06.1)

Databases

postgresql (Version 6.4.2)
postgresql –clients (Version 6.4.2)

Editors

emacs (Version 20.3)
emacs-nox (Version 20.3)
vim-common (Version 5.3)
vim-minimal (Version 5.3)

Engineering

bc (Version 1.05a)

File

file (Version 3.26)
fileutils (Version 4.0)
findutils (Version 4.1)
gzip (Version 1.2.4)
slocate (Version 1.4)
stat (Version 1.5)

Internet

elm (Version 2.5.0)
exmh (Version 2.0.2)
fetchmail (Version 4.7.0, Version 5.0.0)
finger (Version 0.10)
ftp (Version 0.10)
fwhois (Version 1.00)
mailx (Version 8.1.1)
metamail (Version 2.7)
mutt (Version 0.95.4us)
ncftp (Version 3.0beta18)
netscape-common (Version 4.51)
netscape-communicator (Version 4.51)
nmh (Version 0.27)
pine (Version 4.10)
rsh (Version 0.10)
slrn (Version 0.9.5.4)
talk (Versions 0.10, 0.11)
tcpdump (Version 3.4)
telnet (Version 0.10)
tin (Version 1.4_990216)
traceroute (Version 1.4a5)
trn (Version 3.6)
xmailbox (Version 2.5)
xrn (Version 9.01)

Multimedia

ImageMagick (Version 4.2.2)
gnome-audio (Version 1.0.0)
libgr-progs (Version 2.0.13)

Productivity

ical (Version 2.2)

Publishing

ghostscript (Version 5.10)
ghostscript-fonts (Version 5.10)
groff (Version 1.11a)
gv (Version 3.5.8)
mpage (Version 2.4)
printtool (Version 3.40)
rhs-printfilters (Version 1.51)
tetex-xdvi (Version 0.9)
texinfo (Version 3.12f)

System

bind-utils (Version 8.2)
console-tools (Version 19990302)
control-panel (Version 3.11)
gnome-linuxconf (Version 0.21, 0.22)
gnorpm (Versions 0.7, 0.8)
hdparm (Version 3.3)
ipxutils (Versions 1.0, 2.2.0.12)
kernelcfg (Version 0.5)
linuxconf (Versions 1.14r2, 1.14r4)
mkxauth (Version 1.7)
modemtool (Version 1.21)
mt-st (Version 0.5b)
ncpfs (Version 2.2.0.12)
netcfg (Version 2.20)
procps (Version 2.0.2)
psmisc (Version 18)
rdate (Version 0.960923)
rdist (Version 6.1.5)
rhs-hwdiag (Versions 0.35, 0.36)
setconsole (Version 1.0)
setserial (Version 2.15)
setuptool (Version 1.2)
statserial (Version 1.1)
time (Version 1.7)
timeconfig (Versions 2.6, 2.7)
timetool (Version 2.5)
tksysv (Version 1.0)
ucd-snmp-utils (Version 3.6.1)
usermode (Versions 1.6, 1.9)
usernet (Version 1.0.9)

Text

diffutils (Version 2.7)
ed (Version 0.2)
gawk (Version 3.0.3)
grep (Version 2.3)
ispell (Version 3.1.20)
less (Version 332)
m4 (Version 1.4)
sed (Version 3.02)
textutils (Version 1.22)

Base

redhat-logos (Versions 1.0.2, 1.0.5)

redhat-release (Versions 5.9.5.2, 6.0)

Debuggers

gdb (Version 4.17.0.11)

strace (Version 3.1)

Languages

cpp (Version 1.1.2)
egcs (Version 1.1.2)
expect (Version 5.28)
perl (Versions 5.00502, 00503)
perl-MD5 (Version 1.7)
python (Version 1.5.1)
tcl (Version 8.0.4)
tclx (Version 8.0.4)
tix (Version 4.1.0.6)
tk (Version 8.0.4)
tkinter (Version 1.5.1)

Libraries

glibc-devel (Version 2.1.1)

postgresql-devel (Version 6.4.2)

System

kernel-headers (Version 2.2.5)

Tools

ElectricFence (Versions 2.0.5, 2.1)
autoconf (Version 2.13)
automake (Version 1.4)
bin86 (Version 0.4)
binutils (Versions 2.9.1.0.22b, 2.9.1.0.23)
bison (Version 1.27)
byacc (Version 1.9)
cdecl (Version 2.5)
cproto (Version 4.6)
ctags (Version 3.2)
cvs (Version 1.10.5)
flex (Version 2.5.4a)
gettext (Version 0.10.35)
make (Version 3.77)
patch (Version 2.5)
pmake (Version 2.1.33)
rcs (Version 5.7)

Documentation

helptool (Version 2.4)
indexhtml (Version 5.8, Version 6.0)
man-pages (Version 1.23)

System Environment

Base

MAKEDEV (Versions 2.4, 2.5)
SysVinit (Version 2.74)
authconfig (Versions 1.7, 1.8)
basesystem (Version 6.0)
chkconfig (Versions 1.0.4, 1.0.6)
chkfontpath (Versions 1.3, 1.4.1)
crontabs (Version 1.7)
dev (Versions 2.7.3, 2.7.7)
e2fsprogs (Version 1.14)
eject (Version 2.0.2)
etcskel (Versions 1.6, 2.0)
filesystem (Version 1.3.4)
info (Version 3.12f)
initscripts (Versions 3.98, 4.16)
ipchains (Version 1.3.8)
isapnptools (Version 1.18)
kbdconfig (Versions 1.9, 1.9.2)
ld.so (Version 1.9.5)
ldconfig (Version 1.9.5)
lilo (Version 0.21)
logrotate (Versions 3.1, 3.2)
losetup (Versions 2.9, 2.9o)
mailcap (Version 2.0.1)
man (Versions 1.5f, 1.5g)
mingetty (Version 0.9.4)
mkbootdisk (Versions 1.1, 1.2)
mkinitrd (Version 2.0)
mktemp (Version 1.5)
mount (Versions 2.9, 2.9o)
mouseconfig (Versions 3.7, 3.9)
net-tools (Version 1.51)
ntsysv (Versions 1.0.4, 1.0.6)
pam (Version 0.66)
passwd (Versions 0.50, 0.58)
pwdb (Versions 0.56, 0.58)
quota (Version 1.66)
rootfiles (Version 5.2)
rpm (Versions 2.93, 3.0)
setup (Versions 2.0.1, 2.0.2)
shadow-utils (Version 980403)
termcap (Version 9.12.6)
tmpwatch (Versions 1.5.1, 1.7)
utempter (Versions 0.3, 0.5)
util-linux (Version 2.9o)
vixie-cron (Version 3.0.1)
yp-tools (Versions 2.1, 2.2)

Daemons

ORBit (Versions 0.4.2, 0.4.3)
XFree86-xfs (Version 3.3.3.1)
anonftp (Version 2.8)
apache (Version 1.3.6)
bdflush (Version 1.5)
bind (Version 8.2)
caching-nameserver (Version 6.0)
cleanfeed (Version 0.95.7b)
esound (Versions 0.2.9, 0.2.12)
gpm (Version 1.17.5)
inn (Version 2.2)
knfsd (Versions 1.2, 1.2.2)

lpr (Version 0.35)
mars-nwe (Version 0.99pl15)
netkit-base (Version 0.10)
pidentd (Version 2.8.5)
portmap (Version 4.0)
ppp (Version 2.3.7)
procmail (Versions 3.13, 3.13.1)
pump (Versions 0.4, 0.6.4)
routed (Version 0.10)
rusers (Version 0.10)
rwho (Version 0.10)
samba (Version 2.0.3)
sendmail (Version 8.9.3)
sysklogd (Version 1.3.31)
tcp.wrappers (Version 7.6, not installed)
tftp (Version 0.10)
timed (Version 0.10)
ucd-snmp (Version 3.6.1)
wu-ftpd (Versions 2.4.2b18, 2.4.2vr17)
ypbind (Version 3.3)

Kernel

kernel (Version 2.2.5)
kernel-pcmcia-cs (Version 2.2.5)
modutils (Version 2.1.121)

Libraries

XFree86-libs (Version 3.3.3.1)
Xaw3d (Version 1.3)
audiofile (Version 0.1.6)
cracklib (Version 2.7)
cracklib-dicts (Version 2.7)
freetype (Version 1.2)
gd (Version 1.3)
gdbm (Version 1.7.3)
glib (Version 1.2.1)
glib10 (Version 1.0.6)
glibc (Version 2.1.1)
gmp (Version 2.0.2)
gnome-libs (Versions 1.0.5, 1.0.5)
gtk+ (Version 1.2.1)
gtk+10 (Version 1.0.6)
imlib (Version 1.9.4)
libc (Version 5.3.12)
libghttp (Version 1.0.2)
libgr (Version 2.0.13)
libjpeg (Version 6b)
libpng (Version 1.0.3)
libstdc++ (Version 2.9.0)
libtermcap (Version 2.0.8)
libtiff (Version 3.4)
libungif (Version 4.1.0)
libxml (Version 1.0.0)
ncurses (Version 4.2)
newt (Version 0.40)
pythonlib (Version 1.22)
readline (Version 2.2.1)
slang (Version 1.2.2)
words (Version 2)
xpm (Version 3.4j)
zlib (Version 1.1.3)

Shells

ash (Version 0.2)
bash (Version 1.14.7)
sh-utils (Version 1.16)
tcsh (Version 6.08.00)

Desktops

AfterStep (Versions 1.7.75, 1.7.90)
AfterStep-APPS (Version 990329)
AnotherLevel (Versions 0.8, 0.9)
fvwm (Version 1.24r)
fvwm2 (Version 2.2)
fvwm2-icons (Version 2.2)
wmconfig (Versions 0.9.3, 0.9.5)

X Hardware Support

Xconfigurator (Versions 4.1.3, 4.2.3)

X

X11R6-contrib (Version 3.3.2)
XFree86 (Version 3.3.3.1)
XFree86-75dpi-fonts (Version 3.3.3.1)
rxvt (Version 2.6.PRE2)
urw-fonts (Version 1.1)
xinitrc (Version 2.1)

Appendix E

Listing of Man Pages for Linux 6.0

This appendix is a comprehensive listing of man pages for Red Linux 6.0. The appendix lists some 1,800 user commands, system calls, functions, and files without descriptions. This listing does not include man pages for games, kernel internals, and Tcl/Tk. In addition, pthread_....3 man pages are not listed. Red Hat Linux divides the man pages into ten sections. The sections are:

1	User commands
2	System calls
3	Functions and library routines
4	Special files, device drivers, and hardware
5	Configuration files and file formats
6	Games and demos
7	Miscellaneous
8	System administration and maintenance commands
9	Kernel internals
n	Tcl/Tk commands

A

a2p.1
ab.8
abort.3
abs.3
accept.2
access.2
acct.2
acos.3
acosh.3
active.5
actived.8
actsync.8
actsyncd.8
addftinfo.1
addmntent.3
addr2line.1
adduser.8
adjtimex.2
afmtodit.1
afs_syscall.2
aha152x_cs.4
alarm.2
ali.1
aliases.5
alloca.3
alphasort.3
anno.1
answer.1
anytopnm.1
ap.8
apachectl.8
apm.1
apmd.8
apropos.1
apxs.8
ar.1
arch.1
archive.8
arp.8

as.1
ascii.7
asciitopgm.1
ascii-xfr.1
asctime.3
ash.1
asin.3
asinh.3
assert.3
at.1
atan.3
atan2.3
atanh.3
atd.8
atexit.3
atktopbm.1
atof.3
atoi.3
atol.3
atq.1
atrm.1
atrun.8
audiocompose.1
audiosend.1
authconfig.8
autoexpect.1
awk.1

B

badblocks.8
basename.1
bash.1
batch.1
batcher.8
bc.1
bcmp.3
bcopy.3
bdflush.2
bdflush.8
bind.2
bioradtopgm
bison.1
bmptoppm.1
bootparam.7
break.2
brk.2
brushtopbm.1
bsearch.3
bsh.1
bstring.3
btree.3
buildhash.1
burst.1
byacc.1
byteorder.3
bzero.3

C

c++decl.1
c++filt.1
cacheflush.2
cal.1
calloc.3
captoinfo.1m
cardctl.8
cardinfo.1
cardmgr.8
cat.1
catalogs.3
catclose.3
catgets.3
catopen.3
cbrt.3
cccp.1
cdecl.1
ceil.3
cfdisk.8
cfgetispeed.3
cfgetospeed.3
cfmakeraw.3
cfsetispeed.3
cfsetopeed.3
chage.1
charmap.5
charset.1
charsets.4
chat.8
chattr.1
chdir.2
checkalias.1
chfn.1
chgrp.1
chkfontpath.8
chmod.1
chmod.2
chown.1
chown.2
chpasswd.8
chroot.1
chroot.2
chsh.1
chvt.1
ci.1
cjpeg.1
cksum.1
cleanfeed.8
clear.1
cleardbdir.1
clearerr.3
clock.3
clone.2
close.2
closedir.3
closelog.3
cmp.1
cmsg.3
cmuwmtopbm.1
cnfsstat.8
co.1
col.1
colcrt.1
colrm.1
column.1
comm.1

comp.1
compress.1
confstr.3
connect.2
console.4
console.apps.5
console.ctl.5
console.perms.5
console_codes.4
console_ioctl.4
console_ioctls.4
consolechars.8
consolehelper.8
controlchan.8
control-panel.8
convdate.1
copysign.3
cos.3
cosh.3
cp.1
cpio.1
cpp.1
cproto.1
creat.2
create_module.2
createdb.1
createuser.1
cron
crond.8
crontab.1
crontab.5
crosspost.8
crypt.3
cryptdir.1
csplit.1
ctags.1
ctermid.3
ctime.3
ctlinnd.8
ctrlaltdel.8
cu.1
cuserid.3
cut.1
cvs.1
cvs.5
cvsbug.8
cvtbatch.8
cycbuff.conf.5
cytune.8

D

date.1
db.3
dbmmanage.1
dbopen.3
dc.1
dd.1
ddate.1
ddp.4
deallocvt.1
debugfs.8
decryptdir.1
delete_module.2
depmod.1
destroydb.1
destroyuser.1
df.1
diff.1
diff3.1
difftime.3
dig.1
dip.8
diplogin.8
dir.1
dircolors.1
dirname.1
dislocate.1
dist.1
distrib.pats.5
div.3
djpeg.1
dlclose.3
dlerror.3
dlopen.3
dlsym.3
dmesg.8
dn.expand.3
dn_comp.3
dnsdomainname.1
dnsquery.1
doexec.1
domainname.1
dp.8
drand48.3
drem.3
du.1
dummy_cs.4
dump_cis.8
dump2fs.8
dumpkeys.1
dup.2
dup2.2

E

e2fsck.8
e2label.8
echo.1
ecpg.1
ecvt.3
ed.1
edquota.8
efence.3
egcs.1
egrep.1
eject.1
elm.1
elmalias.1
emacs.1
endgrent.3
endhostent.3
endmntent.3
endnetent.3

endprotoent.3
endpwent.3
endservent.3
endusershell.3
endutent.3
english.4
env.1
environ.5
eqn.1
erand48.3
erf.3
erfc.3
errno.3
etags.1
ethers.5
ex.1
exec.3
execl.3
execle.3
execlp.3
execv.3
execve.2
execvp.3
exit.2
exit.3
exmh.1
exp.3
expand.1
expect.1
expectk.1
expire.8
expire.ctl.5
expireindex.8
expireover.8
expirerm.8
expm1.3
exportfs.8
exports.5
expr.1
extcompose.1

F

fabs.3
failog.5
failog.8
false.1
fastmail.1
fastrm.8
fchdir.2
fchmod.2
fchown.2
fclose.3
fcntl.2
fcvt.3
fd.4
fdatasync.2
fdformat.8
fdisk.8
fdopen.3
feof.3
ferror.3
fetchmail.1
fflush.3
ffs.3
fgconsole.1
fgetc.3
fgetgrent.3
fgetpos.3
fgetpwent.3
fgets.3
fgrep.1
file.1
filechan.8
fileno.3
find.1
findaffix.1
finger.1
fingerd.8
finitie.3
fitstopnm.1
flex.1
flex++.1
flist.1
flock.2
floor.3
fmod.3
fmt.1
fmtdump.8
fmvj18x_cs.4
fnmatch.3
fold.1
folder.1
fopen.3
fork.2
formail.1
forw.1
fpathconf.3
fprintf.3
fputc.3
fputs.3
fread.3
free.1
free.3
freopen.3
frexp.3
frm.1
fs.5
fscanf.3
fsck.8
fsck.minix.8
fseek.3
fsetpos.3
fstab.5
fstat.2
fstatfs.2
fstopgm.1
fsync.2
ftell.3
ftime.3
ftl_check.8
ftl_cs.4
ftl_format.8
ftok.3
ftp.1
ftpaccess.5
ftpconversions.5
ftpcount.1
ftpd.8
ftphosts.5
ftpshut.8
ftpwho.1
ftruncate.2

ftw.3
full.4
fuser.1
fwrite.3

G

g3topbm.1
gawk.1
gcc.1
gctags.1
gcvt.3
gdb.1
gemtopbm.1
genksyms.8
geqn.1
get_current_dir_name.3
get_kernel_syms.2
getc.3
getchar.3
getcwd.3
getdents.2
getdirentries.3
getdomainname.2
getdtablesize.2
getegid.2
getenv.3
geteuid.2
getfilename.1
getgid.2
getgrent.3
getgrgid.3
getgrnam.3
getgroups.2
gethostbyaddr.3
gethostbyname.3
gethostid.2
gethostname.2
getitimer.2
getkeycodes.8
getlist.1
getlogin.3
getmntent.3
getnetbyaddr.3
getnetbyname.3
getopt.1
getopt.3
getopt_long.3
getopt_long_only.3
getpagesize.2
getpass.3
getpeername.2
getpgid.2
getpgrp.2
getpid.2
getppid.2
getpriority.2
getprotobyname.3
getprotobynumber.3
getprotoent.3
getpw.3
getpwent.3
getpwid.3
getpwnam.3
getresgid.2
getresuid.2
getrlimit.2
getrusage.2
gets.3
getservbyname.3
getservbyport.3
getservent.3
getsid.2
getsockname.2
getsockopt.2
gettimeofday.2
getty.1
gettydefs.5
getuid.2
getusershell.3
getutent.3
getutid.3
getutline.3
getw.3
getwd.3
ghostscript.1
giftopnm.1
gindxbib.1
glob.3
glob.7
globfree.3
glookbib.1
gmtime.3
gnroff.1
gouldtoppm.1
gpasswd.1
gpic.1
gpm.8
gpm-root.1
gprof.1
grefer.1
grep.1
grephistory.1
grodvi.1
groff.1
groff_char.7
groff_font.5
groff_mm.7
groff_mmse.7
groff_ms.7
groff_out.5
grog.1
grolj4.1
grops.1
grotty.1
group.5
groupadd.8
groupdel.8
groupmod.8
groups.1
grpck.8
grpconv.8
grpunconv.8
gs.1
gsoelim.1
gtbl.1
gtroff.1
gtty.2
gunzip.1
gzexe.1
gzip.1

H

halt.8
hash.3
hasmntopt.3
hcreate.3
hd.4
hdestroy.3
hdparm.8
head.1
herror.3
hexdump.1
hier.7
hipstopgm.1
history.5
host.1
hostname.1
hostname.7
hosts.allow.5
hosts.deny.5
hosts_access.3
hosts_access.5
hosts_options.5
hpcdtoppm.1
hpftodit.1
hsearch.3
htdigest.1
htonl.3
htons.3
htpasswd.1
httpd.8
hwclock.8
hypot.3

I

i82365.4
ibmtr_cs.4
ical.1
icmp.4
icontopbm.1
id.1
ide_info.8
ident.1
identd.8
idle.2
ifconfig.8
ifport.8
ifuser.8
igawk.1
ilbmtoppm.1
imgtoppm.1
in.fingerd.8
in.identd.8
in.ntalkd.8
in.rexecd.8
in.rlogind.8
in.rshd.8
in.talkd.8
in.telenetd.8
in.tftpd.8
inc.1
incoming.conf.5
index.3
indxbib.1
inet.3
inet_addr.3
inet_aton.3
inet_lnaof.3
inet_makeaddr.3
inet_netof.3
inet_network.3
inet_ntoa.3
inetd.8
inetd.conf.5
infnan.3
infocmp.1m
init.8
init_module.2
initdb.1
initigroups.3
initlocation.1
initlog.1
initrd.4
initscript.5
initstate.3
inittab.5
inn.conf.5
inncheck.8
innconfval.1
innd.8
inndf.8
innfeed.1
innfeed.conf.5
innreport.8
innstat.8
innwatch.8
innwatch.ctl.5
innxbatch.8
innxmit.8
insmod.1
insque.3
install.1
installit.1
install-mh.8
intro.1
intro.2
intro.3
intro.4
intro.5
intro.7
intro.8
ioctl.2
ioctl_list.2
ioperm.2
iopl.2
ip.4
ipc.2
ipc.5
ipcalc.1
ipcclean.1
ipchains.8
ipchains-restore.8
ipchains-save.8
ipcrm.8
ipcs.8

ipfw.4
ipfwadm-wrapper.8
ipx_configure.8
ipx_interface.8
ipx_internal_net.8
ipx_route.8
irs.conf.5
iruserok.3
isalnum.3
isalpha.3
isapup.8
isapup.conf.5
isascii.3
isatty.3
isblank.3
iscntrl.3
isdigit.3
isgraph.3
isinf.3
islower.3
isnan.3
iso_8859_1.7
ispell.1
ispell.4
isprint.3
ispunct.3
isspace.3
issue.5
issue.net.5
isupper.3
isxdigit.3

E

J

j0.3
j1.3
jn.3
join.1
jpegtran.1
jrand48.3

K

kbd_mode.1
kbd-compat.8
kbdconfig.8
kbdrate.8
kerneld.8
keymaps.5
kibitz.1
kill.1
kill.2
killall.1
killall5.8
killpg.2
klogd.8
kmen.4
ksyms.1

L

labs.3
last.1
lastb.1
lastlog.8
latin1.7
lchown.2
lcong48.3
ld.1
ld.so.8
ldconfig.8
ldd.1
ldexp.3
ldiv.3
less.1
lesskey.1
lex.1
lfind.3
lgamma.3
libefence.3
libexpect.3
libpq.3
lilo.8
lilo.conf.5
link.2
lispmtopgm.1
listalias.1
listen.2
lkbib.1
llseek.2
lmhosts.5
ln.1
loadkeys.1
locale.5
locale.7
localeconv.3
localtime.3
locate.1
lock.2
lockfile.1
log.3
log10.3
log1p.3
logger.1
login.1
logname.1
logresolve.8
logrotate.8
logwtmp.3
longjmp.3
look.1
lookbib.1
losetup.8
lp.4
lpc.8

lpd.8
lpq.1
lpr.1
lprm.1
lptest.1
lrand48.3
ls.1
lsattr.1
lsearch.3
lseek.2
lsmod.1
lstat.2
lynx.1

M

macptopbm.1
magic.4
mail.1
mailaddr.7
mailcap.4
mailpost.8
mailq.1
mailstats.8
mailto.1
mailto-hebrew.1
make.1
make_smbcodepage.1
makeactive.8
MAKEDEV.8
makehistory.8
makemap.8
malloc.3
man.1
man.7
man.config.5
man2html.1
manpath.1
mark.1
mblen.3
mbstowcs.3
mbtowc.3
mcookie.1
md5sum.1
me.7
mem.4
memccpy.3
memchr.3
memcmp.3
memcpy.3
memfrob.3
memmem.3
memmove.3
memory_cb.4
memory_cs.4
memset.3
merge.1
mesg.1
messages.1
metamail.1
metasend.1
mev.1
mgrtopbm.1
mh-alias.5
mhbuild.1
mh-chart.1
mh-draft.5
mh-format.5
mhl.1
mhmail.1
mh-mail.5
mh-mts.8
mhn.1
mhparam.1
mhpath.1
mh-profile.5
mh-sequence.5
mh-tailor.5
mime.1
mimencode.1
mingetty.8
minicom.1
mkbootdisk.8
mkdir.1
mkdir.2
mke2fs.8
mkfifo.1
mkfifo.3
mkfs.8
mkfs.minix.8
mkinitrd.8
mklost+found.8
mknod.1
mknod.2
mkpasswd.1
mkpasswd.8
mkstemp.3
mkswap.8
mktemp.1
mktemp.3
mktime.3
mlock.2
mlockall.2
mmap.2
mmencode.1
moderators.5
modf.3
modify_ldt.2
modinfo.1
modinfo.1
modprobe.1
more.1
motd.5
motd.news.5
mount.2
mount.8
mouse.4
mouseconfig.8
mpage.1
mpool.3
mprotect.2
mpx.2
mrand48.3
mremap.2
msafer.7
msgchk.1
msgctl.2
msgget.2
msgop.2
msgrcv.2
msgsnd.2
msh.1
msync.2

mt.1
mtvtoppm.1
munchlist.1
munlock.2
munlockall.2
munmap.2
mutt.1
mv.1

N

named.8
named-xfer.8
namei.1
nanosleep.2
ncftp.1
ncftpbatch.1
ncftpget.1
ncftpls.1
ncftpput.1
ncopy.1
ncpmount.8
ncpumount.8
ndc.8
nesend.1
netdevice.4
netlink.4
netreport.1
netstat.8
netwave_cs.4
newalias.1
newaliases.1
newgrp.1
newmail.1
news.daily.8
news2mail.8
newsfeeds.5
newslog.5
newslog.8
news-recovery.8
newsrequeue.8
newsusers.8
next.1
nfs.5
nfsservctl.2
nfsstat.8
nice.1
nice.2
nicknames.5
nisdomainname.1
nl.1
nlmconv.1
nm.1
nmbd.8
nmblookup.1
nmh.1
nnrp.access.5
nnrpd.8
nnrpd.track.5
nntpget.1
nntpsend.ctl.5
nntpsend.8
nohup.1
nologin.5
nprint.1
nrand48.3
nroff.1
nslookup.8
nsswitch.5
ntalkd.8
ntohl.3
ntohs.3
ntsysv.8
null.4
nwauth.1
nwbocreate.8
nwbols.1
nwboprops.1
nwborm.8
nwbpadd.8
nwbpcreate.8
nwbprm.8
nwbpset.1
nwbpvalues.1
nwclient.5
nwfsctrl.8
nwfsinfo.1
nwfstime.1
nwgrant.8
nwmsg.8
nwpasswd.1
nwpurge.1
nwrevoke.8
nwrights.1
nwsfind.1
nwtrustee.1
nwuserlist.1
nwvolinfo.1

O

obsolete.2
oldfstat.2
oldlstat.2
oldolduname.2
oldstat.2
olduname.2
on_exit.3
opeming.3
open.2
opendir.3
outb.2
overchan.8
overview.ctl.5
overview.fmt.5

P

pac.8
pack_cis.8
packet.4
packf.1
pam_console.8
pam_xauth.8
passmass.1
passwd.1
passwd.5
passwd.nntp.5
paste.1
patch.1
patc-metamail.1
pathchk.1
pathconf.3
pause.2
pbmclean.1
pbmlife.1
pbmmake.1
pbmmask.1
pbmreduce.1
pbmscale.1
pbmtext.1
pbmto10x.1
pbmto4425.1
pbmtoascii.1
pbmtoatk.1
pbmtobbnbg.1
pbmtocnuwm.1
pbmtoepsi.1
pbmtoepson.1
pbmtog3.1
pbmtogem.1
pbmtogo.1
pbmtoicon.1
pbmtolj.1
pbmtoln03.1
pbmtolps.1
pbmtomacp.1
pbmtomgr.1
pbmtopgm.1
pbmtopi3.1
pbmtopk.1
pbmtoplot.1
pbmtoptx.1
pbmtox10bm.1
pbmtoxbm.1
pbmtoybm.1
pbmtozinc.1
pbmupc.1
pcinitrd.8
pclose.3
pcmcia.5
pcmcia_core.4
pcnet_cs.4
pcxtoppm.1
pdf2dsc.1
pdf2ps.1
perl50004delta.1
perl.1
perlapio.1
perlbook.1
perlbot.1
perlbug.1
perlcall.1
perldata.1
perldebug.1
perldelta.1
perldiag.1
perldoc.1
perldsc.1
perlembed.1
perltie.1
perltoc.1
perltoot.1
perltrap.1
perlvar.1
perlxs.1
perlxstut.1
personality.2
pf_dumpall.1
pfbtops.1
pftp.1
pg_dump.1
pg_hba.conf.5
pg_passwd
pgmbentley.1
pgmcrater.1
pgmedge.1
pgmenhance.1
pgmhist.1
pgmkernel.1
pgmnoise.1
pgmnorm.1
pgmoil.1
pgmramp.1
pgmtexture.1
pgmtofs.1
pgpverify.8
pi3topbm.1
pic.1
pick.1
pico.1
picttoppm.1
pidof.8
pilot.1
piltoppm.1
pine.1
ping.8
pipe.2
pjtoppm.1
pktopbm.1
plipconfig.8
pmake.1
pmap_dump.8
pmap_set.8
png.5
pngtopnm.1
pnmalias.1
pnmarith.1
pnmcat.1
pnmcomp.1
pnmconvol.1
pnmcrop.1
pnmcut.1
pnmdepth.1
pnmenlarge.1
pnmfile.1
pnmflip.1
pnmgamma.1
pnmhisteq.1
pnmhistmap.1
pnmindex.1
pnminvert.1
pnmmargin.1

pnmnlfilt.1
pnmnoraw.1
pnmpaste.1
pnmrotate.1
pnmscale.1
pnmshear.1
pnmsmooth.1
pnmtile.1
pnmtodif.1
pnmtofits.1
pnmtopng.1
pnmtops.1
pnmtorast.1
pnmtosgi.1
pnmtosir.1
pnmtotiff.1
pnmtoxwd.1
pnpad.1
pnpdump.8
poll.2
popen.3
port.4
portmap.8
post.8
postgres.1
postmaster.1
pow.3
poweroff.8
ppm3d.1
ppmbrighten.1
ppmchange.1
ppmdim.1
ppmdist.1
ppmdither.1
ppmtoyuvsplit.1
pppd.8
pppstats.8
pqlist.1
pqrm.1
pqstat.1
pr.1
praliases.8
prctl.2
prev.1
printcap.5
printenv.1
printf.1
printf.3
printmail.1
proc.5
procmail.1
procmailex.5
procmailrc.5
procmailsc.5
prof.2
profil.3
prompter.1
protocols.5
prunehistory.8
ps.1
ps2ascii.1
ps2epsi.1
ps2pdf.1
psbb.1
pserver.1
psfaddtable.1
psfgettable.1
psfstriptable.1
psidtopgm.1
psignal.3
psql.1
pstree.1
ptrace.2
pullnews.8
pump.8
putc.3
putchar.3
putenv.3
putpwent.3
puts.3
pututline.3
putw.3
pwck.8
pwconv.8
pwd.1
pwunconv.8

Q

qrttoppm.1
qsort.3
query_module.2
quota.1
quotacheck.8
quotactl.2
quotaon.8

R

raise.3
ram.4
ramsize.8
rand.3
random.3
random.4
ranlib.1
rarp.8
rasttopnm.1
raw,4
rawtopgm.1
rcmd.3
rcp.1
rcs.1
rcsclean.1
rcsdiff.1
rcsfile.5
rcsintro.1
rcsmerge.1
rcvdist.1
rcvpack.1
rcvstore.1
rcvtty.1
rdate.1

rdev.8
rdist.1
rdist.8
rdjpgcom.1
re_comp.3
re_exec.3
read.2
readdir.2
readdir.3
readline.3
readlink.2
readmsg.1
readprofile.1
readv.2
readv.3
realloc.3
realpath.3
reboot.2
reboot.8
recno.3
recv.2
recvfrom.2
recvmsg.2
red.1
refer.1
refile.1
regcomp.3
regerror.3
regex.3
regex.7
regexec.3
regfree.3
remove.3
remque.3
rename.2
renice.8
repl.1
repquota.8
res.query.3
res_init.3
res_mkquery.3
res_querydomain.3
res_search.3
res_send.3
resizecons.8
resolver.5
rev.1
rewind.3
rewind.3
rewinddir.3
rexec.1
rexecd.8
rgb3toppm.1
richtext.1
rindex.3
rint.3
rlog.1
rlogin.1
rlogind.8
rm.1
rmail.8
rmdir.1
rmdir.2
rmf.1
rmm.1
rmmod.1
rmt.8
rnews.1
rootflags.8
rotatelogs.8
route.8
routed.8
rpc.rstatd.8
rpc.rusersd.8
rpcgen.1
rpm.8
rpm2cpio.8
rquota.3
rquotad.8
rresvport.3
rsh.1
rshd.8
rtnetlink.4
runlevel.8
runscript.1
rup.1
ruptime.1
ruserok.3
rusers.1
rusersd.8
rvi.1
rview.1
rwho.1
rwhod.8
rz.1

S

s2p.1
samba.7
sash.8
sbrk.2
scan.1
scandir.3
scanf.3
scanlogs.8
sched_get_priority_max.2
sched_get_priority_min.2
sched_getparam.2
sched_getscheduler.2
sched_rr_get_interval.2
sched_setparam.2
sched_setscheduler.2
sched_yield.2
script.1
scsi_info.8
sd.4
sdiff.1
securetty.5
sed.1
seed48.3
seekdir.3
select.2
sem_destroy.3thr
sem_getvalue.3thr
sem_init.3thr
sem_post.3thr
sem_wait.3thr
semctl.2
semget.2
semop.2
send.1
send.2
sendfile.2

sendfiles.1
sendmail.8
sendmsg.2
sendto.2
send-uucp.8
serial_cs.4
services.5
setbuf.3
setbuffer.3
setclock.8
setconsole.8
setdomainname.2
setdprm.8
setegid.2
setenv.3
seteuid.2
setfsgid.2
setfsuid.2
setgid.2
setgrent.3
setgroups.2
sethostent.3
sethostid.2
sethostname.2
setitimer.2
setjmp.3
setkeycodes.8
setleds.1
setlinebuf.3
setlocale.3
setmetamode.1
setmntent.3
setnetent.3
setpgid.2
setpgrp.2
setpriority.2
setprotoent.3
setpwent.3
setregid.2
setresgid.2
setresuid.2
setreuid.2
setrlimit.2
setserial.8
setservent.3
setsid.2
setsid.8
setsockopt.2
setstate.3
setterm.1
settimeofday.2
setuid.2
setup.2
setusershell.3
setutent.3
setvbuf.3
sfdisk.8
sgetmask.2
sgitopnm.1
sh.1
shadow.3
shadow.5
shar.1
shells.5
shlock.1
shmat.2
shmctl.2
shmdt.2
shmget.2
shmop.2
show.1
showaudio.1
showcfont.1
showexternal.1
showkey.1
shownonascii.1
showpartial.1
showpicture.1
shutdown.2
shutdown.8
sigaction.2
sigaddset.3
sigblock.2
sigdelset.3
sigemptyset.3
sigfillset.3
siggetmask.2
siginterrupt.3
sigismember.3
siglongjmp.3
sigmask.2
signal.2
signal.7
sigpause.2
sigpending.2
sigprocmask.2
sigreturn.2
sigsetjmp.3
sigsetmask.2
sigsetops.3
sigsuspend.2
sigvec.2
sigwait.3thr
sin.3
sinh.3
sirtopnm.1
size.1
skill.1
skrinkfile.1
slattach.8
sldtoppm.1
sleep.1
sleep.3
slist.1
slocal.1
slocate.1
slrn.1
sm.8
smb.conf.5
smbclient.1
smbd.8
smbmnt.8
smbmount.8
smbpasswd.5
smbpasswd.8
smbrun.1
smbstatus.1
smbtar.1
smbumount.8
snice.1
snmpbulkwalk.1
snmpcmd.1
snmpd.1
snmpd.conf.5
snmpdelta.1
snmpget.1
snmpgetnext.1
snmpnetstat.1
snmpset.1
snmpstatus.1
snmptable.1
snmptest.1
snmptranslate.1
snmptrap.1

snmptrapd.8
snmpwalk.1
snprintf.3
socket.2
socket.4
socketcall.2
socketpair.2
soelim.1
sort.1
sortm.1
spctoppm.1
split.1
splitmail.1
spottopgm.1
sprintf.3
sputoppm.1
sq.1
sqrt.3
srand.3
srand48.3
srandom.3
sscanf.3
ssetmask.2
st.4
stab.5
startinnfeed.1
stat.1
stat.2
statfs.2
statserial.1
stdarg.3
stderr.3
stdin.3
stdio.3
stdout.3
stime.2
stinit.8
storage.conf.5
storage.ctl.5
stpcpy.3
strace.1
strcasecmp.3
strcat.3
strchr.3
strcmp.3
strcoll.3
strcpy.3
strcspn.3
strdup.3
strerror.3
strfry.3
strftime.3
string.3
strings.1
strip.1
strlen.3
strncasecmp.3
strncat.3
strncmp.3
strncpy.3
strpbrk.3
strptime.3
strrchr.3
strsep.3
strsignal.3
strspn.3
strstr.3
strtod.3
strtok.3
strtol.3
strtoul.3
strxfrm.3
stty.1
stty.2
su.1
subst.1
suffixes.7
sulogin.8
sum.1
swab.3
swapdev.8
swapoff.2
swapoff.8
swapon.2
swapon.8
swat.8
symlink.2
sync.1
sync.2
syscalls.2
sysconf.3
sysctl.2
sysfs.2
sysinfo.2
sysklogd.8
syslog.2
syslog.3
syslog.conf.5
syslogd.8
system.3
sz.1

T

tac.1
tail.1
tailf.1
talk.1
talkd.8
tally.control.8
tally.unwanted.8
tan.3
tanh.3
tar.1
tbl.1
tc574_cs.4
tc575_ch.4
tc589_cs.4
tcdrain.3
tcflow.3
tcflush.3
tcgetattr.3
tcgetpgrp.3
tcic.4
tclsh.1
tcp.4
tcpd.8
tcpdchk.8
tcpdmatch.8
tcpdump.8
tcsendbreak.3
tcsetattr.3
tcsetpgrp.3
tcsh.1

tdelete.3
tee.1
telinit.8
telldir.3
telnet.1
telnetd.8
tempnam.3
term.5
term.7
termcap.5
terminfo.5
termios.3
test.1
testparm.1
testprns.1
tfind.3
tfmtodit.1
tftp.1
tftpd.8
tgatoppm.1
tic.1
tifftopnm.1
time.2
timeconfig.8
timed.8
timedc.8
times.2
tin.1
tixwish.1
tknewsbiff.1
tksysc.8
tload.1
tmpfile.3
tmpnam.3
tmpwatch.8
toascii.3
toe.1m
tolower.3
top.1
touch.1
toupper.3
tput.1
tr.1
traceroute.8
troff.1
true.1
truncate.2
tryaffix.1
tsearch.3
tset.1
tsort.1
tty.1
tty.4
ttyname.3
ttys.4
ttytype.5
tune2fs.8
twalk.3
tzfile.5
tzselect.8
tzset.3

U

udp.4
ul.1
ulimit.3
umask.2
umount.2
umount.8
uname.1
unbuffer.1
uncompress.1
undocumented.2
undocumented.3
unexpand.1
ungetc.3
unicode.7
unicode_start.1
unicode_stop.1
unimplemented.2
uniq.1
unix.4
unlink.2
unmae.2
unsetenv.3
unshar.1
unsq.1
update.8
updatedb.1
updwtmp.3
uptime.1
uselib.2
useradd.8
userdel.8
userhelper.8
userinfo.1
usermod.8
usermount.1
usernet.1
usernetctl.1
userpasswd.1
users.1
usleep.1
usleep.3
ustat.2
utf-8.7
utime.2
utimes.2
utmp.5
utmpname.3
uucico.8
uucp.1
uudecode.1
uuencode.1
uuencode.5
uugetty.1
uustat.1
uux.1
uuxqt.8

E

V

va_arg.3
va_end.3
va_start.3
variables.5
vcs.4
vcsa.4
vdir.1
vfork.2
vfprintd.3
vfscanf.3
vhangup.2
vi.1
videmode.8
view.1
vim.1
vipw.8
vm86.2
vmh.1
vmstat.8
vprintf.3
vscanf.3
vsnprintf.3
vsprintf.3
vsscanf.3
vt-is-UTF8.1

W

w.1
wait.2
wait3.2
wait4.2
waitpid.2
wall.1
watch.1
wavelan.4
wavelan_cs.4
wc.1
wcstombs.3
wctoom.3
whatis.1
whatnow.1
whereis.1
which.1
who.1
whoami.1
whom.1
wish.1
wnewmail.1
write.1
write.2
writelog.8
writev.2
writev.3
wrjpgcom.1
wtmp.5

X

x25.4
xargs.1
xbmtopbm.1
xdvi.1
xferlog.5
ximtoppm.1
xirc2ps_cs.4
xkibitiz.1
xpmtoppm.1
xvminittoppm.1
xwdtopnm.1
xxd.1

Y

y0.3
y1.3
yacc.1
ybmtopbm.1
yes.1
yn.3
ypbind.8
ypcat.1
ypchfn.1
ypchsh.1
ypdomainname.1
ypmatch.1
yppasswd.1
yppoll.8
ypset.8
ypwhich.1
yusplittoppm.1
yuvtoppm.1

Z

zcat.1
zcmp.1
zdiff.1
zdump.8
zeisstopnm.1
zero.4
zforce.1
zgrep.1
zic.8
zmore.1
znew.1

Index

.newsrc file, 66
.slrnrc file, 68
.tinrc file, 68
.trnrc, 68
/, 40
/*, 238
/bin, 20, 40, 239
/bin/mail, 181
/boot, 240
/dev, 40, 156, 229-231, 240-250
/dev/lp*, 92, 231
/dev/modem, 222
/dev/mouse, 230
/dev/null, 41, 230
/dev/printer, 41, 92, 231
/etc, 41, 250
/etc/bin, 24
/etc/catn, 145
/etc/cron.daily, 156
/etc/cron.hourly/, 155
/etc/cron.weekly/, 156
/etc/cron.weekly/makewhatis.cron, 131, 144
/etc/crontab/, 155
/etc/directory, 41
/etc/exports, 75, 123
/etc/fstab, 6, 41, 124, 230
/etc/ftpaccess, 53, 79
/etc/ftpconversions, 53, 79
/etc/ftphosts, 53, 79
/etc/ftpusers, 79
/etc/group, 41, 211
/etc/hosts, 15, 42, 49, 56-57
/etc/hosts.equiv, 92, 231
/etc/hosts.lpd, 92, 231
/etc/http/conf, 87
/etc/inetd.conf, 5, 99
/etc/init, 153
/etc/inittab, 151, 222
/etc/issue, 153
/etc/network, 58
/etc/networks, 150
/etc/news/hosts.nntp, 65
/etc/news/nnrp.access, 65
/etc/nntpserver, 68
/etc/passwd, 42, 139, 211
/etc/printcap, 90, 92, 197, 231
/etc/profile, 42
/etc/rc.d/, 187
/etc/rc.d/init.d/innd, 65
/etc/rc.d/init/nfs, 74, 123
/etc/rc.d/rc.news, 65
/etc/resolv.conf, 58
/etc/sendmail.cf, 15
/etc/services, 42, 57, 189
/etc/shadow, 42
/etc/shells, 139, 217
/etc/skel, 211
/etc/smb.conf, 161
/etc/sysconf/network, 58
/etc/sysconfig, 42
/etc/sysconfig/network, 149
/etc/syslog.conf, 105
/etc/X11, 43
/home, 43, 251-252
/home/ftp, 78
/home/httpd, 187
/home/httpd/html, 188
/home/samba, 161
/home/user, 217
/lib, 43, 253-254
/lost+found, 254
/mnt, 6, 43, 254
/proc, 228, 254
/proc/cpuinfo, 228
/proc/devices, 232
/proc/dma, 228
/proc/interrupts, 229
/proc/ioports, 229
/proc/pci, 228
/proc/scsi/scsi, 234
/pub/contrib, 185
/root, 255
/sbin, 43, 255
/sbin/route, 58, 150
/tmp, 43, 256
/usenet/news.announce.newsusers, 69
/usr, 44, 256
/usr/bin, 16, 20, 44, 67
/usr/bin/netcfg, 149
/usr/dict, 23, 134
/usr/doc, 66, 187
/usr/doc/HOWTO, 142
/usr/lib, 44
/usr/lib/rhs, 44

/usr/lib/slrn, 68
/usr/lin/elm, 12
/usr/local, 44
/usr/local/apache/conf, 186
/usr/local/bin, 44
/usr/local/lib, 44
/usr/local/src, 44
/usr/man, 44, 132, 187
/usr/man/cat, 145
/usr/man/man1, 144
/usr/man/man2, 144
/usr/man/man3, 144
/usr/man/man4, 144
/usr/man/man5, 144
/usr/man/man6, 144
/usr/man/man7, 144
/usr/man/man8, 144
/usr/man/man9, 144
/usr/man/mann, 144-145
/usr/sbin, 20, 187
/usr/sbin/in.ftp, 78
/usr/sbin/pd*, 91
/usr/sbin/tcpd, 58
/usr/share/misc/termcap, 93
/usr/spool, 45
/usr/src, 45
/usr/X11R6, 45
/var, 45, 256
/var/lib/rpm, 45
/var/log, 45
/var/log/messages, 230
/var/log/samba, 161
/var/log/xferlog, 53, 79
/var/spool/*, 92-93, 231
/var/spool/*/lock, 92
/var/spool/*/minfree, 92
/var/spool/output/*/cf*, 91
/var/spool/output/*/df*, 91
/var/spool/output/*/tf*, 91
/varspool*/minfree, 231
[], 132
Pa/var/spool/*/lock, 93

A

ab, 7, 223
accept, 203
access, 205
access.conf, 186, 188
account management definition, 209
accounting rules, 86
acct, 203
Address Resolution Protocol, *see* ARP
adduser, 139
adjtimex, 204
adtimex, 155
Advanced Research Project Agency, *see* ARPA
alarm, 204
alias command, 132
alias function, 16
alt.linux.projects, 62
alt.os.linux, 62
anonftp package, 54, 81
API definition, 191
Apache server, 7
    books, 190
    definition, 185
    features, 185-186
    installing, 186
    man pages, 7
    stopping, 189
    upgrading, 186
    URLs, 189
apachectl, 7
Application Program Interface, *see* API
application server, 2, 89
apropos, 131
apxs, 223
ARAPANET, 97
archie server, 6
archive files, 134
archiving server packages, 351
arp command, 102, 155
ARP definition, 191
ARPA definition, 191
ash, 165
at command, 140
atq, 140
atrm, 140
aumix, 182
aus.computers.linux, 62
authentication, 84
authoritative zone, 2
autoconf, 169
autogroup, 53, 80
automake, 169

B

bulletins, 17
backbone definition, 191
badblocks, 159
banner, 140
base server packages, 354
basename, 165
bash, 165, 179
batch, 140

BBS definition, 191
bc, 170
bg, 137
BGP, 100
    definition, 192
bind, 203
binutils, 171, 180
bison, 170
bit bucket, 230
bootpd, 102, 154
bootptest, 102
Border Gateway Protocol, *see* BGP
bridge definition, 192
Bulletin Board System, *see* BBS

C

caching-only server, 2
cal, 140
calc, 170
cat, 26
cd, 20, 39
CD-ROM driver, 232
cfdisk, 155
cfengine, 170
Challenge Handshake Authentication Protocol, *see* CHAP
CHAP, 112-113
chat, 111
chdir, 202
checker, 170
chgrp, 39, 172
chmod, 22, 53, 80, 132-133, 172-173, 202
chown, 23, 133, 172-173, 202
chroot, 39, 166, 202
chsh, 139
class, 53, 80
Cleanfeed, 7
clock, 154
clock commands, 154
comanche, 223
command operators, 130-131
commands
    adduser, 139
    adtimex, 155
    alias, 132
    apropos, 131
    arp, 102, 155, 233
    at, 140
    atq, 140
    atrm, 140
    autogroup, 53, 80
    badblocks, 159

commands (cont.)
    banner, 140
    batch, 140
    bg, 137
    bootpd, 102
    bootptest, 102
    cal, 140
    cat, 26, 228-229, 232
    cd, 20, 39
    cfdisk, 155, 233
    chgrp, 39, 172
    chmod, 22, 53, 80, 132-133, 172
    chown, 23, 133, 173
    chroot, 39
    chsh, 139
    class, 53, 80
    clock, 154
    compress, 35, 134
    cp, 20, 38, 174
    cpio, 35, 135, 154
    cut, 28
    date, 141, 154
    dd, 28
    debugfs, 159
    delete, 53, 80
    deny, 53, 80
    depmod, 155
    df, 159, 174, 233
    diff, 28-29
    dip, 51
    dir, 39, 174
    dmesg, 137, 230
    domainname, 122
    dsmesg, 106
    dump, 137
    dumpe2fs, 159
    e2fsck, 160
    elm, 12
    expand, 28, 30
    fdisk, 155, 233
    fetchmail, 12
    fg, 137
    file, 27
    find, 23, 25, 133
    fingered, 102
    fold, 28, 30
    free, 136
    fsck, 125, 160
    ftpd, 99-100, 103, 129
    gated, 99-100, 129
    gdc, 102
    grep, 28, 30

commands (cont.)
- groups, 139
- guestgroup, 53, 80
- gunzip, 35-36, 135
- gzip, 36-37, 135
- halt, 137, 141
- help, 167
- host, 99-100, 129
- hwclock, 154
- icmpinfo, 102
- identd, 102
- ifconfig, 99-100, 129, 141
- info, 20, 131
- insmod, 155
- irc, 141
- kbddate, 155, 230, 233
- kill, 138
- kysms, 155
- ldd, 138
- less, 27, 228, 230, 238
- limit, 53, 80
- ln, 21
- locate, 23, 26, 133
- loginfails, 53, 80
- look, 23, 134
- lpc, 90, 92
- lpd, 90, 92
- lpq, 91-92
- lpr, 28, 31
- lprm, 91, 93
- ls, 20, 39, 175, 228, 230, 237
- lsmod, 155
- mail, 12
- man, 131, 142
- mcopy, 37
- mdel, 37
- mdir, 38
- mkdir, 175
- mke2fs, 160
- mknod, 175
- mmap, 233
- modprobe, 155
- more, 27, 153
- mren, 38
- munmap, 233
- mv, 21, 175
- named, 99-100, 129
- netcfg, 141
- netdate, 103
- netset, 99, 101
- netstat, 130, 141, 150
- nice, 138

commands (cont.)
- nl, 28, 31
- nslookup, 99, 101, 129
- overwrite, 54, 80
- pac, 94
- passwd, 139
- passwd-check, 54, 80
- paste, 28, 31
- patch, 28, 32
- path-filter, 54, 80
- pine, 12
- ping, 49, 141
- pppd, 99, 101, 129
- pppstats, 141
- pr, 90-91
- printenv, 136
- printtool, 231
- private, 53, 80
- procmail, 12
- ps, 136, 151
- pstree, 137
- pwd, 39
- quota, 24
- r-, 75
- ramsize, 155, 233
- rarp, 155, 233
- rcp, 76
- rdate, 103, 154
- reboot, 138
- rename, 54, 80
- rlogin, 76
- rm, 21, 176
- rmail, 103
- rmdir, 38, 176
- rmmod, 155
- route, 99, 101, 129
- routed, 99, 101, 129
- rpc.portmap, 122-123
- rpc.yppasswd, 122
- rpcinfo, 122, 125
- rsh, 76, 104
- rstat, 104
- ruptime, 104
- rusers, 77, 104
- rwall, 104
- rwhod, 104
- scsi_info, 234
- sed, 28, 32
- setclock, 154
- setfprm, 141
- setserial, 141, 155, 233
- setup, 234

commands (cont.)
- showmount, 122
- shutdown, 139, 157
- slattach, 105, 155, 233
- sort, 28, 33
- split, 28, 33
- stat, 22
- statserial, 141
- su, 139
- tac, 28, 33
- tail, 27
- tar, 35-36, 136, 153
- tcpdchk, 105
- tcpmatch, 105
- telnet, 141
- top, 137
- touch, 22
- tput, 141
- tr, 28, 34
- traceroute, 106, 160
- tune2fs, 160
- type, 132
- umask, 54, 80
- unalias, 132
- uncompress, 35, 37, 136
- uniq, 28, 34
- unname, 137
- unzip, 35, 37, 136
- upload, 54, 80
- uptime, 141
- vmstat, 141
- w, 141, 161
- wc, 28, 34
- whatis, 131
- whereis, 23, 134
- which, 24, 134
- who, 141
- ypbind, 122
- ypcat, 122
- ypinit, 122
- ypmatch, 122
- yppasswd, 122
- yppoll, 122
- zcat, 27
- zip, 35, 37, 136
- zless, 27
- zmore, 27

communication server packages, 351
communication tools types, 210
comp.mail.elm, 63
comp.mail.imap, 63
comp.mail.mime, 63
comp.mail.misc, 63
comp.mail.pine, 63
comp.mail.sendmail, 63
comp.mail.smail, 63
comp.mail.uucp, 63
comp.os.linux.answers, 62
comp.os.linux.announce, 12, 62
comp.os.linux.hardware, 62, 234
comp.os.linux.misc, 62
comp.os.linux.networking, 62
comp.os.linux.security, 62
comp.os.linux.setup, 62
compress, 35
compress files, 134-135
compress command, 134
Compressed Serial Line Internet Protocol, *see* CSLIP
CONFIG_FIREWALL, 88
CONFIG_IP_ACCT, 88
CONFIG_IP_FORWARD, 88
CONFIG_IP_NOSR, 88
CONFIG_IP_ROUTER, 88
CONFIG_NET_ALIAS, 88
connect, 203
control panel tools
- helptool, 221
- kernelcfg, 222
- linuxconf, 221-222
- modemtool, 221-222
- netcfg, 221-222
- printtool, 221-222
- thsysv, 221-222
- timetool, 221, 223

cp, 20, 38, 172, 174
cpio, 35, 135, 153, 170, 179
cpu information, 228
cracklib, 182
CSLIP definition, 49, 192
customer service definition, 209
cut, 38
cvs, 170, 183

D

daemon definition, 130, 192
daemons
- bootpd, 102, 154
- dhcpcd, 109
- fingerd, 72
- fingered, 102, 154
- ftpd, 79, 99-100, 103, 130, 154
- gated, 99-100, 130
- httpd, 186
- identd, 154
- imapd, 102, 154
- inetd, 103, 154, 188

daemons (cont.)
innd, 65
kerneld, 154-155
lpd, 92, 103, 154
mountd, 126, 154
named, 99-100, 130, 154
nfsd, 126, 154
nnrpd, 65
perror, 161
pop3d, 154
pppd, 99, 101, 111, 130, 154
rdistd, 154
rexecd, 103, 154
ristd, 77
rlogind, 104
routed, 99, 101, 130, 154
rpc.mountd, 74, 122
rpc.nfsd, 74, 122
rquotad, 77
rwhod, 104
syslogd, 103, 105, 154
talkd, 73, 105
tcpd, 105, 154
telnetd, 105
tftpd, 72, 105
tzset, 154
update, 154
ypserv, 154
zdump, 154
zic, 154
daemons man pages, 8
DARPA, 97
database server, 1
database server packages, 351
date, 166
date set, 140-141
date command, 141, 154
dd, 28
debugger server packages, 354
debugs, 159
definition server, 1
DejaGnu, 170
delete, 53, 80
deny, 53, 80
depmod, 155
desktop server packages, 357
device,
files, 230
setup, 234
storage space, 233
df, 159, 172, 174
DHCP definition, 109
dhcpcd, 109
Dial-up IP Protocol Driver, *see* dip
diff, 28-29
diffutils, 171, 182
dig, 9
dip,
definition, 51, 192
using, 51
dir, 172, 174
Direct Memory Access, *see* DMA
directory,
change, 39
copy, 38
create, 38
delete, 38
lists, 39
make, 38
pathname, 39
permissions, 39
remove, 39
root name, 39
directory commands,
cd, 39
chgrp, 39
chroot, 39
cp, 38
ls, 39
mdir, 38
pwd, 39
rmdir, 38
dirname, 166
dld, 170
DMA channel addresses, 229
dmesg, 137
DNS, *see* Domain Name Service, Domain Name System
DNS RFCs, 107
DNS tools
named, 55
nslookup, 55
resolver library, 55
traceroute, 55
dnsquery, 9
documentation server packages, 355
domain definition, 108, 192
domain name server, 108
Domain Name Service, 51, 192
Domain Name System, 16, 106
domainname, 122
DOSEMU, 147
dsmesg, 106
dummy interface, 49
dump, 137, 159
dumpe2fs, 159

Dynamic Host Configuration Protocol, *see* DHCP

E

e-mail,
  agents, 11
  definition, 11
  requirements, 11
  server, 1
e-mail RFCs
  821, 16
  1056, 17
  1123, 17
  1176, 17
  1203, 17
  1211, 17
  1327, 17
  1339, 17
  1343, 17
  1344, 17
  1422, 17
  1423, 18
  1424, 18
  1506, 18
  1711, 18
  1844, 18
  1869, 18
  1893, 18
  1957, 11
  2033, 18
  2045, 18
  2046, 18
  2047, 18
  2048, 18
  2049, 18
  2110, 18
e2fsck, 159-160
echo, 166
ed, 146, 170
editor server packages, 352
editors, 146
efax, 52, 180
EGP, 100
  definition, 192
ElectricFence, 180
electronic mail, *see* e-mail
electronic mail definition, 193
elm, 12-13, 16, 50, 59, 181
emacs, 170
engineering server packages, 352
env, 166
Ethernet,
  boards, 156, 232
Ethernet, (cont.)
  configuration, 56
  definition, 193
  device name, 232
  HOWTO, 148, 156, 233
  network adapters, 148
Ethernet interface, adding, 109-110
execve, 203
exit, 203
exmh, 13, 16, 59, 181
expand, 28, 30
expr, 166
External Gateway Protocol, *see* EGP

F

factor, 166
false, 166
faxing support packaging, 52
fchdir, 202
fchmod, 202, 205
fchown, 202, 205
fcntl, 202
fdisk, 155
fetchmail, 12-13, 16, 59, 181
fetchmailconf, 181, 223-224
fg, 137
file,
  archive, 34 , 37
  compression, 27, 34-36
  copy, 20, 35
  defined, 19, 193
  delete, 21
  display, 20, 27
  executable, 19
  find accessed by date, 24
  find by date, 24
  find by type, 25
  find modified by date, 25
  hidden, 20
  information, 20
  make, 20
  move, 21
  MS-DOS, 37
  ownership, 22
  permissions, 22
  prefix in, 38
  rename, 21
  search, 23-24
  size, 25
  special, 19
  suffixes, 38
  symbolic link definition, 38
  symbolic link information, 22

file, (cont.)
- text, processing, 27-28
- time stamp, 22
- types, 19
- uncompress, 37

file command, 27, 180
file commands
- cat, 26
- cd, 20, 39
- chmod, 22-23
- chgrp, 39
- compress, 35
- cp, 20
- cpio, 35
- cut, 28
- dd, 28
- diff, 28-29
- expand, 28, 30
- file, 27
- find, 23, 25
- fold, 28, 30
- grep, 28, 30
- gunzip, 35-36
- gzip, 36-37
- info, 20
- less, 27
- ln, 21
- locate, 23, 26
- look, 23
- lpr, 28, 31
- ls, 20, 39
- mcopy, 37
- mdel, 37
- mdir, 38
- mkdir, 20
- more, 27
- mren, 38
- mv, 21
- nl, 28, 31
- paste, 28, 31
- patch, 28, 32
- quota, 24
- rm, 21
- sed, 28, 32
- sort, 28, 33
- split, 28, 33
- stat, 22
- tac, 28, 33
- tail, 27
- tar, 35-36
- touch, 22
- tr, 28, 34

file commands (cont.)
- uncompress, 35, 37
- uniq, 28, 34
- unzip, 35, 37
- wc, 28, 34
- whereis, 23
- which, 24
- zcat, 27
- zip, 35, 37
- zless, 27
- zmore, 27

file management, 19
file management definition, 193
file server, 1
file server packages, 352
File Transfer Protocol, *see* FTP
files,
- aliases, 12
- elm.rc, 12
- sendmail.cf, 13

filesystem
- contents, 239
- definition, 193
- tools, 159

fileutils, 171, 180
filter, 16, 84
find command, 23, 25, 133
findutils, 171, 180
finger, 59
fingerd, 8
fingered, 102, 154
firewall definition, 193
firewall server, 5
- definition, 83
- disadvantage, 85
- components, 83
- HOWTO, 86
- networking options, 87
- set up, 86
- types, 83

firewalling information, 85
flock, 202, 205
fold, 28, 30
fontutils, 172
forwarding rules, 87
free, 136
fsck, 125, 159-160
fstat, 202
fstatfs, 204
FTP,
- access commands, 53
- administrative utilities, 54-55

FTP, (cont.)
  definition, 52, 193
  logging commands, 53
  package, 54, 59, 81
  permissions commands, 53-54
  request, 52
  RPM, 77
  security, 53
  server, 3
  service port, 57
  support packages, 54
  utilities, 81
FTP administrative utilities,
  ftpcount, 54
  ftpwho, 54
  ftpshut, 54
FTP commands, 80
  autogroup, 53
  chmod, 53
  class, 53
  delete, 53
  deny, 53
  guestgroup, 53
  limit, 53
  log commands, 53
  log transfers, 53
  loginfails, 53
  overwrite, 54
  passwd-check, 54
  path-filter, 54
  private, 53
  rename, 54
  umask, 54
  upload, 54
FTP server,
  anonymous, 78
  configuration, 79
  daemon, 78
  definition, 78
  packages, 81
  request steps, 78
  security, 79
FTP service,
  definition, 78
  port number, 78
ftpcount utility, 54, 81
ftpd, 8-9, 79, 99-100, 103, 130, 154
ftpshut utility, 9, 54, 81
ftpwho utility, 54, 81

G

gated, 99-100, 130
gateway definition, 194
gateway server, 4, 85
gawk, 147, 170, 182
gcal, 170
gdb, 180
gdbm, 170
gdc, 102
gdk, 170
getdents, 202
getdomainname, 205
getegid, 205
geteuid, 205
getgroups, 205
gethostid, 204
gethostname, 204
getitimer, 204
getlist, 7
getpeername, 204
getpgid, 203
getpriority, 203
getrlimit, 204
getrusage, 204
getsid, 203
getsocketname, 203
getsockopt, 203
gettimeofday, 204
getuid, 205
gftp, 54
gftp package, 81
Ghostscript, 147, 170
Ghostview, 147, 170
glint, 223-224
GNU bc, 148
GNU emacs, 146
GNU Project,
  definition, 169, 194
  distributions, 169-171
  URL, 169
  utilities, 171-172
GNU SQL, 171
GNU tar, 171
GNUplot, 147
gnus, 170
graphic programs, 147
graphics server packages, 351
grep, 28, 30, 171
groff, 171
group, creating, 212
groups, 139, 166
guestgroup, 53, 80
gunzip, 27, 35-36, 135
gzip, 27, 36-37, 135, 148, 171

H

halt, 137, 141, 204
hardware,
  commands, 233
  compatibility, 146, 227
  HOWTO, 227, 234
  knowledge, 227
  man pages, 235
  newsgroups, 234
  processors, 228
  RFCs, 234
hardware commands,
  arp, 155
  cfdisk, 155
  fdisk, 155
  kbdate, 155
  ramsize, 155
  rarp, 155
  setserial, 155
  slattach, 155
hardware requirements,
  inn, 65
  Usenet, 64
helptool, 221
home directory creating, 217
host, 9, 99-100, 130
  definition, 194
host name, 58
hostname, 166
HOWTOs
  3 Button Serial Mouse (mini), 234
  Benchmarking, 257
  Brief Introduction to Alpha Systems and Processors, 234
  Busmouse, 258
  CD-ROM, 259
  Clock (mini), 234
  Configuration, 6, 261
  DNS, 55, 262
  Electronic Mail Administrator, 283
  Electronic Mail User, 285
  Ethernet, 56, 148, 156, 227, 263
  Firewall and Proxy Server, 55, 86, 234, 270
  Hardware Compatibility, 146, 227, 234, 271
  Intranet Server, 149, 274
  IP Masquerade, 85
  IPCHAINS, 276
  IPX, 278
  ISP-Hookup, 55-56, 280
  Keyboard and Console, 281
  Linux Busmouse, 234
  Linux CD-ROM, 234
HOWTOs (cont.)
  Linux CD-Writing, 234
  Linux Electronic Mail, 55
  Linux Ethernet, 234
  Linux I/O Port Programming (mini), 234
  Linux Keyborad and Console, 234
  Linux Net-3, 86
  Linux PCI, 234
  Linux PPP, 55
  Linux Printing, 234
  Linux SCSI, 234
  Linux Serial, 235
  Linux Sound, 235
  Linux WWW, 55
  location, 142
  Mail, 22
  Modem, 286
  MP3, 290
  Multi Disk System Tuning, 292
  Multicast over TCP/IP, 290
  Networking, 295
  Networking Overview, 299
  News, 69
  NFS, 55, 126, 149, 300
  NIS (YP)/NYS/NIS+, 69, 301
  PCMCIA, 302
  Plug-and-Play, 304
  PostSQL, 55
  PPP, 111, 306
  Printing, 93, 308
  Printing-Usage, 93
  Red Hat Linux Kickstart, 282
  RPM, 162, 178, 216, 310
  Samba, 162
  SCSI Programming, 311
  Security, 312
  Serial, 50, 56, 232, 314
  Serial-Programming, 50, 56, 232
  Shadow Password, 318
  Shadow Suite, 46
  SMB, 320
  Software Packages, 320
  Sound, 321
  User-group, 149
  using, 142
  UUCP, 323
  Virtual Services, 324
  VPN Masquerade, 326
  WWW, 327
  X Window User, 329
  XFree86 Video Tunings, 235
httpd, 7-8, 186

httpd.conf, 186-187
hwclock, 154

I

ical, 148, 182
ICMP, definition, 106, 194
icmpinfo, 102
id, 166
identd, 8-9, 102, 154
ifconfig, 99-100, 130
IMAP, 102
imap, 50
imapd, 102, 154
inetd, 8-9, 103, 154
inetd daemon, 5
inetd.conf, 9
inetutils, 172
inews, 183
info, 20, 131
inn, 50, 103
INN, 65
innd, 65
INN-faq_partn, 66
innxbatch, 7
innxmit, 7, 72
input rules, 87
insmod, 155
installit, 223-224
Interactive Mail Access Protocol, *see* IMAP
Internet Control Message Protocol, *see* ICMP
Internet definition, 194
Internet programs
- dip, 50
- elm, 50
- imap, 50
- inn, 50
- pine, 50
- pppd, 50
- sendmail, 50
- tin, 50
- trn, 50

Internet Protocol, *see* IP
Internet Relay Chat, *see* IRC
Internet server, 1
- definition, 47
- man pages, 9
- packages, 52
- prime concern, 48
- programs, 50
- setting up, 48
- services access, 58
- support packages, 59

InterNetNews, 65, 103
intranet,
- definition, 130
- server configuration, 149
- server definition, 47

IO port addresses, 229
iopi, 205
IP address,
- definition, 97, 195
- loopback, 97
- standalone host, 108

IP addresses, name servers, 58
IP definition, 194
IP filtering, 83-84
IP interface configuration, 108
ipfwadm, 84
Ipv6,
- definition, 98
- installation, 98
- RFCs, 98

irc, 141
IRC,
- definition, 195
- support packages, 52

ircii, 52, 180
ircii-help, 52
IRQ addresses, 229
ispell, 148, 171

J

jed, 146
Joe, 146

K

kbdconfig, 223-224
kbdrate, 155, 230, 233
kernel
- definition, 195
- network devices, 229
- structure, 228

kernel 2.2, 163
kernel management commands, 155
kernel upgrade, 162
kernelcfg, 222
kerneld, 154-155
keyboard rate, 230
kill, 138, 203
killpg, 203
ksh, 165
kysms, 155

L

LAN definition, 195

language server packages, 354
ldd, 138
less, 27, 182, 238
libjpeg, 181
libjpeg-devel, 181
libraries server packages, 354
library definition, 195
librpeg6a, 181
libtiff, 183
libtiff-devel, 183
libungif, 181
libungif-devel, 181
libungif-progs, 181
limit, 53, 80
link, 202
inn package, 65
    daemons, 65
    files, 65
    configuring, 65
    hardware requirements, 65
    remote access, 65
Linux user group setup, 149
linux.redhat.applixware, 62
linux.redhat.axp, 62
linux.redhat.devel, 62
linux.redhat.digest, 62
linux.redhat.install, 62
linux.redhat.list, 62
linux.redhat.misc, 62
linux.redhat.pam, 62
linux.redhat.ppp, 62
linux.redhat.rpm, 62
linuxconf, 157, 221-222
listen, 203
ln, 21
Local Area Network, *see* LAN
localhost, 49
locate, 23, 26, 133
log commands, 11
log importance, 210
log transfers, 80
loginfails, 53, 80
logname, 166
look, 23, 134
loopback address definition, 97
lpc, 90, 92
lpd, 90, 92, 103, 154
lpq, 91, 92
lpr, 28, 31, 90-91
lprm, 91, 93
ls, 20, 39, 172, 175, 237
lsmod, 155
lstat, 202
lynx, 52

M

mail command, 12
mail commands
    elm, 12
    fetchmail, 12
    mail, 12
    pine, 12
    procmail, 12
mail packages
    elm, 13, 16
    exmh, 13, 16
    fetchmail, 13, 16
    mailx, 13, 16
    metamail, 13, 16
    mutt, 13, 17
    nmh, 13, 17
    pine, 13, 17
    xmailbox, 13, 17
mail transport agent, 11
mail user agent, 11
mailx, 59, 181
makehistory, 223-224
man command, 131, 142
man page definition, 195
man pages
    ab, 7
    accessing process, 145
    apachectl, 7
    Cleanfeed, 7
    definition, 142
    dig, 9
    divisions, 143
    dnsquery, 9
    exports, 126
    finding, 142
    fingerd, 8
    ftpd, 8-9
    ftpshut, 9
    getlist, 7
    hardware, 235
    host, 9
    httpd, 7-8
    identd, 8-9
    inetd, 8-9
    inetd.conf, 9
    innxbatch, 7
    innxmit, 7
    lpd, 95
    lpq, 95
    lprm, 95

man pages (cont.)
mountd, 126
named, 8-9
navigating, 145
ncpmount, 9
nfs, 126
nfsd, 126
nnrpd, 7-8
nntpget, 7
nslookup, 9
nwfsctrl, 7
nwfsinfo, 7
nwfstime, 7
nwsfind, 7
nwuserlist, 7
portmap, 126
printcap, 95
printing, 143
printmail, 95
pserver, 7
rdistd, 8
Red Hat files, 144
rexecd, 8
rlogind, 8
rotatelogs, 7
rquotad, 8
rshd, 8
rstatd, 8-9
rwhod, 8-9
Samba, 8
search keywords, 145-146
sections, 144
seeing source, 144
slist, 7
smbclient, 8
smbd, 8
string search, 144
talkd, 8
telnetd, 8-9
tftpd, 8
timed, 8
tunelp, 95
writing, 145
Xconfigurator, 9
xferlog, 9
Xserver, 9
ypset, 9
ypwhich, 9
yypoll, 9
masquerading,
definition, 85, 195
HOWTO, 85
masquerading, (cont.)
set up, 86
mcopy, 37
mdel, 37
mdir, 38
memory device map, 233
messaging server, 3, 89
metamail, 59, 181
Midnight Commander, 148
MIME definition, 15, 195
mime.types, 186
mkdir, 20, 172, 175, 202
mke2fs, 159-160
mknod, 172, 175, 202
mmap, 202
modems, 232
modemtool, 221-222
modprobe, 155
module definition, 196
more, 27, 153
mount, 204
mount options, /etc/exports, 75
mount points, 6
mountd, 126, 154
mouse,
generic, 230
kernel ID, 230
mouseconfig, 223-224
mremap, 204
mren, 38
msgget, 203
msgop, 203
msync, 202
MTA, 11
mtools, 171
MUA, 11
multimedia server packages, 352
Multipurpose Internet Mail Extensions, *see* MIME
munmap, 202
mutt, 59, 181
mv, 21, 172, 175

N

name server,
IP addresses, 58
definition, 51
types, 51
named, 8-9, 99-100, 130, 154
nanosleep, 203
ncftp, 54, 59, 81, 180
ncompress, 179
ncpmount, 9
Net::Ping, 73

net-tools, 148, 181
netcfg, 99, 141, 221-222
netdate, 103
Netnews definition, 69
netscape-common, 59
netscape-communicator, 59
netset, 99, 101
netstat, 130, 141
NetWare server man pages, 7
network,
 definition, 129
 services, 1, 129
network adapter, 5
network device names, 149
network devices kernel, 229
network devices supported, 156
network file server, 3
Network File System, *see* NFS
network information server, 3
Network Information System, *see* NIS
network names, 58
 location, 150
Network News Transfer Protocol, *see* NNTP
network RFCs, 164
network shutdown, 157
networking daemons, 154
news distribution policy, 70
news packages
 inn, 65
 pine, 67
 tin, 67
 trn, 67
news reader,
 configuring, 64
 functions, 66
 types, 66
news RFCs 977, 61
news server,
 administrative tasks, 70
 definition, 61
 hierarchy, 63
 policy, 64
news user data, 69
newsgroup server, 4
 man pages, 7
newsgroups,
 comp.os.linux.announce, 12
 controlling authority, 70
 Linux, general, 62
 Linux, Red Hat, 62
 mail, 63
newsrequeue, 223-224
NFS, 3, 73
 characteristics, 121
 commands, 122
 components, basic, 122
 daemons, 122
 definition, 121, 196
 firewall ports, 125
 HOWTO, 125
 integrity, 125
 man pages, 126
 mount options, 124
 mounting, 122
 RFCs, 127
 setup, 149
 start, 125
 stop, 125
 use, 121
 weakness, 121
NFS man pages
 exports, 126
 mountd, 126
 nfs, 126
 nfsd, 126
 portmap, 126
nfsd, 126, 154
nice, 138, 166
NIS, 3, 73
 configuring, 69
 definition, 115, 196
 HOWTO, 69
 man pages, 9
nl, 28, 31
nmh, 59, 181
nnrpd, 7-8, 65
NNTP, 4, 61, 69
NNTP definition, 196
NNTP server,
 alternative, 64
 definition, 64
nntpget, 7
nohup, 166
nslookup, 9, 99, 101, 130
ntpget, 73
ntsysv, 223-224
nwfsctrl, 7
nwfsinfo, 7
nwfstime, 7
nwsfind, 7
nwuserlist, 7

O

offline printing, 91
online, 131

open, 203
output rules, 87
overwrite, 54, 80
ownership, changing, 217

P

pac, 94
package,
  archiving, 179
  building, 216
  definition, 177, 196, 215
  dependency error, 218
  finding, 178
  finding, Web, 216-217
  installing, 178, 217
  querying, 219
  reinstalling, 218
  uninstalling, 179, 218
  updating, 218
  upgrading, 179
  verifying, 179, 220
package types
  archiving, 351
  base, 354
  communication, 351
  databases, 351
  debuggers, 354
  desktops, 357
  documentation, 355
  editors, 352
  engineering, 352
  file, 352
  graphics, 351
  internet, 352
  languages, 354
  libraries, 354
  multimedia, 352
  productivity, 353
  publishing, 353
  system, 353-354
  system environment, 355
  text, 353
  tools, 354
  X, 357
  X hardware support, 357
packages
  anonftp, 54, 81
  aumix, 182
  binutils, 180
  cpio, 179
  cracklib, 182
  cvs, 183
  diffutils, 182
packages (cont.)
  efax, 52, 180
  ElectricFence, 180
  elm, 13, 59, 181
  exmh, 13, 59, 181
  fetchmail, 13, 59, 181
  fetchmailconf, 181
  file, 180
  fileutils, 180
  findutils, 180
  finger, 59
  ftp, 54, 59, 77, 81
  fwhois, 59
  gawk, 182
  gdb, 180
  gftp, 54, 181
  ical, 182
  inews, 183
  inn, 65
  ircii, 52, 180
  ircii-help, 52
  less, 182
  libjpeg, 181
  libjpeg-devel, 181
  librpeg6a, 181
  libtiff, 183
  libtiff-devel, 183
  libungif, 181
  libungif-devel, 181
  libungif-progs, 181
  lynx, 52, 179
  mailx, 13, 59, 181
  metamail, 13, 59, 181
  mutt, 13, 59, 181
  ncftp, 54, 59, 81, 180
  ncompress, 179
  netscape-common, 59
  netscape-communicator, 59
  net-tools, 148, 181
  nmh, 13, 59, 181
  perl, 182
  pine, 13, 59, 181
  playmidi, 182
  python, 182
  rcs, 183
  rpm, 186
  rsh, 59
  sed, 182
  slrn, 59, 182
  sox, 182
  stat, 180
  strace, 180

packages (cont.)
talk, 59
tar, 179
tcl, 182
tcpdump, 59, 148, 181
telnet, 59
textutils, 183
tin, 59, 182
traceroute, 59
trn, 59, 182
which, 180
words, 183
xmailbox, 13, 59
xrn, 59
xxgdb, 180
zip, 179
PAP, 112
Parallel Line Internet Protocol, *see* PLIP
passwd, 139
passwd.nntp file, 73
passwd-check, 54, 80
password,
creating, 211
setting, 218
Password Authentication Protocol, *see* PAP
paste, 28, 31
patch, 28, 32, 148
pathchk, 166
path-filter, 54, 80
PCI motherboard, 228
Perl, 147, 182
permissions, 25-6
changing, 217
commands, 80
perror, 161
pine, 12-13, 17, 50, 59, 66, 181
pine news reader,
characteristics, 67
location, 67
RPM, 69
ping, 49, 141
planning process definition, 209
playmidi 182
PLIP,
definition, 108, 196
interface, adding, 108
Point-to-Point Protocol, *see* PPP
Point-to-Point Tunneling Protocol, *see* PPTP
POP, 11
pop3d, 154
port definition, 197
portmapper, 75
Post Office Protocol, *see* POP
PPP,
components, 111
connection, 111
connection status, 112
definition, 48, 111, 197
HOWTO, 111
kernel support, 112
RFCs, 113
security, 113
setup, 111-112
pppd, 50, 99, 101, 111-112, 130, 141, 154
pppstats 141
PPTP, 4
print commands, 90
print server, 4, 89
print system host ID, 94
printenv, 136, 166
printer,
access, 230
configuring, 93
definition, 90, 197
device name, 231
file description, 231
files, 231
information, 231
line printers, 231
man pages, 95
printtool, 231
reconfiguration, 94
remote host, 231
socket requests, 230
space, minimum, 231
specifications, 231
spool directories, 231
troubleshooting, 95
usage, 94
printer configuration tool, 93
printf, 166
printing HOWTOs, 93
printtool, 221-222, 231
private, 53, 80
process reports, 151
process status commands, 136
processors, 228
procmail, 12-13, 17
productivity server packages, 353
programming languages, 147
protocols,
Usenet, 61
UUCP, 61

proxy, 83-84
    definition, 197
    server, 4, 90
ps, 136, 151
pserver, 7
pstree, 137
ptrace, 203
publishing server packages, 353
pwd, 166
Python, 147, 182

Q

quota, 24
    definition, 197
quotactl, 204

R

r- commands, 75
ramsize, 155
rarp, 155
RARP definition, 197
rc.local, 153
rc.sysinit, 152-153
rcp command, 76
rdate, 103, 154
rdist, 77
rdistd, 8, 154
readdir, 202
readlink, 202
readprofile, 223-224
reboot, 138, 204
Red Hat Package Manager, *see* RPM
remote access commands
    autogroup, 80
    chmod, 80
    class, 80
    delete, 80
    deny, 80
    guestgroup, 80
    limit, 80
    log commands, 80
    log transfers, 80
    loginfails, 80
    overwrite, 80
    passwd-check, 80
    path-filter, 80
    private, 80
    r-, 75
    rcp, 76
    rename, 80
    rlogin, 76
    rsh, 76
    rusers, 77
remote access commands (cont.)
    umask, 80
    upload, 80
remote access daemons
    fingerd, 72
    ftpd, 79
    ristd, 77
    rpc.mountd, 74
    rpc.nfsd, 74
    rquotad, 77
    talkd, 73
    tftpd, 72
remote administration server, 4
    man pages, 8
Remote Procedure Call protocol, *see* RPC
remote server definition, 71
rename, 54, 80, 202
Request for Comments, *see* RFC
resolver definition, 197
restore, 159
Reverse Address Resolution Protocol, *see* RARP
rexecd, 8, 103, 154
RFC definition, 198
RFCs,
    791, 60, 345
    793, 345
    799, 60, 348
    821, 16, 345
    896, 98, 348
    903, 348
    950, 60, 345
    959, 345
    974, 345
    977, 4, 61, 346
    1011, 60, 348
    1027, 348
    1032, 348
    1033, 107, 348
    1036, 348
    1056, 17
    1074, 348
    1090, 348
    1094, 127, 348
    1101, 107
    1104, 348
    1123, 17
    1124, 348
    1155, 99, 346
    1157, 346
    1173, 60, 164, 348
    1175, 164
    1176, 17

RFCs, (cont.)
1180, 60, 99, 348
1183, 107
1196, 72, 102
1203, 17
1206, 348
1207, 348
1208, 164, 348
1211, 17
1234, 346
1241, 348
1242, 164
1244, 348
1267, 348
1288, 72, 102
1302, 164
1327, 17
1332, 60, 113, 346
1339, 17
1343, 17
1344, 17
1346, 164
1349, 60, 346
1355, 164
1383, 107
1421, 346
1422, 17, 347
1423, 18, 347
1424, 18, 347
1425, 347
1441, 164
1463, 164
1498, 164
1506, 18
1513, 347
1524, 347
1527, 164
1535, 107
1536, 107
1552, 347
1565, 347
1566, 347
1579, 87
1598, 347
1611, 107, 347
1612, 107, 347
1618, 113
1638, 347
1661, 60, 113, 346
1704, 60, 348
1706, 107
1711, 18

RFCs, (cont.)
1712, 107
1713, 107
1726 349
1731, 347
1738, 60
1746, 349
1752, 347
1757, 346
1762, 346
1771, 346
1772, 346
1774, 349
1777, 346
1791, 99, 349
1792, 98, 349
1812, 347
1813, 127, 349
1825, 347
1826, 347
1827, 347
1844, 18
1848, 347
1853, 349
1855, 349
1869, 18, 346
1870, 346
1877, 113
1883, 60, 98, 347
1884, 98
1885, 98
1886, 98, 107, 347
1887, 98
1888, 98
1893, 18
1912, 107
1925, 164
1929, 347
1938, 347
1944, 164, 349
1955, 349
1957, 11, 346, 349
1958, 60, 349
1963, 60, 349
1968, 347
1983, 60, 349
1984, 349
1994, 347
2002, 347
2007, 164, 349
2011, 347
2012, 347

RFCs, (cont.)
- 2013, 348
- 2023, 113
- 2026, 60, 349
- 2030, 349
- 2033, 18, 349
- 2045, 18, 346
- 2046, 18, 346
- 2047, 18, 346
- 2048, 18, 346
- 2049, 18, 346
- 2052, 107
- 2057, 60, 349
- 2063, 349
- 2064, 349
- 2065, 101, 107, 347
- 2072, 349
- 2078, 348
- 2084, 60, 349
- 2107, 349
- 2110, 18
- 2119, 349
- 2136, 107, 348
- 2137, 348
- 2142, 348
- 2151, 60, 99, 349

RIP, 100
- definition, 198

ristd, 77
rlogin command, 76
rlogind, 8, 104
rotatelogs, 7
RPC,
- daemons, 74
- definition, 73
- version importance, 75

rm, 21, 172, 176
rmail, 104,
rmdir, 172, 176, 202
rmmod, 155
route, 99, 101, 130
- definition, 198

routed, 99, 101, 130, 154
router, 84
router balancing, 148
Routing Information Protocol, *see* RIP
routing status, 58
routing definition, 198
RPC definition, 198
rpc.mountd, 74, 122-123
rpc.nfsd, 74, 122-123
rpc.portmap, 74, 122-123
rpc.yppasswd, 122
rpcinfo, 122, 125-126
RPM, *see also* package
- definition, 162, 177, 198
- documentation, 217
- features, 215
- help, 216
- HOWTO, 177
- information sources, 178
- modes, 215
- version number, 216

RPM types
- archiving, 351
- base, 354
- communication, 351
- databases, 352
- debuggers, 354
- desktops, 357
- documentation, 355
- editors, 352
- engineering, 352
- file, 352
- graphics, 351
- internet, 352
- languages, 354
- libraries, 354
- multimedia, 352
- productivity, 353
- publishing, 353
- system, 353-354
- system environment, 355
- text, 353
- tools, 354
- X, 357
- X hardware support, 357

rquota, 77
rquotad, 8, 77
rsh command, 59, 76, 104
rshd, 8
rstat, 104
rstatd, 8-9
rule set, 84
rup, 77
ruptime, 104
rusers, 104
rusers command, 77
rwall, 104
rwhod, 8-9, 104

S

Samba (SMB server), 5
- components, 161
- definition, 161

Samba (SMB server) (cont.)
 files, 161
 information, 161
 man pages, 8
scanner set, 95
script,
 definition, 167
 running, 167
SCSI address parameters, 233
SCSI controller, 6
scsi_info, 223, 234
security risk using root, 208
sed, 28, 32, 182
sendmail,
 compiling, 14
 configuration file, 14
 definition, 13, 198
 functions, 13-14
 installing, 14
 spamming, 15
 upgrade need, 15
sendmsg, 203
sendto, 203
seq, 166
serial communication devices, 50, 232
Serial Line Internet Protocol, *see* SLIP
server,
 application, 89
 definition, 199
 firewall, 83
 hard drive requirements, 5
 inetd, 188-189
 maintenance rule, 187
 messaging, 89
 news definition, 61
 print, 89
 proxy, 90
 remote, 71
 standalone, 188
 testing, 187
server types,
 Apache Web server, 7
 application, 1
 archie, 7
 caching-only, 1
 database, 1
 definition, 1
 domain name, 1
 e-mail, 1
 file, 1
 firewall, 4
 FTP, 3
server types, (cont.)
 gateway, 4
 Internet, 1
 messaging, 3
 NetWare, 7
 network file server (NFS), 3
 network information server (NIS), 3
 newsgroup, 4
 print, 4
 proxy, 4
 remote administration, 4
 Samba (SMB), 5
 security, 4
 three-tier client/server, 1
 UUCP, 5
service,
 definition, 1, 199
 examples, 1
 name, 57
 start, 151
 stop, 151
Session Message Block (SMB), *see* Samba
setclock, 154
setdomainname, 205
setegid, 205
seteuid, 205
setfprm, 141
setfsuid, 205
setgroups, 205
sethostid, 204
sethostname, 204
setitimer, 204
setpgid, 205
setpriority, 203
setregid, 205
setreuid, 205
setrlimit, 204
setserial, 141, 155
setsockopt, 204
settimeofday, 204
setuid, 205
setup, 223-224
Shadow Suite, 46
shell,
 definition, 167
 operators, 167
 commands, find, 167
shellutils, 172
showmount, 122, 127
shutdown, 139, 157
sh-utils, 165-166
Simple Mail Transfer Protocol, *see* SMTP

slattach, 105, 155
sleep, 166
SLIP definition, 199
slist, 7
smbclient, 8
SLIP,
 connection, 106
 definition, 49, 106
 loading, 106
 support, 106
slrn, 59, 66, 182
slrn news reader,
 .slrnrc file, 68
 characteristics, 68
 RPM, 69
smail, 171
SMB, *see* Samba
smbd, 8
SMTP, 2
 definition, 16, 199
 sendmail, 13
socket call, 203
socketpair, 204
sort, 28, 33
sox, 182
spamming, 15
split, 28, 33
spool definition, 91, 199
srm.conf, 186, 188
standalone host IP address, 108
stat, 22, 180, 202
statfs, 204
statserial, 141
storage space check, 159
strace, 180
stty, 166
su, 139, 166
swap, 223-224
symlink, 202
sysctl, 204
sysfs, 204
sysinfo, 204
syslogd, 103, 105, 154
system administrator,
 becoming, 210
 definition, 207
 management point, 208
 requirements to be, 207
 tasks, 208, 211
system calls,
 access management, 205
 call processing, 203
 creating, 201
system calls, (cont.)
 definition, 201
 directory management, 202
 domain management, 205
 file management, 202
 filesystem management, 204
 group management, 205
 prototype, 201
 socket management, 203
 timers, 204
 user management, 205
system crashes, 157
system environment server packages, 355
system server packages, 353-354
system update strategy, 162

T

tabs, 171
tac, 28, 33
tail, 27
talkd, 8, 73, 105
tar, 35-36, 136, 153, 179, 182
tcl, 182
tcl/tk, 147
TCP, definition, 199
TCP/IP, 49, 155
 commands, 99
 definition, 97, 199
 RFCs, 99
TCP/IP commands
 ftpd, 99-100, 130
 gated, 99-100, 130
 host, 99-100, 130
 ifconfig, 99-100, 130
 named, 99-100, 130
 netset, 99, 101, 130
 nslookup, 99, 101, 130
 pppd, 99, 101, 130
 route, 99, 101, 130
 routed, 99, 101, 130
TCP/IP daemons
 ftpd, 99
 gated, 99
 named, 99
 pppd, 99
 routed, 99
 tcpd, 105
tcpd, 105, 154
tcpdchk, 105
tcpdump, 59, 148, 181
tcpdmatch, 105
tcsh, 165
tee, 166

telnet, 59
telnet command, 71, 141
telnet commands, 72
telnet options, 71
telnetd, 8-9, 105
terminology,
- API, 191
- ARP, 191
- ARPA, 191
- backbones, 191
- BBS, 191
- BGP, 192
- bridge, 192
- CSLIP, 192
- daemon, 192
- dip, 192
- DNS, 192
- domain, 192
- EGP, 192
- electronic mail, 193
- Ethernet, 193
- file, 193
- file management, 193
- filesystem, 193
- firewall, 193
- FTP, 193
- gateway, 194
- GNU Project, 194
- host, 194
- ICMP, 194
- internet, 194
- Internet, 194
- IP, 194
- IP address, 195
- IRC, 195
- kernel, 195
- LAN, 195
- library, 195
- man page, 195
- masquerading, 195
- MIME, 195
- module, 196
- NFS, 196
- NIS, 196
- NNTP, 196
- package, 196
- PLIP, 196
- port, 197
- PPP, 197
- printer, 197
- proxy, 197
- quota, 197

terminology, (cont.)
- RARP, 197
- resolver, 197
- RFC, 198
- RIP, 198
- route, 198
- routing, 198
- RPC, 198
- RPM, 198
- sendmail, 198
- server, 199
- service, 199
- SLIP, 199
- SMTP, 199
- spool, 199
- TCP, 199
- TCP/IP, 199
- TFTP, 199
- URL, 200
- Usenet, 200
- UUCP, 200
- WWW, 200

termutils, 172
test, 166
texinfo, 172
text server packages, 353
textutils, 172, 183
TFTP, 71, 105
- definition, 199

tftpd, 8, 72, 105
three-tier client/server, 1
thsysv, 221-222
time set, 140-141
time call, 204
timeconfig, 223, 225
timed, 8
times, 203
timetool, 221, 223
tin, 50, 59, 66, 182
tin news reader,
- .tinrc, 68
- characteristics, 67
- RPM, 69
- started, 68

tools
- ab, 223
- apxs, 223
- comanche, 223
- fetchmailconf, 223-224
- glint, 223-224
- helptool, 221
- installit, 223-224

tools (cont.)
kbdconfig, 223-224
kernelcfg, 222
linuxconf, 221-222
makehistory, 223-224
modemtool, 221-222
mouseconfig, 223-224
netcfg, 221-222
newsrequeue, 223-224
ntsysv, 223-224
printtool, 221-222
readprofile, 223-224
scsi_info, 223-224
setup, 223-224
swap, 223-224
thsysv, 221-222
timeconfig, 223, 225
timetool, 221, 223
usermount, 223, 225
userpasswd, 223, 225
Xconfigurator, 223, 226
tools server packages, 354
top command, 137
touch, 22
tput, 141
tr, 28, 34
traceroute, 59, 106, 160
Transmission Control Protocol, *see* TCP
Transport Control Protocol/Internet Protocol, *see* TCP/IP
Trivial File Transfer Protocol, *see* TFTP
trn, 50, 59, 66, 182
trn news reader,
.trnrc file, 68
characteristics, 68
RPM, 69
true, 166
truncate, 202
tty, 166
tune2fs, 159-160
tview, 171
type command, 132
tzset, 154

U

umask, 54, 80, 202
umount, 204
unalias command, 132
uname, 137, 166
uncompress, 35, 37, 136
Uniform Resource Locator, *see* URL
uniq, 28, 34
UNIX-to-UNIX CoPy Protocol, *see* UUCP
unlink, 202
unzip, 35, 37, 136
update, 154
upload, 54, 80
uptime, 141, 166
URL definition, 52, 200
Usenet,
definition, 61, 200
hardware requirements, 64
having, 64
logical parts, 61
program types, 62
setup, 69
user, adding, 211
usermount, 223, 225
userpasswd, 223, 225
users, 166
ustat, 204
utilities, 147-148
ftpcount, 54
ftpwho, 54
ftpshut, 54
utilities, file,
chgrp, 172
chmod, 172
chown, 172
cp, 172
df, 172
dir, 172
ls, 172
mkdir, 172
mknod, 172
mv, 172
rm, 172
rmdir, 172
utilities, general,
binutils, 171
diffutils, 171
fileutils, 171
findutils, 171
fontutils, 172
inetutils, 172
shellutils, 172
termutils, 172
texinfo, 172
textutils, 172
UUCP, 61, 104
definition, 200
server, 5
UUCP network,
contribution, 150

UUCP network, (cont.)
definition, 150
disadvantage, 150
primary users, 150
uux command, 73

V

Vim, 146
vmstat, 141

W

w command, 141, 161
wait, 203
wc, 28, 34
wdiff, 171
Web server definition, 185
whatis, 132
whereis, 23, 134
which, 24, 134, 180
who, 141, 166
whoami, 166
words, 183
workstation, 6
World Wide Web, *see* WWW
WWW,
definition, 200
server RFCs, 59
server setup, 58-59
service port, 57
setting up for, 58

X

X hardware support server packages, 357
X server packages, 357
X server setup, 6
Xconfigurator, 9, 223, 226
xferlog, 9
xfig, 147
xfm, 148
xinfo, 171
xmailbox, 59
xon, 73
Xpaint, 147
xrn, 59
Xserver, 9
XV, 147
xxgdb, 180

Y

yes, 166
ypbind, 122
ypcat, 122
ypinit, 122
ypmatch, 122
yppasswd, 122
yppoll, 122
ypserv, 154
ypset, 9
ypwhich, 9
yypoll, 9

Z

zcat, 27
zdump, 154
zic, 154
zip, 35, 37, 136, 179
zless, 27
zmore, 27
zsh, 165

Other Books from Wordware Publishing, Inc.

Communications/General

The Complete Communications Handbook
Demystifying ATM/ADSL
Demystifying EDI
Demystifying ISDN
Demystifying TCP/IP (3rd Ed.)

Demystifying Virtual Private Networks
Developing Internet Information Services
Digital Imaging in C and the World Wide Web
Learn Advanced Internet Relay Chat
Learn Internet Relay Chat (2nd Ed.)
Learn Microsoft Exchange Server 5.5 Core Technologies
Writing and Publishing with Your PC

Applications/Operating Systems

Learn ACT! 3.0 for Windows 95
Learn ACT! 3.0-4.0 for the Advanced User
Learn ACT! 2000 for the Advanced User
Learn AutoCAD in a Day
Learn AutoCAD 12 in a Day
Learn AutoCAD LT 97 for Windows 95/NT

Learn AutoCAD LT 98
Learn AutoCAD LT 2000
Learn AutoCAD LT 2000 for the Advanced User
Learn AutoCAD LT 2000 for Architects
Learn Linux 3-D Graphics Programming

Applications/Operating Systems

Learn Lotus 1-2-3 Rel. 5 for Windows in a Day
Learn Microsoft Access 2.0 for Windows in a Day
Learn Microsoft Access 7.0 for Windows 95 in a Day

Learn Microsoft Excel 7.0 for Windows 95 in a Day
Learn Microsoft Excel 2000 VBA Programming
Learn Microsoft FrontPage 97
Learn Microsoft Office 95
Learn Microsoft Office 97
Learn Microsoft Office 2000
Learn Microsoft PowerPoint 7.0 for Windows 95 in a Day
Learn Microsoft Publisher 2000 for the Advanced User
Learn Microsoft Word 6.0 for Windows in a Day
Learn Microsoft Word 7.0 for Windows 95 in a Day
Learn Microsoft Works 3.0 for Windows in a Day
Learn Peach Tree Accounting
Learn P-CAD Master Designer
Learn Red Hat Linux Server Tips
Learn Red Hat Linux OS Tips
Learn Visio 5.0
Learn Visio 5.0 for the Advanced User

Learn Visio 2000
Learn Visio 2000 for the Advanced User
Learn Visio 2000 for the Masters
Learn to Draw with Visio 2000
Learn Windows 95 in a Day

Applications/Operating Systems

Learn Word 2000 VBA by Example
Learn Word 2000 VBA Document Automation
Learn WordPerfect 5.2 for Windows in a Day
Learn WordPerfect 6.0 for Windows in a Day
Visio 4 for Everyone
Visio 2000 Developer's Guide: Software Patterns
Windows NT Server 4.0/2000: Testing and Troubleshooting

Programming

Advanced 3-D Game Programming with DirectX 7.0
Collaborative Computing with Delphi 3
CORBA Developer's Guide with XML
Data Warehousing with MS SQL 7.0
Delphi Developer's Guide to OpenGL
Delphi Graphics and Game Programming Exposed! with DirectX

Designing Arcade Computer Game Graphics
Developer's Guide to Computer Game Design
Developer's Guide to Delphi Troubleshooting
Developer's Guide to HP Printers
Developer's Guide to Lotus Notes and Domino R5
Developer's Guide to Oracle Tools
Developer's Workshop to COM and ATL 3.0
Developer's Workshop to COM+
Developer's Workshop to COM and Visual Basic 2000
Developing Enterprise Applications with PowerBuilder 6.0
Developing Utilities in Visual Basic 4.0

Programming

The HTML Example Book
Iterative UML Development using Visual Basic 5.0
Iterative UML Development using Visual Basic 6.0
Iterative UML Development using Visual C++ 6.0
Learn ActiveX Development using Visual Basic 5.0
Learn ActiveX Development using Visual C++ 6.0
Learn ActiveX Scripting with Microsoft Internet Explorer 4.0
Learn ActiveX Template Library Development with Visual C++ 6.0
Learn Advanced HTML 4.0 with DHTML

Learn Advanced JavaScript
Learn Advanced JavaScript Programming
Learn C in Three Days
Learn C++ in Three Days
Learn Computer Game Programming with CDX and DirectX 7.0
Learn Computer Game Programming with DirectX 7.0
Learn Encryption Techniques with BASIC and C++
Learn Graphics File Programming with Delphi 3
Learn Microsoft Active Desktop Programming using Windows 98
Learn Microsoft SQL Server 7.0

Learn Microsoft SQL 7.0 Care and Maintenance
Learn Microsoft Transaction Server Development using Visual C++ 6.0
Learn Microsoft Visual Basic in Three Days
Learn the MFC C++ Classes
Learn Object Pascal
Learn OLE DB Development with Visual C++ 6.0
Learn Oracle 8i
Learn Pascal
Learn Pascal in Three Days
Learn Personal Oracle 8.0 with Power Objects 2.0
Learn SQL

Programming

Learn Visual Basic 5.0 in Three Days

Learn Visual C++ in Three Days

Lotus Notes Developer's Guide

Nathan Wallace's Delphi 3 Example Book

Practical Guide to SGML Filters

Practical Guide to SGML/XML Filters

Real-Time Strategy Game Programming using DirectX 6.0

Real-Time Strategy Game Programming using DirectX 7.0

Squirrel's Computer Game Programming in C

Tomes of Delphi: Algorithms and Data Structures

Tomes of Delphi: Win32 Core API—Win 2000 Ed.

Tomes of Delphi: Win32 Database Developer's Guide

Tomes of Delphi: Win32 Graphics Programming

Tomes of Delphi: Win32 Shell API—Win 2000 Ed.

Tomes of Delphi: Win32 Multimedia API

Tomes of Delphi 3: Win32 Core API

Tomes of Delphi 3: Win32 Graphical API

The Visual Basic 4.0 Example Book

The WordBasic Example Book

Networking/Internet

CORBA Networking with Java

DCOM Networking with Visual J++

Learn Internet Publishing with Microsoft Publisher 97

Learn Internet Publishing with Microsoft Publisher 98

Learn Lotus Domino

Practical Guide to Intranet Client-Server Applications using the Web

redhat®

The Revolution of Choice

On the CD

The companion CD-ROM contains Red Hat Linux Publisher's Edition, version 6.1.

The root directory is organized as follows:

doc	various FAQs and HOWTOs
dosutils	installation utilities for DOS
images	boot and ramdisk images
misc	source files and install trees
Srpms	Red Hat Package Manager

There are two separate boot images for booting your system. You will need one to boot your system into the Red Hat installation and upgrade process. For CD-ROM and hard drive installs, use the boot.img file. NFS, ftp, and http installations require the bootnet.img file. In addition, installs that require a PCMCIA adapter need the pcmcia.img file. All of these can be found in the images directory.

Please see the README files on the CD for more information.

This book includes a copy of the Publisher's Edition of Red Hat Linux from Red Hat Software, Inc., which you may use in accordance with the GNU General Public License. The Official Red Hat Linux, which you may purchase from Red Hat Software, includes the complete Official Red Hat Linux distribution, Red Hat Software's documentation, and 90 days of free e-mail technical support from Red Hat Software on issues other than installation. You may purchase Official Red Hat Linux and technical support from Red Hat Software through the company's web site (www.redhat.com) or its toll-free number 1-888-REDHAT1.

Warning: Opening the CD package makes this book nonreturnable.